Women, Crime and Criminal Justice

Women, Crime and Criminal Justice

Allison Morris

Basil Blackwell

Copyright © Allison Morris 1987

First published 1987

Basil Blackwell Ltd
108 Cowley Road, Oxford, OX4 1JF, UK

Basil Blackwell Inc.
432 Park Avenue South, Suite 1503
New York, NY 10016, USA

British Library Cataloguing in Publication Data
Morris, Allison
    Women, crime and criminal justice.
    1. Crime and criminals   2. Female
    offenders   3. Criminal justice,
    Administration of
    I. Title
    364   HV6030
    ISBN 0-631-15444-2
    ISBN 0-631-15445-0 Pbk

Library of Congress Cataloging in Publication Data
Morris, Allison.
    Women, crime, and criminal justice.

    Bibliography: p.
    Includes index.
    1. Female offenders.   2. Women – Crimes against.
3. Women correctional personnel.   4. Women prisoners.
5. Criminal justice, Administration of.   I. Title.
HV6046.M63   1987   364'.088042   87-5207
ISBN 0-631-15444-2
ISBN 0-631-15445-0 (pbk.)

Typeset in 11 on 12pt Atlantic
by Pioneer Associates, Perthshire.

Contents

Preface

In 1981 I wrote that there had been little research in criminology on women. That is no longer the case. Recent years have seen a tremendous growth in the literature on women as offenders, defendants, prisoners and criminal justice professionals, especially in the United States. I have tried to bring together these diverse sources (both published and unpublished), highlight themes, identify inconsistencies and draw attention to gaps in our knowledge. Clearly, there is still a need for research.

In writing this book, my intention has been to create an awareness of the special problems, needs and contributions of women in the criminal justice system and to explore how attitudes and preconceived stereotypes of the social roles of women have affected women in the criminal justice system in a variety of ways. Although my main concern throughout is with women, my objective is to demonstrate that consideration of women is of fundamental, not marginal, significance for criminology.

Finally, my thanks to students, colleagues and friends who discussed with me the issues which form the focus of the book and who commented on some or all of the chapters, in particular, Stan Brodsky, Loraine Gelsthorpe, Lorna Smith, Nigel Walker and Chris Wilkinson. Errors and omissions are, of course, my responsibility. I am also grateful to the secretarial staff of the Institute of Criminology, especially Pat Cochrane and Pam Paige who struggled with various drafts of the chapters.

1

Criminology and Women

Introduction

It is not uncommon for criminological textbooks, even critical reviews, to contain nothing at all on women (see, for example, Taylor, Walton and Young, 1973). It goes without saying that if texts do not cover women, courses do not either. In a paper presented at the 1983 meeting of the American Society of Criminology, Moyer demonstrated that only 21 per cent of American four-year criminology or criminal justice programmes had courses which were concerned in any way with women and crime; and that even these were never core or required courses. Much the same would be true in Britain. Texts and courses appear sexless, as if the subjects were neutral or neuter. The language refers to 'people', 'criminals', 'defendants' and 'prisoners', but it is actually about men. This collective amnesia is no mere literary convention, as Rock (1977) has argued, for sexism in language indicates sexism in theory and practice.

Criminology, then, like most academic disciplines (Spender, 1981), has been concerned with the activities and interests of men. The reasons for this are fairly obvious. Historically, it reflects the interests of its founding fathers (cf. Lombroso and Ferrero, 1895) and, until recently, it was almost completely a male profession. This meant that attention was focused away from women and from areas of concern to women (Oakley, 1981).

It is easy to rationalize this neglect. Female offenders represent a small proportion of arrested offenders and create few social problems; they tend to be petty property offenders. But criminology has long recognized the benefits of studying the exception. In the 1950s and 1960s attempts were made to explain the 'good' boy in the delinquent area (Reckless et al., 1957; Scarpitti et al., 1960). More recently, countries with low crime rates were examined with a view to providing clues to understanding the crime rates in other countries (Clinard, 1978; Adler, 1983). Investigating the absence of crime in certain groups is therefore just as important as investigating its presence in others. Exploring why women commit fewer crimes than men (if indeed they do) could arguably provide clues for dealing with men's criminality.

Theories of criminality have been developed from male subjects and validated on male subjects.[1] Thus they are 'man made'. There is nothing wrong with this *per se*. But the theories have tended to be generalized to all criminals, defendants and prisoners.[2] It is assumed that the theories will apply to women; many do not (Leonard, 1982). 'Man' has also been regarded as the prototype in theory construction. A clear example of this is found in Freudian theory: the penis is viewed as central to the Oedipus complex and to the subsequent development of both men and women. For men, it is the presence of the penis, for women the absence. Thus women's recognition that they do not have a penis is viewed as *the* critical experience for them; it is used to explain their sense of inferiority, passivity and dependence.

Relying on male subjects or on men's experience has two implications. It means that, first, these theories are really special theories about *men's crime* and, secondly, that doubts must arise about a particular theory's validity as a general theory if it does not apply to women. A theory is weak if it does not apply to half of the potential criminal population; women, after all, experience the same deprivations, family structures and so on that men do. To study only men or boys to assess whether or not delinquency springs from, for example, poverty makes little sense. Similarly, to refer to the 'subcultural style' of working-class boys as a solution to the problems of redevelopment, housing, depopulation and community solidarity begs an important question: how do working-class *girls* solve these problems? Theories of crime should be able to take account of both men's and women's behaviour and to highlight those factors which operate differently on men and women. Whether or not a particular theory helps us to understand women's crime better is of fundamental, not marginal, significance for criminology.[3]

I can demonstrate this by taking a few criminological theories and exploring what happens when women *are* considered. I am not concerned with a general critique of these theories;[4] that is not the point. Rather, my purpose is two-fold: to identify the extent to which the theories or, more accurately, the theorists have been blind to women, and to assess the consequences for the theories of ignoring women. There are two inter-related questions: do the theories explain women's crime? and do the theories explain differential crime rates? It is obviously not possible to discuss every theory in detail. What follows is necessarily selective. (See also Leonard, 1982.)

Ignoring Women

Criminologists have linked area of residence to criminal behaviour. The earliest proponents of this view were Shaw and McKay (1942). They plotted the residences in Chicago of over 60,000 adjudicated and institutionalized male delinquents between the years 1900 and 1940. The majority lived in the transitional, inner-city areas: near the centre of the city the rate of official delinquency per 100 boys was 24.5; in outer areas it was 3.5. Residences were subsequently plotted in other areas (Philadelphia, Boston, Cincinnati, Cleveland and Richmond) and up to 1966. The findings were the same: official delinquents were concentrated in the overcrowded, deteriorated parts of the cities. Shaw and McKay stressed that this was due to the nature of the areas themselves — characterized by social disorganization, physical deterioration, racial and ethnic segregation, and a high incidence of social ills — not to the nature of the individuals. Crime was presented as providing the social and economic advantages which had been denied the residents of the area.[5] The residents, however, are referred to explicitly in male terms. Shaw and McKay wrote:

> Role problems of the adolescent male probably are more serious than are the problems of other age groups. With the exception of the school, for which he may not be adequately prepared, no meaningful conventional institutional setting is available for him in urban communities. If the adolescent male fails in school or drops out, or for other reasons finds school roles unsatisfactory or unplayable, he finds himself in an institutional void. He is not

wanted in industry or commerce, he is too young for military service, and odd jobs traditionally available to his age group are decreasing in numbers. (1969: 383)

Only a few pages in Shaw and McKay's book are devoted to female delinquents. Although there were some similarities in the findings — for example, in general, the same areas had high rates of both male and female delinquency — there were also differences: female delinquents were more concentrated in a few areas and the bulk of female delinquency was described as sexual. The significance of these differences for Shaw and McKay's theory was ignored.

Research in Britain has not found the same zonal pattern that exists in some American cities, but the general argument that certain areas within cities have higher delinquency rates than others is broadly supported (see, for example, Morris, 1957; Mays, 1954). In a detailed project carried out by Baldwin and Bottoms (1976) in Sheffield, 17 per cent (211) of the sample of offenders were female, but the bulk of the analysis was 'for convenience' (1976: 83) confined to male offenders. Regression analyses were carried out for five sub-samples including the sample of female offenders; from this, certain factors were highlighted, in particular, the significance of social class. The results for the sample of female offenders, however, were described as 'relatively disappointing' (1976: 119); social class explained only a small part of the variance in their delinquency rates and no other variable was significant. Two explanations for this were offered: the small size of the sample or 'a fundamentally different correlational pattern for females' (1976: 119). Neither explanation was explored further; nor was the significance for the findings on the male samples (who, after all, lived in the same neighbour-hoods). This perspective has referred generally to the need for re-education and the reconstruction of social values (see, for example, Morris 1957: 197—9); in this, the differential crime rates of men and women are ignored.

A linked perspective has been to view delinquent behaviour as a normal reaction to the norms and values of lower-class culture. Miller (1958), for example, believed that lower-class men had certain 'focal concerns'. He described these as trouble, toughness, smartness, excitement, fate and autonomy. He argued that simply by satisfying these values, men became involved in delinquency (for example, in fighting, gambling and drinking); that illegal behaviour was the expected response to certain common situations in lower-class life (for example, a threat to one's status) and that even when alternatives were available, crime was seen as offering more immediate results with less effort.

Miller's theory has been criticized because it does not adequately take into account middle-class delinquency.[6] Equally important is the question of how well the theory can account for female delinquency. Millers article focused on male delinquency and, according to Leonard (1982: 134), 'his thesis simply breaks down when applied to women'. Leonard's reason for rejecting Miller's explanation is her belief that women are unlikely to be as concerned as men with the focal concerns identified by Miller. She writes, 'once again, a sociologist has described a situation . . . in this case the focal concerns of an entire culture . . . which neglects to consider half the population' (1982: 134). I am not convinced that these concerns are irrelevant for women. The contexts in which they are played out may differ, but trouble, toughness, smartness, excitement, fate and autonomy are, as Matza and Sykes (1961) argue, concerns for all of us. Campbell's (1984) description of female gang members in New York certainly provides evidence of the similarity of their behaviour to that of male gang members. Both smoked 'grass', drank, fought, stole and 'partied'. More recently, Campbell (1986: 33) interviewed schoolgirls about fighting (which they were involved in more frequently than generally believed) and concluded that 'it may be no more than a demonstration of certain qualities (toughness, determination and positive self-concept)'. However, Miller's theory cannot take account of men and women's differential involvement in gangs or criminal behaviour, and, therefore, remains deficient. Similar points can be made with respect to British research which has also promoted the idea that delinquency is a culturally accepted form of behaviour in certain socially disadvantaged areas (such as that described by Mays (1954) in Liverpool and by Willmott (1966) and Downes (1966) in the East End of London).

Other theorists have emphasized the impact on crime rates of the structural inequalities which exist because of social class.[7] Merton (1938), for example, adapted Durkheim's notion of anomie — meaning a breakdown of laws or rules — to suggest that two elements in American culture interact to lead to potentially anomic conditions. These two elements are culturally defined goals (like wealth and success) and approved means to obtain these (that is, through work or education). According to Merton, American society tends to over-emphasize the goals without sufficient attention to the means. The pressure on all to succeed is strong, and failure to achieve this is seen as rooted in individual responsibility rather than in social sources. Such pressures are not apparent in caste systems (as in India) and are less apparent in class systems (as in Great Britain). With respect to the United States, Merton wrote, 'a cardinal American virtue — ambition — promotes a cardinal American vice — deviant behaviour' (1959: 146).[8]

Merton recognized class inequalities. He neglected, however, the structural inequalities which exist through sex. Logically, within Merton's theoretical framework, there should be at least as much crime by women as by men since opportunity structures are less open to them. There are two ways out of this dilemma: either women are socialized not to aspire to these goals or women's goals are different from men's.

Merton's major emphasis was on monetary success. Leonard (1982: 57) argues that 'he has forgotten at least half the population with this formulation'. She agrees with Ruth Morris (1964) that the goals of women are different from those of men: they are relational (the achievement of successful relationships with others) rather than financial. Such a view is based on stereotypical beliefs rather than on evidence.[9] Measures of men's and women's motivation to achieve show no real differences in score. (See Deaux, 1976 for an elaboration of this.)

In schools, girls achieve well initially; reduced achievement occurs for many only after they reach adolescence. This seems due partly to pressure on girls to adhere to traditional role definitions and partly to the internalization of the low expectations which our culture holds for them. But this does not mean that the goal or aspiration to succeed is abandoned; rather, it may mean that women experience conflict in these aspirations. Sharpe (1976), for example, asked schoolgirls what career they would like to follow. Their choices bore no relation to the *actual* distribution of women's work.

Horner (1970) introduced the concept of 'fear of success' and this is also relevant here. She suggested that many people, particularly women,[10] avoid success because they expect negative consequences if they do succeed. For women, these might include feelings of being 'unfeminine', a fear of being socially rejected by men or conflicts between a job and a family. Overall, Horner found that 65 per cent of the women she tested, but only 10 per cent of the men, told stories that indicated a fear of success. Later studies, however, show high figures for fear of success amongst men (Alper, 1974) and that fear of success depends on the particular situation (Deaux, 1976) rather than on the sex of the individual. For example, Weinreich-Haste (as reported in *New Society*, 30 August 1984: 218), gave 'story cues' to a sample of girls and boys about a young man or woman (matched to the respondent's own sex) who was training to be a nurse or an engineer and asked them to continue the story. The girls were more likely than the boys to describe success or recovery from failure in their stories; the boys were more inclined to describe failure. Weinreich-Haste concludes that there may have been more change in what is expected of girls than of boys; that is, girls may now be encouraged to succeed and to work in unusual fields. Thus, while earlier investigators saw achievement motivation as primarily a male phenomenon, more recent research suggests that women do strive to achieve. Stereotypes persist because of cultural time-lags and because few women have actually achieved responsible and powerful positions. Most women are concentrated in low-paid and low-status jobs. This, arguably, could also lead to an anomic situation. The fact that women may experience frustration in these ways was not considered by anomie theorists.

Merton also claimed that different goals could be substituted within his framework. If marriage is the apex of relational goals, most women achieve this; their goal is accessible. Hence one can argue that women do not experience the types of pressure and frustration experienced by men in the economic sphere. Leonard (1982: 59) concludes from this that anomie theory could explain women's low crime rate; simply being married and having children is all that they expect. She writes: 'women have very low aspirations and their goals are extremely accessible' (1982: 59). But the situation is more complex than this. Many marriages end in divorce and it is estimated that half of all marriages are touched by wife abuse. Because of the romanticized and idealized notions of marriage, it is plausible that the reality does result in frustration.

Leonard gets into further difficulties when she attempts to analyze the crimes which women appear to commit within her newly constructed goals/means (relationship/marriage) framework. Prostitution and shoplifting, she argues, are 'certainly not alternative means to the goal' (1982: 60). Thus she concludes that the framework simply does not work. Yet research on shoplifting (Argenent, 1981) points to the fact that items stolen by girls include clothes, cosmetics, jewellery and toiletries — which easily fits within a framework of attempting to improve desirability on the marriage market. Also, rather than consider prostitutes as retreatists (because they reject the accepted goals and means for women) or rebels (because their primary goal is financial success rather than marriage), as Leonard does, it makes more sense to discuss their crimes (and other crimes committed by women, for example, fraud and forgery) as part of Merton's *original* economic model. Providing for their children, for example, is commonly cited by prostitutes as a common motivation for their prostitution. It is only by accepting relationships rather than financial success as women's primary goal that Leonard can conclude, in her discussion of anomie, that '*nothing* helps us explain why women deviate in the way they do' (1982: 61, my emphasis). Leonard also seems puzzled that crime is more common among working-class women. The substitution of economic for relational goals readily explains this. But a question unanswered by anomie theorists remains: why is women's recorded crime rate not higher than men's?

Despite their sociological stance, these theories deny the meaning of actions for the actors themselves and ignore individual choice. (See Taylor, Walton and Young, 1973 for a detailed critique.) The theories are primarily concerned with one central issue: whether or not differences between criminals and non-criminals can be identified. The labelling or social reaction perspective is focused instead on the social reactions to delinquency. Writers in this school (for example, Becker, 1963; Lemert, 1972) believe crime to be normal and that if people persist in crime it is due to the negative effect of the police, courts and institutions on them. Exposing people to the criminal justice system is viewed as essentially counter-productive. By stigmatizing, punishing and criminalizing, it compounds the problem. Individuals become delinquent, therefore, not because of their behaviour or because they were predisposed to do so but because they are so labelled by someone in a position of power.[11]

Generally, this literature has also ignored women. For example, in Bryan's work (1973) on prostitutes, the pimps provided much of the information, and in Ball's ethnography of an abortion clinic (quoted in Millman, 1975), the female clients were neglected. Smart (1976) criticized this perspective for that reason. Rock (1977), however, responded by arguing that Becker's marihuana user was only 'nominally male' and that this was a mere literary convention — Becker's marihuana user was also not black, homosexual, a dwarf or a giant. This is a surprising statement since it suggests that the specific characteristics of the offender are irrelevant. As Smart replied in turn: 'The material conditions under which women and men . . . exist are not identical and these structural factors need to be accounted for in analyses of . . . deviant behaviour' (1977: 398). The sociology of deviance, therefore, remained male-oriented and male-defined;[12] only male deviants were interesting (Downes, 1978).

Conflict theorists explain differences in labelled criminality by reference to the relative powerlessness of certain groups; for example, the young and blacks. Such an explanation is problematic, however, when applied to women, for they are both powerless and not labelled as criminal as frequently as men. Rather than question the validity of this proposition, Turk explained sex differences as follows:

> The greater likelihood of female than male agreement with legal norms far outweighs relative powerlessness as a factor in accounting for lower female criminality rates . . . when we also recognise that a female's patterns of activity tend to be more restricted than those of males — implying both less opportunity to violate norms and less exposure to law enforcement — the conclusion is suggested that power, whatever its relation to sex may be, is of negligible explanatory value. (1969: 195)

But what evidence is there that women have more favourable attitudes to legal norms? Turk's own evidence is contradictory. For example, he found (1969: 155) that women were more critical of the police than men. This he called 'surprising' as it did not fit the facts (one would expect criticism of the police to lead to higher crime rates). Turk attempted to explain this paradox by suggesting (1969: 161) that these critical attitudes stem from the ineffectiveness of the police and the consequent threat to the maintenance of legal norms. That is, women, having a greater commitment to legal norms, are more concerned about the failure of law enforcement. But again we have to ask what evidence there is for this. Turk's theory fails to explain women's criminality and his attempt to offer an alternative explanation is strained, confused and empirically weak.

Box (1983) reverses Turk's argument and uses powerlessness to explain women's apparent lack of crime. By this he means that women are rarely in a position to commit crime, have few resources or opportunities to do so and experience a level of surveillance and social control which inhibits the commission of crime. Powerlessness, then, is used to explain crimes by men by one theorist and the lack of crime by women by another. There is no logic in this.

Marxist theorists not only said little explicitly about crime (cf. Bonger, 1916); they also said little explicitly about women. Engels, for example, painted a graphic picture of the 'comfortless, filthy house . . . ill-furnished . . . [in which] no domestic comfort is possible'. He recognized that both husband and wife were likely to work, and went on: 'What family life is possible under such conditions? Yet the working-*man* cannot escape from the family' (quoted in Cain and Hunt, 1979: 179, my emphasis). If these demoralizing influences acted on the working man more powerfully than usual, crime was said to be the result: 'Life has nothing to offer *him*; *he* is deprived of virtually all pleasures. Consequently *he* does not fear the penalties of law. Why should *he* restrain *his* wicked impulses? Why should *he* not take at least a part of this property for *himself*?' (quoted in Greenberg, 1981: 48, my emphasis). The impact of these conditions on women was not discussed, yet they were as oppressed[13] and as powerless as any within capitalism. Moreover, the sympathetic portrayal of men by Engels contrasts sharply with the language used to portray the effects of industrial conditions on women: 'The moral consequences of the employment of women in factories are even worse . . . not calculated for the favourable development of the female character . . . the language used . . . is characterised . . . as "indecent", "bad", "filthy" etc. . . . three-fourths of young factory employees . . . were unchaste' (quoted in Cain and Hunt, 1979: 181 – 2).

Modern Marxist theorists, on the other hand, have written extensively on crime (for example, Taylor, Walton and Young, 1973 and 1975) but they too have said little about women. Sex is not considered any more systematically in radical or critical criminology than in traditional criminology (cf. Klein and Kress, 1976). Such theorists neglect women as firmly as did their forebears. Heidensohn (1985) goes on to say that this is particularly devastating as she expected more of them. There are references in critical criminology to women's oppression in capitalist society and even suggestions for treating sexism as a crime, but the differential crime rates of men and women and the significance of this are not discussed. Taylor, Walton and Young (1973), for example, argue that only the acceptance of Marxist methods can fill the 'blank spots' left by other attempts to construct social theories of deviance. They are unaware of their own 'blank spot': women. There is not one word on women in their text and, despite a sharp critique of criminology, they do not notice the relevance or applicability to women of the theories reviewed. Hartmann (1981: 10) sums up such theorists' difficulty this way: 'marxist categories, like capital itself, are sex blind' (cf. the discussions in Sargent, 1981).

Some criminologists have taken account of criticisms of the male dominance of the subject, but it is usually no more than a token gesture. Hall and Scraton (1981), for example, in a review article of current debates in critical criminology, refer to the emergence of a feminist criminology but thereafter ignore any significance that this might have for the issues raised. For instance, reference is made to the economic marginalization of black youth (1981: 484), but not to the economic position of women generally or of black girls in particular. Similarly, they refer to the 'poor taking advantage of the poor' (1981: 485), but take no cognisance of men taking advantage of women. The point is not that 'women' should be discussed for the mere sake of it, but that their inclusion would enrich theoretically the points being explored by Hall and Scraton. Another example is Young's review of 'models of criminology' in the same text, in which he systematically compares theories 'on the central questions which any theory of order and criminality must tackle' (1981: 305). Young dutifully refers to 'he/she' and 'him/her' throughout. But the relevance or significance of gender for the theories reviewed is never explored. To borrow from Rock (1977), the use of such language *is* a mere literary convention. It has no impact on Young's subject matter.

A variant of this is Box's approach. The contrast between the first (1971) and second (1981) editions of *Deviance, Reality and Society* is interesting. There is nothing at all on women in the first. In the second, about a page on self-report studies by girls is included in the chapter on the social distribution of criminal behaviour, two 'caveats' — each no more than one and a half pages — are added to two further chapters and a small note on female inmates is added to another chapter. This is better than nothing. But women are presented as afterthoughts, not as integral to the arguments being developed in the chapters. Thus women appear as 'by the way' and peripheral. For all intents and purposes, they are not really there. (See also McRobbie and Garber's (1976) critique.)[14]

Misrepresenting Women

This is not to say that women are always ignored in criminological texts or theorizing. Sometimes women are represented or, more accurately, misrepresented[15] in superficial ways with brief, stereotypical and uncritical references to 'menopausal shoplifters' or to a 'new breed of aggressive female criminals'.[16]

Historically there is no doubt that men and women were seen as fundamentally and qualitatively different creatures. Women were seen as pure, passive, dependent, submissive, selfless, caring and gentle, but also as childlike, narcissistic, emotional, jealous, malicious, deceptive, sexual and unstable.[17] These images of women were reflected in images of criminal women.[18] The negative qualities inherent in all women were simply more apparent in criminal women for they had not been 'neutralized' by such factors as piety and maternity. Lombroso and Ferrero (1895), for example, referred to the 'innocuous and semi-criminal personality' present in all women. The criminal woman, though acknowledged to be a rarity, was also often viewed as worse than her male counterpart. Mary Carpenter, for example, wrote: 'When a woman has thrown aside the virtuous restraints of society, and is enlisted on the side of evil, she is far more dangerous to society than the other sex' (1864: 32). And Hartman quotes a newspaper article on Constance Kent who was accused in 1860 of murdering her half-brother: 'It was a wanton murder, not done by the hand of a man, for there was a *finesse* of cruelty about it that no man, we believe, however depraved, could have been guilty of: but it is the revengeful act of a woman . . . morbid, cruel, cunning' (1977: 126, emphasis in the original). In similar terms, according to Adam, the female criminal was: 'almost entirely devoid of any gentle or redeeming trait; some are in baseness, cunning, callousness, cruelty and persistent criminality far worse than the worst male offender known to the law' (1914: 3– 4). He also believed that the cruellest forms of crime were committed by women.

Somewhat paradoxically, there was an alternative imagery: the criminal woman was not really a woman. The maternal instinct in criminal women, for example, was viewed as weak because, according to Lombroso and Ferrero, 'psychologically and anthrop-ologically she belongs more to the male than the female sex' (1895: 153). The author of an article on 'The Criminal' in *Westminster Review* for July 1898 wrote in similar terms: 'criminal women approximate very much in physical character to men; they are usually of a masculine type' (p. 87). Freud (1925 and 1933) also believed criminal women to be neurotic, maladjusted, sexual misfits who were not content with their roles of wife and mother. Their behaviour was said to result from a failure to develop healthy feminine attitudes and from a wish to be a man. On occasions, these two images — the female criminal had the worst characteristics of women and all the qualities of men — were combined. Again to quote Lombroso and Ferrero (1895), 'as a double exception, the criminal woman is consequently a monster'.

This imagery of women and criminal women is not just of historical relevance; idealized and simplified stereotypes of appropriate behaviour for men and women persist and continue to influence criminological theory. The thrust of Freda Adler's argument, for example, was that in the 1970s women were behaving more like men — 'virilized', in her terms (1975: 87). She referred to 'the increasing number of women who are using guns, knives, and wits to establish themselves as full human beings, as capable of violence and aggression as any man' (1975: 15). And sociologists of deviance, though critical of conventional criminology in many respects, continued to view criminal women as acting like stereotypical women: they fell in love with deviant men, were out of control of their emotions, or used sex exploitatively but not that differently from other women (Millman, 1975). These stereotypes also influence current practice in the criminal justice system. As recently as June 1986, Mr Justice Boreham, while sentencing two women convicted of conspiracy to cause explosions, described Martina Anderson as a hard, cynical young woman 'stripped of humanity' and Ella O'Dwyer as having 'sunk to the depths of inhumanity' (*Guardian*, 24 June 1986). And much of the emphasis in women's prisons is to re-form the women in a domestic mould: to train them to be good wives and mothers.

In fact, these stereotypical images affect discussions of women and crime in a number of ways. They are used to explain:

> the lack of criminal behaviour in women (through the particular nature of their socialisation and through the restrictions imposed on them in marriage and in the family);
>
> why women engage in criminal behaviour (for example, under-socialization or role frustration);
>
> the types of crimes women commit (for example, prostitution and shoplifting) and the nature of their participation (for example, as assistants or instigators);
>
> the labelling of certain women as criminal (for example, where women have breached role expectations by acting aggressively);
>
> the rejection of certain women as victims (for example, assaults on hitchhikers, though not explicitly justified, are to be expected);
>
> the responses to both female offenders and female victims in the criminal justice system; and
>
> the kind of work in the criminal justice system thought appropriate for women.

I critically examine the impact of these images in subsequent chapters. For the moment, two brief examples will suffice to demonstrate my point. Pollak (1961) explained women's low crime rate, as reflected in the official statistics, with reference to their inherently deceitful nature which he rooted in their ability to conceal their lack of sexual arousal. He took no account of the way in which sexuality is structured by culture or of power relationships between men and women. (See Smart, 1976 for an elaboration of this.) A further example is the large number of rape allegations which are treated as unfounded by the police. In part, this stems from assumptions about women generally and about the rape victim in particular — 'she asked for it', 'rape is impossible' and so on. Little evidence exists for these claims (Clark and Lewis, 1977).

Another point needs to be made here. These stereotypical conceptions tend to idealize white and middle-class characteristics and ignore racial and class dimensions. 'Being a woman' is not a clear, single conceptual category; prospects, situations and experiences differ. Nevertheless, in the criminological literature, the term 'woman' tends to be synonymous with 'white woman': for example, in discussions of women's lower official crime rate or of women's lenient treatment by the courts. Focusing on gender *per se* blinds us to these different experiences and to the significance of the interaction of gender with such factors as race, class and age. Experience of racial prejudice, for example, is an integral part of 'being black' and black women's experiences of crime and in the criminal justice system obviously differ from white women's because of this. I attempt to explore these issues in subsequent chapters; data are not always available, however. In the criminological literature, 'being black' tends to be synonymous with 'being a black man'. Pitts (1986), for example, in his discussion of 'black young people and juvenile crime', ignores girls. Writings on class and crime have also focused on men.

A Feminist Criminology?

There have, of course, been changes in criminology since the mid-1970s — primarily due to an increase in the number of women writing about and carrying out research on women and crime — and a 'feminist criminology' is said to have emerged. This phrase, however, begs many questions, not least what it is and what it can contribute.[19] This lack of clarity is demonstrated in the debate between Greenwood (1981) and Smart (1981). Does feminist criminology include criminologists who are feminist, female criminologists or criminologists who study women? Or does it depend on the topic researched, the politics of the researchers or the method of research? A concrete example of the confusion is provided by Heidensohn's (1985) discussion of the association between the women's movement and crime which she presents as part of the contribution of feminist criminology. She discusses the work of Adler (1975) and Simon (1975) who assert this association and then the critiques of their work by Box (1983) and Steffensmeier (1978). It is not at all clear from Heidensohn's text who the 'feminist criminologists' are. Initially I assumed she meant Box and Steffensmeier, but it seems that Heidensohn meant Adler and Simon, as she concluded: 'in the least helpful way to women offenders . . . one branch of feminist criminology has at last made female crime visible' (1985: 160). The label 'feminist criminology', therefore, confused rather than clarified the issue.

Another example of this is Carlen's (1985) statement that attempts to establish a feminist criminology have not been very successful. She gives two reasons for this: first, many feminist writers have viewed crime as essentially a male activity and, secondly, attempts to identify a global theory of crime (which would apply to both men and women) or a special theory of women's crime are theoretically unsound. As support for her first proposition, Carlen cites Adler (1975) and Simon (1975), as did Heidensohn (1985). My response is the same. The writings of Adler and Simon do not constitute a feminist criminology. Carlen's second argument is really a criticism of criminology generally (which, in any case, has been notoriously unsuccessful in these endeavours) rather than of feminist criminology – however constituted – in particular.

In 1976, Smart discussed the possibility of formulating a feminist criminology. By 1981, she viewed the task as redundant. There were, she wrote, 'more important goals to achieve than the one of constructing a sub-discipline to rank alongside other criminologies' (1981: 86). Heidensohn (1985) agrees with this. She concluded her text by stating that the best way of understanding women and crime is not through feminist criminology but through 'using insights into the role, position and social control of women which can be derived from other studies of women's oppression' (1985: 197). It is true that social control mechanisms can operate differently on men and women and that there are some which only women experience; for example, the double standard of morality and such ideological constructs as 'lady' and 'nice girl'. The impact of these in the criminal justice system is considered in subsequent chapters. It is also common to assert that women are controlled through informal mechanisms (or in the private sphere) and that men are controlled through formal mechanisms (or in the public sphere) (Hagan, Simpson and Gillis, 1979; Smart and Smart, 1978). This is an over-simplification. Men and women are both controlled by such mechanisms as the family, marriage, work and concepts of 'masculinity' and 'femininity'. Moreover, focusing on the social control of women leaves unresolved the question of women's crimes and raises, by implication, the spectre of pathological reasons for their criminality. I agree with Smart for a different reason: feminism can inform criminology and should, therefore, be an element of the mainstream discipline.

Feminism, however, is not one thing; it is not a unified set of principles and practices. At the very least, 'radical', 'socialist' and 'bourgeois' feminism can be distinguished. Nor is criminology a unified set of principles and practice. Thus *a* feminist criminology cannot exist. Feminists who are criminologists reflect the tensions and differences which exist within these perspectives. Some argue that women and men should be dealt with equally in the criminal justice system (for example, Moulds, 1980); others believe that there are differences between men and women which justify differential treatment (for example, Smart and Brophy, 1985). Some reject the notion of fundamental differences between men and women (for example, Adler, 1975); others argue that women's personality is different from men's (for example, Gilligan, 1982). Feminism informs my approach in a number of ways. It makes me anti-positivist, aware of the sexism of conventional 'wisdom', conscious of the need to make women visible and reject the supposed neutrality of the discipline. I know whose side I am on; I know what it is to be afraid, to feel oppressed. My concern, therefore, lies unequivocally with women — whether as victims, offenders, prisoners or policewomen — and I am writing explicitly as a woman.[20] To paraphrase Ann Jones (1980: xvi) the story of women and crime is the story of women. But my intention is not merely to insert 'women' into discussions about crime or the criminal justice system. Although this book is about women, and the experiences of women are central to it,[21] it is also both a correction of, and a complement to, the criminology of men. The study of women and crime ultimately contributes to our knowledge about crime.[22] For example, sexual violence will be better understood by attempting to understand both the offender's and the victim's experience. I am not proposing an androgynous criminology because that would ignore gender, but rather a criminology which considers gender important and alongside such factors as race, age and class.

2

Gender Differences in Crime

Introduction

There is a tension in the literature on women and crime about the appropriate focus of concern. Two distinct questions are often intermingled: why do women commit crime? and why do women not commit crime? These questions presuppose that there is a clear picture of women's crimes; there is not. This chapter explores three prior questions:

> Are there differences in the amount of crime committed by men and women?
> Are there differences in the kind of crimes committed by men and women?
> Are there recent changes in the amount and kind of crimes committed by women?

The answers to these questions are not straightforward and depend, in part, on the data source referred to. I will examine three such sources: official statistics, self-report studies and observational and experimental research.

How Much Crime?

Sex differences in crimes have been described as so sustained and so marked as to be, perhaps, the most significant feature of recorded crime (Wootton, 1959; Heidensohn, 1985). Certainly, historical records reveal a disparity between the sexes (Beattie, 1975; Wiener, 1975[1]) and more recent statistics in a variety of jurisdictions demonstrate that recorded crime is overwhelmingly a male activity (Hindelang, 1971; Farrington, 1981; Christiansen and Jensen, 1972). For example, Wadsworth (1979) found in the British National Survey that 18 per cent of men but only 2.5 per cent of women had been convicted or cautioned before their 21st birthday and Farrington (1981), using Home Office statistics, calculated that 12 per cent of men but only 2 per cent of women were likely to be convicted of an offence by the age of seventeen and that 44 per cent of men but only 15 per cent of women were likely to be convicted of offences at some time in their lives.

In 1985, in England and Wales,[2] a mere 17 per cent of those found guilty or cautioned for a notifiable offence were female.[3] The percentage of women arrested for crime-index offences in the United States is broadly similar (US Department of Justice, 1984). Women also have fewer previous convictions than men. A recent Home Office Statistical Bulletin (1986a) indicated that a much higher proportion of convicted women are first offenders than is so for men: 60 per cent of the women convicted in 1982 were first offenders compared with 35 per cent of men convicted in that year.

Other factors, of course, influence the male:female ratio in recorded crime, notably the nature of the offence committed: women are more involved in some crimes than others. Table 2.1 demonstrates this.

Factors such as age, class and race also affect the male:female ratio in crime, yet it is difficult to obtain these data, especially for the same sample. The official statistics in England and Wales

TABLE 2.1   MALE: FEMALE RATIO FOR SELECTED OFFENCES

Offence	*Male: female ratio*
Violence against the person	9:1
Burglary	26:1
Robbery	14:1
Theft and handling	3:1
Fraud and forgery	3:1
Shoplifting	1.5:1
Prostitution	0:13, 354

Source: Home Office, 1986a

provide data on sex and age. Table 2.2 shows that certain age-groups are more involved in recorded crime than others.

The English criminal statistics give no information on the race or class of offenders. (Recent prison statistics, however, indicate that black women are over-represented there (Home Office Statistical Bulletin, 1986b). In the United States, arrests for crime-index offences are recorded by the age, race and sex of offenders, but not as cross-tabulations. Thus the interaction of age, race and sex cannot be examined.

So far I have assumed that the picture suggested by the criminal statistics is valid. It may not be. First, there are many technical problems in the construction of the criminal statistics. Law-enforcement practices vary from one area to another, from one year to another, and so on (Wiles, 1970; Box, 1981). But more important than this, the recording of an event in the criminal statistics is the outcome of a sequence of social and psychological processes. First, the act must be perceived by someone, for example, the victim; then it must be classified or defined as an event of a certain kind (an assault, a joke, an argument and so on). Assuming it is defined as a criminal act, the individual must then decide whether or not to report it to the police. There are many reasons for not so reporting: triviality of the offence, a belief that the police could do nothing, embarrassment, fear, laziness and the like (Hough and Mayhew, 1983 and 1985). If it is reported to the police a separate process of redefinition takes place. If they agree that the act is illegal or worth bothering about, the act is recorded in the criminal statistics (McCabe and Sutcliffe, 1978; Chatterton, 1983). At each stage, there is a wastage element: collectively this represents 'the dark figure' of crime — crimes not

TABLE 2.2   MALE: FEMALE RATIO FOR NOTIFIABLE OFFENCES, BY AGE

Age (years)	*Male: female ratio*
10 to 14	3:1
14 to 17	4:1
17 to 21	7:1
All ages	5:1

Source: Home Office, 1986a

reported by victims or observers to the police and crimes not recorded by the police. The dark figure of crime is large. The British Crime Surveys estimated that the crime rate was three to four times larger than that recorded (Hough and Mayhew, 1983 and 1985), although it varied enormously according to the type of crime.

To determine the sex of the offender another step must be taken: detection. Only 35 per cent of indictable offences were cleared up in England and Wales in 1985. Observational studies of police officers (Piliavin and Briar, 1964; Reiss, 1971) demonstrate the extent to which they rely on cues derived from dress, demeanour, on what they know or believe about the individual's previous record, and on stereotypical conceptions of 'bad' or 'troublesomeness' in their decision whether or not to arrest. Sex may, directly or indirectly, be a factor taken into account in this decision. This is discussed further in chapter 4. The point here is that crime and the criminal statistics are constructed and we have to consider whether they are constructed in ways which conceal or misrepresent crimes committed by women.

Pollak (1961) argues that discrepancies in the criminal statistics are more apparent than real. There are three planks to his argument. First, he suggests that the behaviour of men is criminalized more readily than the behaviour of women. It is difficult to think of examples of this. Mannheim (1965) suggests that if quarrelling and lying were criminal offences this would alter the statistical picture, but Mannheim is making an unfounded and stereotypical assumption about women. There is no evidence of which I am aware that such acts are more common amongst women. Certain offences in England and Wales can currently be committed only by men: for example, the definition of rape and indecent exposure both refer to the penis. But in many states in the United States, rape has been redefined as sexual battery and its legal definition is sex-neutral. Also, an English woman who sexually assaults a man or exposes her body is committing an offence: indecent assault, conduct likely to lead to a breach of the peace or whatever. Pollak, therefore, goes too far − similar behaviour by *either* sex can be regulated by the criminal law. On the other hand, there are examples of offences in which the legal definition is sex-neutral, but which are *enforced* primarily against one sex. Prostitution and status or 'moral danger' offences (a category which conceals a concern about the sexual activity of adolescent girls) are examples of this. The dominance of women in these categories reflects differences not in the behaviour of the sexes, but in social responses to that behaviour. For example, the clients of prostitutes are often ignored in the policing of prostitution (though this is changing, at least in some states in the United States).

Pollak's second argument is that women are more prominent than men in the dark figure. He sees women as inherently deceitful and cunning and, therefore, as more able to conceal their crimes. As 'evidence', he points to the large dark figure in abortion, theft by prostitutes and child abuse. This is a valid point (though it is not at all certain that these offences are more often committed by women). But the assumption that the dark figure of men's crime is low is simply not plausible. There are clearly large dark figures in certain male-dominated offences: wife assault and rape, for instance.

A linked view is that women instigate rather than perpetrate criminal acts and remain in the background because of this. Lucas, for example, believed that influencing every criminal there was some woman who, unseen, had 'helped to write the most startling pages in the annals of crime' (1926: 88). Earlier, Adam (1914: 15) referred to women's 'ascendancy' and 'mastery' over men: 'the leading spirit in the criminal enterprise'.[4] These claims lack empirical support and, like Pollak's views, have their roots in the supposedly deceitful and cunning nature of women.

Pollak further suggests that victims tend not to report female offenders to the police[5] and that, consequently, female offenders are more likely to remain in the dark figure. Victimization surveys[6] provide a means for exploring the nature of the dark figure and for assessing the extent to which official statistics are reliable. Hindelang (1979) examined American victimization data between 1972 and 1976. He found that the victims of female offenders did report them to the police less often than was true for the victims of male offenders.[7] When respondents were asked if they had reported their crimes to the police, half of those victimized by men, but only one-third of those victimized by women, said yes. But Hindelang also found that the crimes committed by men were more serious than those committed by women. For example, men dominated in such offences as commercial robbery, and this was always referred to the police. The importance of the nature of the offences was also highlighted in an earlier project by Hindelang (1974). The decision whether or not to report shoplifters to the police was related to the value of the object stolen, what was stolen and the method of theft. The implication from this was that the lower referral rates of women to the police could be explained by the fact that they stole items of less value and in a non-professional way. Gibbens and Prince's (1962) research found much the same for a sample of men and women convicted of shoplifting in London in the 1960s. Taken together, these projects indicate that it is mainly *minor* offences which remain in the dark figure rather than *women's* offences. (See also Hough and Mayhew, 1985.)

On the other hand, certain offenders may be more readily reported to the police than others. Statistics produced by the Metropolitan Police (Home Office Statistical Bulletin, 1983) showed that, where victims of crimes against the person were able to classify the ethnic appearance of the offender, the offender was identified as black in a higher proportion of cases than would have been expected from the ethnic composition of the population. This could mean that black offenders tend to commit this kind of offence; but it could also mean that black offenders are more readily reported to the police than white offenders. Stevens and Willis (1979: 37) lend some support to this suggestion. Their data on reported crimes of violence showed that white victims were more willing to report to the police crimes which left them uninjured when the offender was black. This research did not consider the sex of offenders but it is possible that victims also more readily report to the police black female offenders. Young (1980) found this to be so in the United States.

Criminologists have also attempted to explore the dark figure of crime by studies of self-admissions of delinquent behaviour (Short and Nye, 1958; Gold, 1970; Wise, 1967; Jensen and Eve, 1976; Hindelang, 1971; Mawby, 1980; Campbell, 1981; Riley, 1986).[8] These suggest that although the male:female ratio in criminal behaviour is much closer, it is still predominantly a male activity. For example, Riley and Shaw (1985) surveyed a sample of 14- and 15-year-olds. They showed that while the admission rates were quite close — 49 per cent of the boys and 39 per cent of the girls admitted offending in the past year — delinquency was more prevalent among boys. Self-report studies also indicate that the male:female ratio for frequent delinquency is several times higher than for occasional delinquency (Hindelang, 1971; Sarri, 1983). This is consistent with the official picture of crime.

Self-report studies have explored the relationship between crime and race, and crime and social class (for a review, see Box, 1981) and these findings also confirm to some extent the reliability of the official statistics (Elliott and Ageton, 1980). However, few studies have considered race, class, age and gender simultaneously. What we can say from American data is that black and working-class girls commit more offences than white and middle-class girls (Ageton, 1983a), that black girls are less delinquent than black boys and that white girls are less delinquent than white boys (Jensen and Eve, 1976).

One reason suggested for the apparent sex differences in criminal behaviour is that men and women have different opportunities to commit crime. Simon (1975), for example, argued that the propensities of men and women to commit crimes do not differ, but that women have not had the same opportunities as men to do so. There are now a few experimental studies which examine what happens when people have the opportunity to act dishonestly.

Farrington and Knight carried out a number of what are called 'lost letters' experiments (1979 and 1980). In these, a series of letters were dropped, in which certain conditions were manipulated: the amount of money enclosed, the form of the money (cash or postal order) and the apparent victim (an old lady or an affluent man). The characteristics of the person who picked up the letter were observed and the experimenters knew from a code number whether a particular letter was posted or retained. Stealing was most common when cash was involved and the victim was an affluent man. Female subjects, however, were as likely to steal as male subjects. There was one exception: where larger amounts of money were involved. Nearly half of the male subjects stole in this situation compared with less than a quarter of the female subjects. Though these findings are interesting, such experiments are not simply tests of honesty: factors such as forgetfulness or laziness may have influenced the behaviour. Thus we need to know more about the context of the actions and the meaning of them for the actors. We need also to know more about the interaction of sex with such factors as class, age and race.

Another kind of experiment conducted by Farrington and others (1977 and 1980) was offering money to persons in the street and asking whether or not they had dropped it. Here, more than a third dishonestly claimed that the money was theirs, and women were slightly, but not significantly, more likely than men to accept the money. According to Farrington et al., the subjects could not have genuinely believed the money to have been theirs, but it is possible that the female subjects were more likely to accept the money for reasons other than dishonesty. Their socialization, for example, may have made them more willing to please, more deferential, more receptive to the suggestions of others (particularly where the questioner was male) than men. Again, the context and meaning of the action is important.

In part, Simon's (1975) argument is that women are no more moral than men. Studies of moral attitudes to such items as gambling, smoking, lying, stealing, pre-marital sex and drugs, however, present contradictory findings: Wright and Cox (1971) found virtually no difference in attitudes between the sexes. Maccoby (1967), on the other hand, cites eight studies and in all but one of them girls or women were found to have a stronger moral code than boys or men. Similar contradictions are apparent in research on cheating. Medinnus (1966) found that boys cheated more than girls on a ray-gun task, but Grinder (1961) found no such difference on self-reported rates of reading. Feldman (1977) concluded his review of this literature by suggesting that men's and women's responses to temptations are much less clear than the official statistics on crime would lead us to expect. These studies indicate that opportunities and particular social contexts are important in affecting both men's and women's criminal behaviour.

What Kind of Crime?

The male:female ratios in recorded crime already referred to tell us something about the kind of crimes committed by men and women. Table 2.3 provides further detail. From this, it is apparent that, overall, women are more likely to be involved in property

TABLE 2.3 PERCENTAGE OF OFFENDERS FOUND GUILTY AT ALL COURTS, OR CAUTIONED, BY TYPE OF OFFENCE, SEX AND AGE

	Men					Women				
Offence	*All ages*	*10–14*	*14–17*	*17–21*	*21 and over*	*All ages*	*10–14*	*14–17*	*17–21*	*21 and over*
Violence against the person	10	4	8	12	12	6	3	8	7	5
Sexual offences	2	1	2	1	2	a	a	a	a	a
Burglary	17	20	22	21	11	3	4	4	5	2
Robbery	1	a	1	1	1	a	a	a	a	a
Theft and handling stolen goods	50	69	60	47	45	79	91	84	70	75
Fraud and forgery	4	1	1	3	7	6	1	2	9	9
Criminal damage	3	4	3	3	2	1	1	1	1	1
Other (incl. motoring offences)	13	a	3	11	20	5	a	a	7	8
TOTAL	100	99	100	100	100	100	100	99	99	100

a Less than half of one per cent.
Source: Home Office, 1986a

offences than in violent offences. But this is so for men too. Also, just as there are probably variations in the amount of crime committed by women depending on their class, race and age, common sense tells us that there will also be variations in the kind of crimes committed by women in different classes, races and age-groups. This has not yet been fully investigated and the data are patchy, but table 2.3 demonstrates slight variations in recorded crimes according to age. For example, 8 per cent of offences attributed to 14- to 17-year-old girls were offences of violence against the person, compared with only 3 per cent for the 10 to 14 age-group. Von Hentig (1940), in an analysis of American data, found that black women exhibited higher rates of homicide and aggravated assault than white women. More recent data from self-report studies of delinquency confirm this with respect to assaults (Jensen and Eve, 1976; Ageton, 1983a); and Laub and McDermott (1985) reached similar conclusions from an analysis of victimization data. Self-report studies of delinquency also indicate that black girls are less involved than white girls in drug and alcohol use and in defying parental authority (Cernkovich and Giordano, 1979) and in minor theft (Jensen and Eve, 1976). Working-class girls in Ageton's (1983a) sample also reported considerable involvement in violent crime.

Recorded statistics tell us nothing about the 'quality' of crime. Legal labels conceal a wide variety of activities and so it is difficult to tell from them whether women's crime is less serious than men's. Research can help answer this question. Studies of shoplifting, for example, suggest that women steal fewer items and items of less value than men (Buckle and Farrington, 1984) and are viewed less often than men as 'commercial' or 'professional' shoplifters (Cameron, 1964; Gibbens and Prince, 1962; Hindelang, 1974). Franklin (1979) found much the same in her study of embezzlement: 81 per cent of the women, compared with 50 per cent of the men, embezzled less than $150. Violence by women also differs from that committed by men. Victims are most often members of the woman's family or those with whom she has an affectionate relationship. In McClintock's (1963) analysis of convicted violent offenders, most of the women (who made up less than 7 per cent of the sample) were convicted of attacks on their own families or neighbours. (See also Gibson and Klein, 1961 and 1969; McClintock and Avison, 1968; Gelles, 1979.) In a different context, Campbell (1984) found that fights by female gang members were primarily the result of domestic or romantic disputes.

McClintock and Avison (1968) suggested further differences, namely that women were involved in their criminal activities with male offenders, rather than on their own or with female associates, and that their role was more passive than men's, for example, keeping watch.[9] These claims have not been fully investigated and some research rebuts them. Block (1979), in an interesting account of women in organized crime in New York in the 1930s, lists a series of influential female criminals who, though sometimes married to men in organized crime, themselves played active roles. He asserts that organized crime was not as sexually segregated as traditional accounts suggest. Fortune et al. (1980) found that a third of their imprisoned female robbers had acted on their own, or with female accomplices, and although most terrorist operations are directed and executed by men (Russell and Miller, 1978), there are clear exceptions. Ulrike Meinhof founded the Baader—Meinhof group and the majority of the members of that organization were said to be female. A number of women involved with the IRA have been convicted of terrorist offences in England and have been sentenced on a par with male terrorists. This indicates that the courts viewed them as playing an active and independent part in the offences.

The offence most commonly attributed to women, especially to girls, is shoplifting. In 1985, half of the women sentenced for indictable offences in the magistrates' courts were shoplifters compared with 16 per cent of men. The percentages for juveniles were similar: for 10- to 14-year-olds it was 53 per cent of girls compared with 20 per cent of boys, and for 14- to 17-year-olds it was 44 per cent and 14 per cent respectively. And although prostitution now makes up only a small part of women's crime, the number of recorded offences related to prostitution is much higher for women than for men (9,161 women but *no* men were found guilty of such offences in 1985). Such figures have led researchers to link women's crime to women's traditional role, that is, to describe such offences as role-expressive (Smart, 1976). Put simply, the argument is that women shop and so shoplifting is an extension of their normal role; that women exchange sex in marriage for security and so prostitution is again an extension of their normal role. Thus assumptions about women's behaviour influence assumptions about the crimes they commit.

I will examine in chapter 3 the adequacy of this kind of explanation. In brief, it is questionable how helpful it is to categorize such offences as predominantly 'masculine' or 'feminine',[10] and to then go on to describe these crimes as simply functions of 'masculinity' or 'femininity' confuses complex processes. For the purposes of this chapter, all we need to determine is whether women are in fact more involved in prostitution and shoplifting than men. Clearly, women are more commonly labelled prostitutes or criminalized in the interaction,[11] but the actual behaviour objected to requires two persons, usually one man and one woman, and the female prostitute services a number of male clients. Moreover, according to Allen (1980), in the United States male prostitution is as common as female prostitution. More men than women, therefore, are 'involved' in prostitution. Similarly, shoplifting is not numerically more common amongst women and girls than men and boys, even in the criminal statistics[12] and, if we take into consideration the sex of those who use stores, there is even less reason to call shoplifting a woman's crime. The claim that shoplifting is an offence committed mainly by women is a myth, but one which persists.[13]

Research also suggests that women may be over-represented in recorded offences of shoplifting. Buckle and Farrington (1984), for example, summarized a series of observational studies on shoplifting which produced interesting, though conflicting, findings. In brief, research in the United States (Astor, 1971) and in Ireland (Marks, 1975) produced higher rates of shoplifting than research in England (Group 4, 1972; Buckle and Farrington, 1984) and the American and Irish research also found that women had higher shoplifting rates than men. This is in contrast to the British findings: in Buckle and Farrington's study, men were twice as likely to shoplift as women. Shoplifting, of course, was rarely observed by them. Out of 503 shoppers, only nine shoplifted: four men and five women. As a percentage of those observed, however, it was 2.8 per cent of men and 1.4 per cent of women. These numbers are very small, but the research has been replicated elsewhere and the findings were similar (Buckle and Farrington, unpublished). This raises the issue that women may figure to a great extent in shoplifting statistics because store detectives, sales-persons and the like *expect* women to shoplift because of preconceived notions of 'menopausal' or 'kleptomaniac' women and thus they *observe* women more carefully. This obviously increases women's chances of detection.

Some support for the suggestion that women are over-represented amongst detected shoplifters comes from another source: self-report studies of delinquency. Campbell (1981) contrasted her findings on girls' admission rates with those of West and Farrington's (1973) for boys. In response to the question, 'Have you taken things from big stores or supermarkets when the shop was open?', 12 per cent of the girls and 28 per cent of the boys responded positively. The disparity was similar with respect to taking things from 'little shops': 20 per cent and 40 per cent respectively. The male:female ratio for juveniles cautioned or sentenced for shoplifting in 1985, on the other hand, was 1.7:1.

While official data give the impression of different patterns of delinquency involvement by boys and girls, self-report delinquency data suggest quite the opposite. Generally, they suggest that the pattern of boys' and girls' delinquency is broadly similar. They also suggest, however, that boys are more involved in serious offences than girls. For example, Sarri (1983) found that whereas the male:female ratio for alcohol use, marihuana use and truancy was about 1:1, in more serious offences, the ratio widened. For example, in theft of up to $500, it was 8.5:1.

Riley and Shaw's (1985) survey of 14- and 15-year-olds presents a similar picture for England, as table 2.4 demonstrates. Riley and Shaw attempted to explain their findings by arguing that for offences which there was a more or less equal opportunity to commit, the prevalence rate was as high among girls as boys. But for those acts which were more likely to occur as part of an unstructured group activity, the prevalence rate was higher for boys — about 3:1. Thus they are suggesting that differential opportunities shape not only the amount of crime committed by men and women, but also its nature. (See also Hoffman-Bustamente, 1973.)

The criminal statistics show higher rates of violence among men than women and it is commonly believed that men are more aggressive than women. (See Rutter and Giller, 1983 for a review.) Fighting by girls, however, is much more common than it is thought to be. Campbell (1986) asked a sample of schoolgirls

TABLE 2.4   SEX DIFFERENCES IN SELF-REPORTED OFFENDING
(MALE:FEMALE RATIOS BASED ON NUMBER ADMITTING HAVING
COMMITTED THE OFFENCE AT LEAST ONCE IN THE PAST 12 MONTHS)

Offence	*Male: female ratio*
Damaged seats on buses or trains	0.4:1
Written or sprayed paint on buildings	0.6:1
Stolen something from family or relatives	0.9:1
Made hoax 999 call	1.0:1
Travelled on bus or train without paying correct fare	1.1:1
Shoplifted something worth less than £1	2.1:1
Smashed bottles in the street	2.6:1
Carried a weapon	2.8:1
Bought stolen goods	3.3:1
Broke windows in an empty house	3.6:1

Source: Riley and Shaw 1985

about their experience of fighting. Almost all admitted to having been involved in a fight: just over a quarter had been involved in more than six fights.[14] On the other hand, only a few had ever been involved with the police over their fights and even fewer had been referred to the juvenile court for their behaviour. The majority rejected the statement 'I think fighting is only for boys.'

Observational studies of aggressive behaviour tend to confirm the criminal statistics and show men to be more aggressive than women. However, Caplan (1975) disputes this simple conclusion in a fascinating review of the literature on male/female differences in antisocial behaviour. While it is true that a considerable body of research points to differences between boys and girls in violent behaviour there is also research which finds no differences. Caplan highlights the fact that it is only when an adult is present that differences in violent behaviour appear. For example, Madsen (1968) observed pre-school children's aggressive behaviour after they viewed a film of a model behaving aggressively. No adult was present. Although the nature of the aggression displayed by the boys and girls differed (the girls were less imitative), the amount of aggression displayed did not. On the other hand, Bandura et al.

(1966) found that when an adult asked children to imitate the aggressive behaviour they had just seen in a film, the boys imitated more aggressive behaviour in the presence of the experimenter than the girls. Similarly, Martin et al. (1971) showed children an aggressive model and then involved them in play either with an adult or peer observer or with no observer. Girls were generally less aggressive than boys but the inhibiting effect of the adult observer was greater for girls. This raises an interesting question: are girls, in fact, less aggressive? Or are boys and girls, at least in their early years, equally aggressive? Girls may learn that adults do not approve of such behaviour *for them*. If this is so, girls would be more easily influenced than boys by the presence of an adult, who, presumably, would be critical of their aggression. I return to this point in chapter 3.

Changes in Crime

In the 1960s and 1970s, there was concern about increases in women's crime and changes in its nature. It was suggested by some (Adler, 1975) that a new breed of violent female criminal was emerging. Adler linked these changes to the women's movement and I will discuss this in chapter 3. For the moment, I wish to examine the statistical basis of the claim.

It is always problematic to contrast criminal statistics over time, because this magnifies the problems mentioned earlier with respect to interpreting annual criminal statistics. However, if we look at the number of persons found guilty or cautioned per 100,000 population, this has increased for all age-groups in England and Wales over the past 20 years[15] and the rate of increase is higher for women than for men. Table 2.5 shows this. Overall, the rate of known offending for men has almost doubled over this period; for women it has more than doubled. However, there are considerable differences between the sexes in the rate of increase within different age-groups. For example, the known rate of offending of 10- to 14-year-old boys has increased only slightly; the rate for girls in this age-group has increased almost threefold. In the 14 to 17 age-group, the rate for boys in 1985 is almost twice that in 1965; for girls it is almost three times larger. On the other hand, for those aged 21 and over, the rate of increase

TABLE 2.5 NUMBER OF PERSONS FOUND GUILTY AT ALL COURTS, OR CAUTIONED FOR INDICTABLE OFFENCES, PER 100,000 POPULATION

	Men					Women				
Year	All ages	10–14	14–17	17–21	21 and over	All ages	10–14	14–17	17–21	21 and over
1965[a]	1,262	2,741	4,481	3,594	681	184	397	683	333	125
1975[a]	2,072	3,522	7,861	6,689	1,101	398	894	1,514	889	248
1985	2,297	3,231	8,128	7,241	1,328	443	1,048	2,018	1,055	254

[a] For these years the figures represent numbers of offenders found guilty or cautioned per 100,000. The criminal statistics no longer present this data but it is broadly equivalent to the number of persons found guilty or cautioned per 100,000.

Source: Home Office, 1986a and 1978

is much the same for both men and women. (See also Home Office Statistical Bulletin, 1985.) The overall ratio of men to women cautioned or found guilty changed over this period from 7:1 to 5:1[16] but this is primarily due to changes in cautioning practice. The overall ratio of men's to women's convictions remained relatively stable (Box and Hale, 1983; Smart, 1979).

The concern was not just about increases in women's crime; it was about changes in the nature of the crimes committed by women. If we take recorded offences of 'violence against the person', for example, the number committed by women increased by 58 per cent between 1975 and 1985; the comparable figure for men was 40 per cent. Percentage increases, however, are misleading. Relatively small numerical increases in women's crime can appear as substantial percentage increases. Also, the absolute number of crimes committed by men remained much higher than that committed by women. In the example just given, the number of men found guilty or cautioned for offences of 'violence against the person' in 1985 was 50,900 compared with 5,600 women. Moreover, the male:female ratio for crimes of violence changed only slightly, from 10:1 to 9:1.

Evidence of a new breed of female criminal is also absent in the United States. Darryl Steffensmeier and his colleagues examined the criminal statistics over various periods of time in three major articles (1978, 1979 and 1981). In relation to violent crime, they concluded that offences involving violence by women did increase, but that the male level of violence was increasing at a broadly similar pace and violence was still predominantly a man's crime. The findings were similar with respect to property crimes. Property crimes by women increased, but only in larceny/theft and fraud/embezzlement was the pace faster than property crimes by men. Even so, absolute differences in the number of crimes continued to exist and women's property crimes lagged behind those of men. Women were still typically non-violent, minor property offenders. In the third article, Steffensmeier and Cobb examined arrest patterns for the period from 1934 to 1979. From this, they argued that the apparent increases in crime reflected changes in law-enforcement practices rather than changes in women's behaviour. And, again, they argued that the profile of the female offender had changed little. Johnson (1986) found much the same in Canada.

Though such exercises are useful in rebutting the kinds of argument presented by Adler, there are dangers too. Criminal statistics are notoriously unreliable. By discussing rather than dismissing their significance, we give them a credence and credibility which they do not have. Smart (1979), for example, in trying to explain away apparent increases in women's crime (she refers to small numbers, the lack of an historical perspective, etc.) fell into this trap. It enabled Walker (1981) and Austin (1981) to attack both her statistical expertise and her interpretation of the statistics. Thereby the thesis she was attempting to reject — the existence of a new breed of female criminal — was brought back into the mainstream of discussions.

The most that we can say from the criminal statistics is that there are more women involved now *in the criminal justice system* than there were 20 or so years ago. A more difficult question is what this means. Are activities which previously remained in the dark figure now being more readily reported to the police by victims? Have the attitudes of criminal justice professionals towards female offenders changed? Are women more willing to commit crimes? The significance of the increase is not clear and it is probably a mixture of all three of these propositions. Self-report studies, however, can offer some guidance for, if admission or victimization rates remain stable while statistics increase, this suggests that the explanation for the increase lies not in changes in women's criminal behaviour, but in victims' and police practices. There is some support for this.

Gold and Reimer (1975) administered self-report delinquency questionnaires to a sample of American boys and girls in 1967 and 1972. Apart from increases in drug use, the delinquency of girls had not increased in contrast with the picture in the official statistics. Similarly, Steffensmeier and Steffensmeier (1980) contrasted arrest statistics and self-report findings. They found that there was an increase in the number of arrests of girls for larceny, but that the number of larcenies admitted by girls had remained stable. Hindelang (1979) contrasted the estimated percentage of offenders reported by victims to have been female for the years 1972 and 1976. He found no change for violent offences, again in contrast to the official statistics.

Concern about women's crime is not new. Worsley (1849: 116) referred to the 'alarmingly increased proportion of female crimes since 1840'. In 1826, there were, he claimed, 20 women for every 100 men convicted; in 1846, it had risen to 26.5. An article in *The Economist* in 1858 quoted figures for the number of persons committed or bailed for trial, as shown in table 2.6, and commented with alarm that 'while the male committals have decreased between one-sixth and one-seventh, the female committals have not decreased by so much as one-sixtieth part'. In 1857, women made up 28 per cent of those convicted summarily and 21 per cent of those committed for trial by jury, a considerably higher figure than now. Many of these women would probably have been convicted of offences related to prostitution and drunkenness, but, nevertheless, such figures caution us against taking too narrow a view of 'increases in women's crime'.

In a different context, Pearson (1983) has shown that moral panics about young working-class boys occur repeatedly. He traces a history of what he calls 'respectable fears' which consistently and unfavourably compare the present generation with previous 'golden ages', and he identifies the '20 years' rule': the fact that things now are perceived to be worse than 20 years ago. This is relevant for discussions of women's crime too. Morris and Gelsthorpe (1981) have suggested that concerns about women's crime represent a means by which much wider social anxieties are articulated and expressed. A moral panic about women's crime has repercussions not only for female offenders but for women generally. This is discussed further in chapter 3.

Conclusion

Pulled together, what does all this mean? Official statistics indicate

TABLE 2.6   NUMBERS OF PERSONS COMMITTED OR BAILED FOR TRIAL, 1848–57

	Males	*Females*
5 years from 1848 to 1852	112,825	27,623
5 years from 1852 to 1857	94,887	27,207

Source: The Economist, 11 September 1858

that there are differences between men's and women's criminality, but these are unreliable because they have been constructed in ways which may misrepresent men's and women's criminality. Smith and Visher (1980) reviewed 44 self-report delinquency studies and argued that they were generally supportive of the conclusions drawn from the official statistics though they qualified them to some extent. In brief, self-report delinquency studies indicate that the differences between men's and women's criminality are 'real', particularly with reference to serious and persistent criminal behaviour, though less than apparent from the official statistics. But these studies may also be unreliable. (See Box, 1981 for a review.) Samples are small and unrepresentative, and questions tend to concentrate on trivial offences. This may mean that self-report studies and official statistics measure different kinds of criminality (Elliott and Ageton, 1980). It is possible also that respondents conceal or exaggerate their involvement in crime. More importantly, these tendencies may be linked to gender — girls may be more likely to conceal offences than boys, and boys may be more likely to exaggerate than girls. That is, there may be differences in the willingness to *report* delinquent activities. There is some evidence to support this suggestion (Erickson and Smith, 1974; Morris, 1965).

Observational and experimental data, in contrast to official statistics and self-report studies, indicate that, given the opportunity and the appropriate social context, women may be as capable of dishonesty or aggression as men. But there are only a few observational studies of criminal behaviour, and experimental studies often put people into artificial situations. Clearly, research needs to explore further differences between men's and women's criminal behaviour.[17] Research also needs to explore further the interaction of gender with such factors as race, class and age. In the United States, the rates of offending of white men and black women are closer than those for black women and white women (Laub and McDermott, 1985). In Lewis's words, 'the black women's sex and race operate in contradictory ways' (1981: 94). The issue of gender differences in crime, therefore, is more complex than Wootton (1959) and Heidensohn (1985) claim. Some, but not all, women are involved in crime to a limited extent.

Depending on the final outcome of this research, quite different and, more importantly, quite difficult questions arise. Should we take the crime rate from the official statistics as 'real' and explain why women are less criminal than men? Or should we take the self-report and observational data as 'real' and explain why women are protected from criminalization? These questions raise further questions. If more women than men are non-criminal, why is this so and why do certain women commit criminal offences? And, if more women than men are protected from criminalization, why is this and why are certain women criminalized?

Put another way, should we attempt to explain women's criminality or women's conformity? According to Leonard (1982), each theory explaining crime contains in it an explanation of conformity; she argues that a theory which cannot explain both is inadequate and logically unsound. Heidensohn makes much the same point:[18] 'If we start from the broader issues of conformity and control and observe and analyse how these affect *all* women . . . we can then learn rather more about those who become involved in crime . . .' (1985: 199, emphasis in the original).

I disagree with both of these writers. Explanations for conformity and criminality can be linked: for example, women may be socialized into a certain kind of role — passive, dependent, gentle and so on — which is far removed from the stereotype of criminality; criminal women, therefore, may be those who are under- or badly socialized, or who reject that socialization. (For an example of this kind of explanation, see Richardson, 1969.) But explanations for conformity and criminal behaviour need not be linked. Women can be socialized in a particular way, but nevertheless commit crimes. Female prisoners, for example, score very high on traditional femininity scales (Widom, 1981) and prostitutes in McLeod's (1982) sample referred to their 'work' as fitting in well with child-care arrangements. Their responsibilities as mothers, therefore, were important to them. Moreover, Leonard and Heidensohn assume that all women are socialized in the same way. They are not. Black women, for example, are socialized to be self-reliant, independent and resourceful (Lewis, 1975; Bryan et al., 1985). Working-class children are also said to be socialized differently from middle-class children (Trasler, 1965).

Criminal behaviour is not peculiar to any particular social class, age-group or sex; the same explanatory principles should be relevant for each or should at least be able to take account of any differences in criminal behaviour. The next chapter discusses the adequacy of some 'explanatory principles' offered for women's crime.

3

Theories of Women's Crime

Biological and Psychological Explanations: a Critique

Biological determinism was the dominant theory of criminality for both sexes in the nineteenth and early twentieth centuries. For men's crime, explanations have shifted towards theories with a more sociological basis, for example, subcultural or labelling theory.[1] But for explanations of women's crime, biological determinism is not a matter of history; it continues to dominate theory and practice. Klein's claim in 1973 that 'the road from Lombroso to the present is surprisingly straight' (1973: 7) remains valid. For example, Gove (1985) refers to the stability of men's and women's crime rates over time and place as evidence of biological differences. He attributes women's lower rate of criminal behaviour to their 'affiliative nature, their physique and to their lack of assertiveness, all of which have a biological base' (1985: 138). Wilson and Hernstein reached much the same conclusion: 'the best guess centres on the difference in aggression and perhaps other primary drives that flow into the definition of sex roles' (1985: 124). In this section, I do not intend to describe in any detail the work of those writers who stress biological interpretations of women's crime; for a critique of earlier writers, see Smart (1976), Campbell (1981) and Heidensohn (1985). Rather, I criticize biological determinism at a more general level and examine the reasons for the continued appeal of this kind of explanation for women's crime.

It is perhaps not surprising that women's crime is often viewed as biologically based since biology is commonly assumed to determine women's lives generally, hence Freud's widely quoted phrase 'anatomy is destiny' (1924: 178).[2] Clearly, there are chromosomal and hormonal differences between men and women. We all have 23 pairs of chromosomes, 22 homologous pairs of autosomes and the sex chromosomes. If the fertilized egg has an XX chromosomal structure, the child will be female; if the chromosomal structure is XY, it will be male.[3] The main hormone in men is testosterone and the main hormones in women are oestrogen and progesterone. These also shape whether a child will be male or female. But neither chromosomes nor hormones shape what is defined as 'masculine' and 'feminine'.

The significance of this is best demonstrated by studies of hermaphrodites. Ellis, in a review article based on 84 such cases, concluded that their role 'accords primarily not with his or her internal or external somatic characteristics, but rather with his or her masculine or feminine upbringing' (1945: 120). Later research (for example, Money et al., 1955) confirmed this, but it was subsequently questioned by Imperato-McGinley et al. (1979). Wilson and Hernstein (1985), influential writers on the biological basis of criminal behaviour, rely on Imperato-McGinley et al.'s research for their argument and so it is necessary to consider it further.

Imperato-McGinley et al.'s observations were based on a group of people in the Dominican Republic who were genetic male pseudo-hermaphrodites due to an enzyme deficiency which results in ambiguity in the external genitalia of the male fetus. The individuals were raised as girls. At puberty, under the influence of their own testosterone, they experienced phallic growth and deepening of the voice. Of the 18 subjects investigated, 17 changed their gender identity at puberty from female to male. This change was interpreted as being due to the increased level of testosterone but Ehrhardt is critical of such a conclusion:

> One needs to ask whether they really had a female gender identity in childhood and whether the rearing experience was unambiguously female. . . . Perhaps villagers and the parents of these individuals recognised some ambiguity in the children's genitalia from birth which may have given them a special status. (1985: 86)

This seems quite likely. Imperato-McGinley et al. even refer to the fact that these children had a special name in the villages: 'penis at 12'. This does not indicate an entirely normal socialization.

Differences between the sexes are fewer than was once believed.

In Maccoby and Jacklin's (1975) review of differences between men and women for 83 dimensions, they highlight exaggeration, misinterpretations and myths. Weisstein (1971) has also been critical of theories which assert that differences have biological or psychological roots; she refers to them as theories without evidence. It is certainly true that much of the research on differences between men and women has been influenced by the social expectations of the (usually male) researcher and that, consequently, the resulting observations are not necessarily 'scientific' or 'objective'. Moreover, while the 'average' woman may differ from the 'average' man on a variety of dimensions, these dimensions fall on a continuum and the overlap between the two sexes is considerable. Some women, for example, are stronger than some men and, in mental tests, some girls will score higher than some boys. This overlap is concealed in the presentation of apparent differences between the sexes (especially when means are used) and so, in the process of investigation, differences become magnified. Different research methodologies also produce different results (Caplan, 1975) and some differences occur for statistical reasons. Oakley (1981: 60) quotes one study in which 35 categories of behaviour were rated. Seven per cent of the differences between men and women achieved the 5 per cent level of significance and, as she points out, this is hardly greater than the number that would have been expected to occur by chance. Research which sets out to examine differences may, therefore, exaggerate and reinforce the differences and neglect similarities. Furthermore, a study which finds no differences may be disregarded; it is difficult to publish results in which there are no significant differences. Thus stereotypes are perpetuated. I am not suggesting here that there are no differences between men and women; there clearly are (Gilligan, 1982). The point is that these differences have been overstated for some attributes and, more importantly, assumed to have a biological foundation. Debates about differences in men's and women's levels of aggression demonstrate this.

Aggression and Biology

The only differences which stood up to testing in Maccoby and Jacklin's (1975) review were aggression, verbal ability and spatial or mathematical ability. The supposed difference in aggression is obviously of interest to us because of the prevalence of men in detected crimes of violence (cf. Campbell, 1986), but we need to examine whether such a difference is sex- or gender-based, that is, whether it is determined by biological factors (for example, through hormonal differences) or by social or cultural factors (for example, through learning). Maccoby and Jacklin believe the difference to have a biological foundation and they present four reasons for this.

First, they argue that men are more aggressive than women in all human societies for which evidence is available. This is not so. Anthropologists like Margaret Mead (1935)[4] have demonstrated that qualities we think of as naturally 'masculine' and 'feminine' have been turned upside down in some cultures, or differentiate both men and women in yet others.[5] From Mead's writings we know that amongst the Mundugumur, both sexes were aggressive whereas, among the Arapesh, both were gentle and unaggressive.

Secondly, Maccoby and Jacklin argue that differences in aggression are found early in life, at a time when there is no evidence that differential socialization pressures have been brought to bear by adults. But socialization starts from birth. Research has shown that subjects respond differently to a baby depending on whether they believe the baby to be male or female. Also the research by Caplan (1975), referred to in chapter 2, suggests that the presence or absence of an adult affects the demonstration of aggression by girls. This suggests that they learn early in life that such behaviour is unacceptable for them.

Their third argument is that aggression is related to levels of sex hormones and can be affected by experimental administration of these hormones. Testosterone has been cited (Rutter and Giller, 1983) as a major explanation for violence in men. However, both men and women have 'male' and 'female' hormones in varying amounts, and even within one sex the variation in the amount of each set of hormones is great. Hormone levels also vary for any one person in moments of stress, on different days and at different times of life.

Nevertheless, research indicates that if male monkeys are castrated at birth they will be less aggressive than non-castrated monkeys; and if female monkeys are fetally androgenized or given testosterone at birth they will be more aggressive than normal female monkeys. Research also indicates that aggressive monkeys have higher testosterone levels than less aggressive monkeys (Rose et al., 1971). And a similar study by Kreuz and Rose (1972) of men in prison showed that the men with the higher testosterone levels had committed the more violent and aggressive crimes. But these same researchers found that providing a male monkey with an opportunity to dominate actually increased his testosterone level (Rose et al., 1972). This suggests that aggressive behaviour can affect the production of the hormone. The same may be so for humans.

Assuming that the difference in aggression is due to hormones is further complicated by the fact that girls and boys have very similar hormonal patterns before puberty yet differences in aggression appear before then. It seems likely that this again is explained by reference to differential socialization experiences. Indeed, even in animals, there seems to be a learning process. Cats, for example, can be trained to accept mice and then retrained to kill them. It is not clear, therefore, that hormonal differences *per se* explain the apparent difference in aggression.

Maccoby and Jacklin's final argument is that similar differences in aggression exist in all subhuman primates. There are, however, wide variations among primates in many aspects of behaviour, including aggression. In gibbons, for example, there are minimal sex differences in aggression; in baboons there are extreme differences. Also, social contexts are important. Many female primates (and other animals for that matter) are aggressive in defence of their young. Indeed, what is often ignored in this controversy is that some of the theorists who argued for biologically based aggressiveness did not argue for sex-based differences. Lorenz (1969), for example, believed female animals, including female humans, to be often more aggressive than males because of what he called 'brood defence', that is, aggression in defence of the young. As Sayers (1982: 72) points out, it was later writers who extended Lorenz's claim and who took the position that biology had rendered males naturally more aggressive than females.

Each of Maccoby and Jacklin's arguments can be questioned, yet belief in the biological basis of differences in aggression remains strong. Wilson and Hernstein (1985: 121), for example, conclude their discussion by saying that while aggression is often situationally controlled and the forms which it takes are shaped by learning, 'the durability, universality and generality of the relative aggressiveness of males cannot plausibly be blamed entirely on arbitrary sex roles'. They believe the constitutional (that is, biological) sex differences in aggression to be of a magnitude sufficient not only to explain differences in the commission of violent crime, but possibly also in the commission of crimes generally.

The points raised to rebut Maccoby and Jacklin's conclusion are equally valid with respect to Wilson and Hernstein's. Patterns of behaviour — including aggression — are culturally determined and learned. 'Woman' is constituted differently in different historical periods, cultures, races and classes. Put more explicitly, differences between men and women are often gender rather than sex differences and are maintained through differential socialization. The dualism inherent in contrasts between nature and culture, between the biological and the social, is untenable and unscientific. Archer (1976), for example, argues that the nature/nurture debate is obsolete; all characteristics derive from both.

Menstruation and Crime

A different kind of biological theory is the supposed link between the menstrual cycle and criminal behaviour. Negative associations with menstruation have a long history. Pliny, for example, described menstrual blood as: 'fatal poison, corrupting and decomposing urine, depriving seeds of their fecundity, destroying insects, blasting garden flowers and grasses, causing fruits to fall from branches, dulling razors' (quoted in Sayers, 1982: 111).[6] It is not surprising, therefore, that menstruation was also linked early on to women's criminal behaviour (Lombroso and Ferrero, 1895; Ellis, 1894). Cooke (1945: 459), for example, quotes the finding that 84 per cent of violent crime by women in Paris was committed just before or during menstruation; Gibbens and Prince (1962) claimed that in their sample of shoplifters the offence usually took place just before menstruation and, more recently, Marsh (1981: 98) stated that '80% of all female crime occurs paramenstrually'. Writers like Freud (1924) and Pollak (1961) attributed the underlying reason to revenge; menstruation was said to remind women of their inferior status.

The main modern advocate of a link between menstruation and crime (or other deviant or 'problematic' behaviour) is Katherina Dalton. One of her earliest projects (1960a) concerned the effect of menstruation on the school-marks of 217 girls in a boarding school. She found that marks fell (compared with the previous week) for just over a quarter of the girls when they were pre-menstrual, for a further quarter when they were menstruating and for only 10 per cent during the post-menstrual week. However, one can reverse these 'findings': more than half of the girls did not show any change in their marks in the pre-menstrual week and, for 17 per cent, their marks improved. The figures were similar for the menstrual week. Thus 'no change' was the most common occurrence and, especially in the menstrual week, the proportion whose marks improved was almost as high as the proportion whose marks fell. Dalton (1960b) also recorded the behaviour of 350 boarding-school girls. Two hundred and seventy-two breaches of the school rules were recorded, primarily forgetfulness, lack of punctuality and talking in class. An even distribution of breaches would have meant that 14 per cent were recorded in the first four days of a 28-day cycle; the actual figure was 29 per cent. However, Dalton also found that prefects were more likely to punish girls during their own menstruation. The results, therefore, may reflect *their* behaviour as much as the girls' if Dalton's hypothesis is valid. In subsequent research, Dalton (1977) found that over half the female admissions to four London teaching hospitals for accidents occurred in the paramenstruum and that about half the female admissions to a psychiatric hospital occurred during the same period (Taylor and Dalton, 1983).

Specifically with reference to crime, Dalton (1961) presented data on a sample of female prisoners; 156 of those interviewed had committed their offences during the previous 28 days. The menstrual cycle was divided into seven four-day periods (days 1–4 represented menstruation and days 25–8 the pre-menstruum). Table 3.1 shows the relationship of the date of the offence to the menstrual cycle of these women.

Nearly half of all the crimes were committed by the women during menstruation or in the pre-menstruum. On a normal distribution, only 29 per cent of the crimes would be expected

TABLE 3.1   TIME OF CRIME OF 156 REGULARLY MENSTRUATING
WOMEN

Day of cycle	Number	Percentage
1 – 4	41	26.3
5 – 8	13	8.3
9 – 12	20	12.8
13 – 16	21	13.5
17 – 20	19	12.2
21 – 24	7	4.5
25 – 28	35	22.4
TOTAL	156	100.0

Source: Dalton, 1961

during these eight days. Dalton also discussed the effects of pre-menstrual tension (PMT).[7] This was said to be present in more than a quarter (43) of this sample and almost two-thirds of them (27) had committed their crime during the time of their PMT symptoms (these were tiredness, headaches, bloatedness, mastitis and mood changes). In the same article, Dalton presented a graph (replicated here as figure 1) which purports to show an association between negative behaviour and menstruation. Similar conclusions were reached by Ellis and Austin (1971) from their research in the women's prison in North Carolina.

But all is not as it seems. There are many confusions in the literature: pre-menstrual tension, menstruation and menstrual discomfort are all referred to as if they were the same, and the pre-menstrual and menstrual weeks are sometimes used inter-changeably. Phrases such as 'pre-menstruum' and 'paramenstruum' are often not defined or are defined in so broad a way that a reasonable proportion of women would be expected to be in that phase. Also, such simple statistical analyses are not appropriate; few women have 28-day cycles. Moreover, it is widely accepted that stress or anxiety (caused, for example, by detection) can induce menstruation. Cause and effect, therefore, are difficult to disentangle. So the meaning of the figures is unclear. Given also that women spend almost half of their lives in the menstrual or

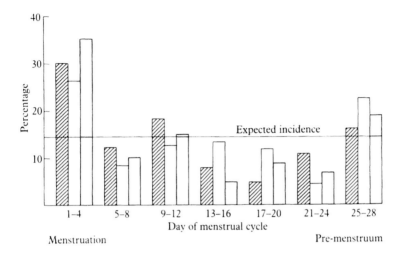

FIGURE 1
Source: Dalton, 1961

pre-menstrual phase, the figures cited are not that surprising. Showing that women who commit crimes are more likely to be in a certain part of their menstrual cycle does not mean that women generally in this phase are more likely to commit crimes. Furthermore, there is counter-evidence. For example, Epps (1962) interviewed 200 women in Holloway prison soon after their admission. Fourteen per cent admitted to PMT symptoms (in this project, these were feelings of irritability, depression or tension). Less than half of them had committed their offences during the paramenstruum.

Also, much of Dalton's data is retrospective and, therefore, unreliable. Women know that their behaviour can often be excused by reference to the menstrual cycle (in part, because 'strange' behaviour is expected then). They might thus believe that they are less likely to be punished for criminal acts during their menstrual cycle. Mills' (1940) notion of the 'vocabulary of motives' is relevant here. He suggested that there exist accounts for behaviour which are popularly acceptable as excuses and which in effect encourage that behaviour. Problems associated with the menstrual cycle seem to fit with this. Parlee (1982) asked a small sample of women to fill in questionnaires daily for three months. They were unaware that they were participating in a study of menstruation. They reported few fluctuations in mood. On a retrospective menstrual-distress questionnaire, on the other hand, the same subjects said that they experienced increases in anxiety, irritability, depression and tension in the pre-menstrual phase. Thus daily logs of symptoms do not corroborate retrospective reports. Parlee explains this by suggesting that retrospective studies produce stereotyped beliefs about the psychological concomitants of menstruation, that is, menstrual awareness influences the symptoms reported. Daily reports, on the other hand, appear to reflect more closely actual psychological changes throughout the cycle.

AuBuchon and Calhoun (summarized in *New Society*, 28 March 1985: 491) report similar findings. They told nine men and nine women that they were interested in any psychological changes occurring in people over a period of eight weeks. Nine other women were specifically told that the research was aimed at examining mood changes before and during menstruation. The results showed that the women in the second group reported significantly worse moods during menstruation. In contrast, the other women reported very little fluctuation in moods and their scores were similar to those of the men.[8] AuBuchon and Calhoun concluded that the self-reports of depression and aggression due to menstruation were influenced by social expectations. Thus menstruation *per se* may not affect women's lives, but rather its social construction.

Despite the lack of clear evidence for an association between menstruation and crime, the criminal courts have been fairly receptive to it. Indeed, they have been receptive to evidence of menstrual disorders as evidence of abnormality for a long time.[9] Edwards (1984: 86) cites a case of arson in 1833 in which the defendant was found to be insane on account of amenorrhoea. In another case, a theft, the woman was dealt with as insane on account of the 'personality changes and eccentricities' associated with her menstruation.

In 1980, Sandra Craddock pleaded not guilty to the murder of a fellow barmaid. Her plea of guilty to manslaughter due to diminished responsibility caused by PMT was accepted. During a three-month deferment for sentence, she underwent progesterone therapy which appeared to lead to improvement in her behaviour. The judge subsequently imposed a probation order with a condition of continued treatment.[10] Christine English also successfully pleaded guilty to manslaughter. (She had crushed a former lover against a telegraph pole with her car.) The judge accepted that the offence had been committed in 'exceptional circumstances', namely that English was suffering from PMT. He imposed a conditional discharge and a 12-month period of disqualification from driving. Menstrual factors have also been accepted in mitigation of penalty. Edwards (1982: 476) describes the case of Nicola Owen, convicted of arson in 1978. The medical evidence was that she was suffering from PMT and the judge imposed a probation order with a condition of treatment.

Why do biological theories have such an appeal? In the nineteenth century, the biological make-up of women was used as an ideological pretext for justifying and continuing the dispossession of women from social and political life. Sayers (1982) demonstrates that in discussions on the education of women much was made of the effect which education would have on women's reproductive ability. It was believed that it would ruin both the health of women and their children and hence that education would be bought 'at the price of a puny, enfeebled race' (Maudsley, 1874: 482). Similarly, it was argued that emancipation would debase and degrade women. The appeal of biological determinism, therefore, was that it justified the status quo and it did so 'objectively'. It reinforced and maintained traditional roles: if it is 'natural', it cannot be changed. But nature is not responsible for these associations; they are a consequence of patriarchal thought. As Millett (1971: 58) put it, 'patriarchy has a . . . tenacious or powerful hold through its successful habit of passing itself off as nature'. It is the *use* made of biological differences — and the implicit assumption that one (the male) is 'better' than the other (the female) — which is invidious, not the differences *per se*.

Mental Illness and Crime

There is an apparent paradox in the literature on women, crime and mental illness: mental illness is presented as an alternative to criminal behaviour for women, but it is also presented as an explanation of their criminal behaviour. In this first view, it is suggested that women become mentally ill whereas men become criminal; that is, there is a functional equivalence between the two. Turk (1969: 143), for example, suggested that mental illness was a kind of 'alternative "arrest" category for women' and Chesler (1972) wrote that the kinds of behaviour which are considered 'criminal' and 'mentally ill' are sex-stereotyped and that each sex is conditioned accordingly. More recently, Barrett and McIntosh (1982), two feminist writers, suggested that since more men than women are convicted of criminal offences, and since more women than men are treated for neuroses and depression, this may reflect different responses to similar stresses. The second view is that when women do commit criminal offences they do so for pathological or irrational reasons.[11] Criminal activity by men, on the other hand, is more likely to be viewed as normal, explicable or rational.

The criminal statistics are consistent with the statistical basis of the first view: men commit more crimes than women. The ratio is currently about 5:1. In the mental-health area, statistics suggest that the ratio of men to women is about 2:3. About 60 per cent of those admitted to mental hospitals in England and Wales are female. The figure for the United States is much the same (Chesler, 1972; Russo and Sobel, 1981). The number of women among patients with mental disorders does, however, vary according to age, marital status, educational level, social class, race, historical period and diagnosis (Smart, 1976; Rutter and Giller, 1983; Bryan et al., 1985). That is to say, certain women, for example, black, working-class and older women, are over-represented in the figures.[12] But these figures do not reflect reality; rather, they reflect the particular ways in which the statistics have been constructed. That is, they reflect differential patterns of socialization, differential expectations of behaviour and differential opportunity structures: in short, stereotypical images of men and women.

I have already demonstrated this with respect to the construction of the criminal statistics. Mental-health statistics are constructed in a similar way. The behaviour must be perceived and then defined as a certain kind of behaviour. The individual (an observer or oneself) must then decide whether or not to involve a GP (or other professional). There may be reasons for not doing so — embarrassment, fear or laziness. Once reported, the GP (or other professional) may redefine[13] the behaviour (for example, prescribe tranquillizers) or refer to a specialist (for example, a psychiatrist) who then makes a further series of decisions — whether or not the situation is treatable, and whether treatment should be in-patient or out-patient. Thus there is likely to be a large dark figure of mental illness, that is, mental illness which is unrecognized, unreferred, undiagnosed and unhospitalized. Brown and Harris (1978), for example, found a large number of their control sample of women with symptoms of an equivalent degree of depression to those diagnosed as clinically depressed. This suggests that we could reverse the ordinary way of thinking about mental-health statistics from:

mental illness ➤ control by psychiatric agencies ➤ statistics

to

control by psychiatric agency ➤ mental illness ➤ statistics.

This is not to suggest that mental illness is *caused* by psychiatric intervention or that there is no such thing as mental illness, but rather to suggest that it is by this process that a particular state is labelled 'mental illness'; that is, it takes on this character within the social contexts created by psychiatry. An experiment by Rosenhan (1973) demonstrates this point nicely. A group of people voluntarily admitted themselves to mental hospitals (their presenting symptom was that they heard voices) and then they behaved normally. Staff continued to describe the behaviour (for example, note-taking) as symptomatic. Interestingly, the patients recognized that the subjects were not mentally ill!

With respect to the ratio of women to men, a far more important point is the suggestion that definitions of mental health reflect stereotypes and that the standard of mental health in our culture is masculine. Broverman et al. (1970), for example, gave a questionnaire to clinicians in which they had to rate certain bipolar traits as representing healthy male, healthy female or healthy adult behaviour. The results were that, for all the clinicians, the concept of a healthy man approximated to that of a healthy adult. However, the concept of a healthy woman differed; she was described as excitable, submissive, emotional, dependent: the opposite of the healthy adult (see also Broverman et al., 1972). What this means is that if clinicians adhere to this standard of mental health, women are likely to be viewed as unhealthy adults, *simply because they are women.* Chesler puts it more generally: 'What we consider madness, whether in women or in men . . . is either the acting out of the devalued female role or the total/partial rejection of one's sex role stereotype' (1972: 56). The influence of role stereotypes is also apparent in diagnostic categories. Women feature in the vaguer, catch-all categories (for example, neurosis and depression rather than alcoholism) and in those which focus on emotional states (Russo and Sobel, 1981; Hiller, 1982). This process is made considerably easier by the lack of consistent or objective diagnostic criteria.[14] There is some evidence that mental-health professionals tend to label men as suffering from antisocial personality disorders and women as suffering from hysterical personalities, even when they have identical clinical features. There is also evidence that black women are over-represented in psychiatric hospitals. Bryan et al. (1985) suggest that this is not because black women experience more stress; rather it is due to the way in which agencies respond to the women's anger, frustration or emotion.

So far I have stressed the influence on the construction of the statistics of conceptions of health, of professionals' (including psychiatrists') views of appropriate behaviour and of diagnostic categories. Also influential is the effect of family labelling. It seems that wives are committed to psychiatric hospitals by husbands more readily than are husbands by wives. There is also less social tolerance of 'unacceptable' behaviour by women and psychiatric commitment can be a response to this. Certainly, there are many nineteenth-century examples of the institutional-ization of women who rejected conventional roles. Chesler (1972: 16) described this as a penalty 'for being "female" as well as for desiring and daring not to be'. Parents still do this with rebellious daughters.

A further influence on the statistics' construction is self-labelling. The encouragement of 'help-seeking' behaviour, emotionality and expressiveness among women means that they may more readily consult professionals, express distress and define themselves as depressed (Horwitz, 1977). (We can contrast this with the stereotype of the man who is expected to 'grin and bear it'.) There is also greater tolerance for that help-seeking behaviour by women. (We can again contrast this with the male stereotype in which such behaviour might be viewed as 'cissy' or 'unmasculine'.) Feminist writers (for example, Procek, 1981) have recently added a further dimension: mental illness as a form of resistance, like going on strike; women are presented as using mental illness in a conscious, rational way to control others in their families and to force them to share domestic responsibilities.

The functional equivalence thesis depends on accepting both the criminal and mental-health statistics at face value. We cannot. As Busfield writes:

> Data on psychiatric morbidity . . . do not provide a sound basis for generalizations about the comparative incidence or prevalence of mental illness among men and women . . . not only may the constitution of the category of mental illness differ for the groups we are attempting to compare, but in practice the boundaries of the particular types of conditions that are embraced within the general term may vary also. (1983: 111)

I am not suggesting that women commit as many crimes as men or that men become mentally ill as frequently as women. There are differences in the opportunity structures of men and women and the objective conditions of life may differ so that women are more likely than men to feel unhappy or depressed (Gove and Tudor, 1972). But if more women than men are viewed as 'mad' it is hardly surprising that the second view — female offenders are 'madder' still — is expressed.

Female offenders are, according to the statistics, less numerous than male offenders and so it is readily assumed that there must be 'something wrong' with them. (I discuss in subsequent chapters the effect this assumption has on the processing of female defendants in the criminal justice system.) Hence the apparent paradox — that mental illness is presented as both an alternative to and an explanation of crime — is resolved. But the second view is as questionable as the first.

This connection between madness and crime has a long history.

Griffiths (1884: 255) quoted the ex-deputy governor of Millbank as saying that 'it was often difficult to draw the line between madness and outrageous conduct among women prisoners'. Quinton (1910: 42) also refers to the governor at Millbank who 'seemed to have an idea that all women were mad'. Research since has pointed to supposedly high rates of psychiatric abnormality among women in prisons (Goodman and Price, 1967; Gibbens, 1971; D'Orban, 1971; Eysenck and Eysenck, 1973; Worth, 1981). The 1967 Holloway Survey, for example, found that almost half of the women were suffering from some form of psychiatric disorder and that a quarter had previously been admitted to psychiatric hospitals (Gibbens, 1971). Eysenck and Eysenck (1973: 596) believed that: 'Crime is so unusual an activity for women that only the most unusually high P [psychotism] scores overcame the social barriers involved.' They described female prisoners as 'psychiatrically ill to a marked degree' (1973: 696).

The most recent survey of psychiatric disorder among female prisoners was carried out by Turner and Tofler (1986) at Holloway prison. From a random sample of 708 women, they found that 18 per cent had a history of psychiatric disturbance. Given the early removal of some overtly disturbed women from the original sample (63 in all), Turner and Tofler view this as an under-estimate. If other behaviours like suicide attempts and drug use are included, about half the sample had a history of psychological disorder. Two points can be made here. First, even if we accept that these rates of disorder are high, it means that about half the female prisoners show *no* sign of disorder (it is also disputable whether drug use should be so included). Secondly, the psychiatric morbidity of male prisoners is as high as it is for female prisoners. Gunn et al. (1978) found that close to a half of a random sample of male prisoners had had in-patient and/or out-patient treatment. On the other hand, 18 per cent of those admitted to special hospitals in 1979 were female (DHSS, 1984) − considerably higher than the percentage received into prisons − and a significantly greater proportion of female offenders were dealt with as mentally disordered by the various procedures under the Mental Health Act (Walker, 1965; Home Office, 1986b; Home Office, 1986c).

Studies of institutionalized offenders are, however, notoriously suspect. Certain kinds of offenders may be selected for official processing in the first place and then, subsequently, selected for certain kinds of dispositions. For example, research now indicates that coming from a 'broken home' leads to official processing as an offender rather than to delinquency itself (Shacklady-Smith, 1978; Datesman and Scarpitti, 1980). In Maguire and Shapland's (1980: xv) words, 'sentences may be reflecting a belief . . . that crime in women is primarily the result of inadequacy, sickness or emotional problems'. Their selection, then, confirms the beliefs of subsequent decision-makers and so the cycle continues. In this way, we construct the 'female criminal' and the 'female prisoner'.

Women's Sexuality and Crime

Suspicion of women probably has biblical origins (for example, the story of the temptation of Eve). St Paul argued for the restriction of women's freedom so that they could not use their sexuality to ensnare men and, in their handbook for witch-hunters, Kramer and Sprenger (1486; 1971 edn: 46—7) referred to women as 'beautiful to look upon, contaminating to touch'. Once awakened, their carnal lust was viewed as insatiable. Thus it was primarily woman, not man, whom, it was believed, the devil used as an instrument for his evil designs. Woman was either a 'madonna' or a 'whore'.

Such imagery is not only of historical relevance; women are used to being characterized and categorized on the basis of beliefs about their sexuality. Robins and Cohen, for example, refer to the fact that their teenage male interviewees classified all girls 'into the *familiar* two categories: the slags who'd go with anyone and everyone . . . and the drags who didn't but whom you might one day think about going steady with' (1978: 58, my emphasis).[15]

Women's sexuality has been used to explain their involvement in prostitution and status or moral danger offences. It is true that the characteristics of institutionalized populations often confirm this impression. For example, in Cowie et al.'s (1968) sample, only 81 out of the 322 girls had been institutionalized for criminal behaviour. And of the Glueck's (1934) 500 criminal women, one-quarter were first given custodial sentences for prostitution and over one-half had been prostitutes before their admission to the reformatory. But the over-representation of women and girls in these populations is a product of differential social responses and differential policing. Richardson (1981), for example, documents how social workers view sexual behaviour as indicative of individual pathology in girls, and as normal in boys (except where boys are involved in homosexuality). Chesney-Lind (1973) goes further and suggests that female juvenile delinquency is 'sexualized'; that is, the girl's criminal acts may be ignored and she is processed through the courts as 'in moral danger'. (This is discussed further in chapter 4.) Schofield (1968), on the other hand, indicates the 'normality' of adolescent sexual experimentation. He estimated that by the age of eighteen, 34 per cent of boys and 17 per cent of girls are sexually experienced and that something over 350,000 boys and girls aged under 20 had experienced pre-marital intercourse. (This figure is likely to be considerably higher now.) Moreover, Schofield found that sexually experienced girls did not have less favourable backgrounds than other girls. For example, there was no difference in the number who came from broken homes. Sexual experience among teenage girls, he writes, is 'closely associated with a desire for freedom and independence from the family, . . . they were not debauched' (1968: 233).

Psychoanalytic explanations of prostitution or sexual behaviour among girls refer to the Oedipal syndrome and the repression of early sexual love for the parent. Freud (1925 and 1933) suggested that because this attachment was frustrated by the incest taboo, subsequent sexual partners became mere surrogates. Further, because sexual partners were surrogates, complete satisfaction was unobtainable and so the individual continually searched for new partners. Theorists have variously described the prostitute as masochistic, infantile, excessively dependent, confused in her gender-role identity, aggressive, frigid, sex-crazed and so on (Rolph, 1955; Gibbens, 1957; Greenwald, 1958; Choisy, 1962). Two main themes emerge from this literature. First, such writers tend to equate women's sexual activity with pathology. Al-Issa (1980: 216), for example, described the prostitute as 'craving for sex'. The second theme is that there must be something abnormal about a woman who turns to prostitution. The Wolfenden Committee, for example, wrote:

> We believe that whatever may have been the case in the past, in these days, in this country at any rate, economic factors cannot account for it (prostitution) to any large or decisive extent . . . there

must be some additional psychological element in the personality of the individual woman who becomes a prostitute. (1957: para. 223)

Many of the magistrates interviewed by Smart echo these themes. They viewed prostitution as the result of some unresolved personality problems and prostitutes as 'quite beyond the pale' (1985: 54). To quote a few:

> I think one of the main things is that you find that very often they come from disturbed family backgrounds.
>
> I think a lot of them seem to lack love.
>
> I think also inadequate girls . . . you know — problem families. (1985: 59)

About 90 per cent of the women in Gebhard's (1969) sample, on the other hand, gave money as their prime motivation. Eileen MacLeod (1982) paints a picture of considerable social disadvantage among her Midland sample of street prostitutes. She concludes that their involvement in prostitution was a reasonable choice in the face of difficult economic and social circumstances. Other factors mentioned by James's (1976) interviewees were independence, excitement and a dislike of routine jobs.

With respect to girls, Blos wrote that: 'It seems delinquency is an overt sexual act, or to be more correct, a sexual acting out' (1957: 232). In a later paper (1969: 100), he contrasts the infinite variety of boys' delinquency with girls' 'extraordinary limited delinquent repertoire . . . sexual acting out, vagrancy . . . and stealing of the kleptomaniac type'. He described these activities as 'perversion'. The actions of the adolescent delinquent boy, on the other hand, were attempts at '*progressive* development' (my emphasis). Herskovitz (1969: 89) also saw sexual behaviour as the 'predominant expression of delinquency among girls in our society' and he described the sexually active girl as 'psychologically maladjusted' (1969: 92). He noted that 'we pay little attention to the boy who is very active sexually' (1969: 89).

Sociologists have also stressed women's sexuality. Cohen (1955), for example, saw female delinquency as primarily sexual and his different explanation for male and female delinquency was dependent on that belief.[16] He suggested that women's status depended on marriage to a successful man and that, therefore, the sexes had different problems of adjustment:

> In short, people do not simply want to excel, they want to excel as a
> man or as a woman, that is to say, in those respects which, in their
> culture, are symbolic of their respective sex roles . . . Even when
> they adopt behaviour which is considered disreputable by
> conventional standards, the tendency is to be disreputable in ways
> that are characteristically masculine and feminine. (1955: 138)

The boys' delinquent subculture, therefore, was viewed by Cohen
as completely inappropriate for girls' problem of adjustment
because: 'It is, at best, irrelevant to the vindication of the girls'
status as a girl, and, at worst, because it positively threatens her in
that status in consequence of its strongly masculine symbolic
function' (1955: 143– 4). He continued: 'A primary determinant
of the female's "peace of mind" and feeling of security is her
assurance of her sexual attractiveness' (1955: 144). Her problem,
therefore, was whether to give or withhold sexual activity. She
may want attention and company, but if she gives too much, she
loses status. Thus Cohen wrote that the 'problem of explaining
female sexual delinquency may be viewed as a problem of
accounting for choices and compromises between these socially
structured alternatives' (1955: 147).

Riege (1972) agreed with Cohen and viewed a girl's 'most
highly ego-involved region' as her relationship with the opposite
sex. It is in this that 'she finds her fulfillment *as a girl*' (1972: 71,
emphasis in original). Riege went on to suggest that feelings of
rejection or not being loved, particularly by the father, led to
running away, truanting and aggressive behaviour 'in an attempt
to re-establish self-esteem'. Girls can accomplish this, she argued,
through contacts with the opposite sex which provide a substitute
for parental love.

A variant of this kind of approach is the work of Ruth Morris
(1964 and 1965). She asserted that more than half of female
delinquents were involved in sexual delinquencies. This led
directly to her theory. Since relationships were more important
for girls than boys, she hypothesized that if girls had problems in
maintaining positive personal relationships they would turn to
delinquency.[17]

To test this, Morris (1964) matched a sample of white
delinquent girls (that is, girls with two or more police contacts)
with groups of male delinquents, male non-delinquents, and
female non-delinquents for class, intelligence, age and grades in

school. She then presented data which purported to show that delinquent girls came more often from broken homes or from homes with family tensions, and more often lacked grooming skills. These factors were important in Morris's view because broken homes cut girls off from a parental relationship and thus from models for establishing and maintaining a happy and stable marital relationship. Tense family situations similarly provided unsatisfactory relationships and no model for establishing good relationships. The dating relationship was also considered important and Morris hypothesized that poor personal appearance would limit the likelihood of dates and would thus encourage delinquency.

Morris's data is full of paradoxes. It is true that delinquent girls came from broken homes more often than non-delinquent girls. But the majority came from unbroken homes. Further, it is now recognized that family structure is a factor which is likely to lead to official rather than unofficial processing, especially with respect to status offenders which the majority of Morris's female delinquents were (Datesman and Scarpitti, 1980). Her figures were, therefore, likely to have been an artifact resulting from the different types of delinquency for which boys and girls were processed.

Morris also developed an overall attractiveness scale, and delinquent girls scored lower on this, primarily as a result of poor grooming rather than 'inherent' characteristics. Such a scale is inevitably very subjective, and 'unattractiveness' may also be a factor leading to referral to the police or courts. More important, though, for the purposes of Morris's argument, is the paradoxical finding that the delinquents of both sexes reported more frequent dating. According to Morris, the answer to this probably lay in the quality of the dates which delinquent girls obtained (1964: 88) and in the number of sexual favours bestowed in order to obtain these dates. This claim lacks evidence, ignores the meaning of the date to the girl and is circular; it amounts to no more than the proposition: sexual delinquents are sexual.

Overall, the analyses of these writers do not work. First, they completely ignore property crimes committed by girls.[18] Moreover, the negativistic beháviour of male delinquents is viewed as the expression of contempt for standards which they cannot meet. But the majority of girls, including sexually active girls, do marry; they can meet the standards of success for women which these writers set out. Further, the boys' delinquency provides them with status in the eyes of the peer-group. This is not so for sexually active girls. Girls must learn to achieve sexual attractiveness without demonstrating active sexuality. 'Having plenty of boy friends' is approved of; 'being obsessed with boys' is not. There is a vast range of activities and ways of appearing which are viewed negatively: *too* much make-up, *too* tight jeans, *too* low a blouse and so on (Hudson, 1979). The essence of these theorists' discussion is that men and women have different goals. Leonard, a feminist writer, agrees: 'they experience different expectations (marital status versus occupational achievement)' (1982: 133). In this, Leonard adopts the same dated, stereotypical and sexist position. There may be differences in emphasis between men's and women's expectations, but they are not fundamentally different. Gilligan (1982: 159), for example, refers to highly successful and achieving women who did not mention their academic and professional distinction in describing themselves; their identity was defined rather in the context of a relationship. For men, this was not so. This difference is clearly important, but it is a difference *in emphasis*. The women had, after all, aspired to, and achieved, professional distinction.

Women's sexuality has also been used to explain non sex-related offences.[19] The Gluecks wrote that the women in their sample were a 'sorry lot': 'the major problem in (their) delinquency and criminality . . . is their lack of control of their sexual impulses' (1934: 299). In Pollak's (1961) terms, it is woman's ability to conceal her lack of sexual arousal that lies at the root of women's criminal behaviour. West described girls who stole as 'sexual rebels' (1967: 198) and Konopka suggested that whatever the girl's offence — shoplifting, running away, truancy — 'it is usually accompanied by some disturbances . . . in the sexual area' (1966: 4). Kleptomania is rare, but women are reputedly more often affected by it than men. In the psychoanalytic literature, this is linked to women's sexuality. For example, Zavitzianos writes:

> Female castration anxiety and other pregenital anxieties push kleptomaniacs to steal in order to compensate for the loss of a penis and various other libidinal gratifications and ego needs of childhood

. . . common to all forms of kleptomania are the conflicts over masturbation and the search for a symbolic object. (1983: 156)

Al-Issa (1980: 179) refers to evidence that 'occasionally women discover that laying hands on certain objects . . . with an intent to steal results in sudden orgasm'.[20] Even terrorism by women has been explained with reference to women's sexuality. Cooper refers to erotomania as a primary cause of female terrorism and goes on: 'The key to female terrorism undoubtedly lies hidden somewhere in women's complex sexual nature . . . Clearly, the sexual relationships of women terrorists have considerable influence on what they do and why they do it' (1979: 154). It is as if women could not hold strong political views or act on them.

Sex Role and Crime

In chapter 1, I outlined the stereotypical characteristics of men and women which exist in our culture, and earlier in this chapter I questioned the extent to which these are biologically determined. The impact of differential socialization cannot be ignored. Girls are more closely supervised and more strictly disciplined than boys, and informal sanctions are imposed more consistently and for more minor deviations from accepted standards. While boys might be encouraged to conform, often they are rewarded for flaunting conventional standards (sexual experimentation among male teenagers, for example, is condoned if not actively encouraged).

This process of differential socialization starts at birth. Parents respond differently to babies, depending on what sex they believe the child to be, and certain culturally designated behaviours are rewarded or punished (for example, aggression) depending on the sex of the child. As early as three years old, children have clear gender identities though the process of socialization continues beyond this, both directly and indirectly (through advertising, books and school curriculum). This has obvious implications for understanding women's criminality, or the apparent lack of it.

The notion of 'sex role' is, however, somewhat more complex than that outlined. Eichler (1980: 21) identifies ten possible versions of it and is critical of its everyday usage as 'unidimensional, polarized and reified'. She explains that this usage has equated the ideal sex role with actual sex roles, has equated men's perception with men's and women's actual behaviour and has ignored women's perception. Discussions of sex role also tend to omit references to race and class differences in socialization. Black girls, for example, are encouraged to be assertive, responsible and independent (Sharpe, 1976), and Trasler (1965) used differences in middle-class and working-class socialization practices to explain the apparent prevalence of criminality in working-class children. He did not, however, explore gender differences. There is also the danger of substituting social for biological determinism, of substituting 'role is destiny' for 'anatomy is destiny'. (For a fuller critique of sex roles see Smart, 1976.) But it is this over-simplified and everyday usage which has influenced the criminological literature. Oakley, for example, suggests that: 'One might reasonably conclude that the patterns of male and female crime are tied to cultural patterns of masculinity and femininity so that the type and amount of crime committed by each sex express both sex typed personality and sex typed social roles' (1972: 68). She continues: 'Criminality and masculinity are linked because the sort of acts associated with each have much in common . . . the dividing line between what is masculine and what is criminal may at times be a thin one' (1972: 72).[21] Crime is, in this way, seen both as a contradiction and an expression of women's traditional role.

The contradiction is the belief that women are socialized not to commit crime; those who do must have experienced faulty socialization (Morris, 1964 and 1965; Richardson, 1969). This alleged relationship between poor socialization and women's criminality has not, however, been much tested. The emphasis in research has tended to be on the family, particularly the effect of a broken home on girls. However, evidence that 'broken homes' lead to delinquency is lacking (Datesman and Scarpitti, 1980), and other researchers (Shover et al., 1979; Thornton and James, 1979) have found that very little delinquency is accounted for by role differences. Conversely, the supposedly different socialization of black women has been used to explain their greater involvement in crime. In the dominant culture, the traits of independence, responsibility and assertiveness which they demonstrate are gender-specific and black women who display these so-called 'masculine' traits may be viewed as crime-prone.

Two offences traditionally associated with women — shoplifting and prostitution — have been linked to expressions of women's role. I questioned the statistical basis of this association in chapter 2. It can also be more generally criticized. Explanations offered for shoplifting tend to differ according to the sex of the offender. Women are often thought to shoplift as a result of subconscious motivations (kleptomania), depression (for example, resulting from the menopause) or poverty (for example, mothers on welfare who steal food). Accounts presented for men, on the other hand, refer more frequently to peer-group pressure and the search for excitement. Argenent's (1981) review indicates that a whole variety of similar motives exist for both sexes: addiction, poverty, excitement, personal problems, and so on. Thus a simple link with women's role is inappropriate. All women shop, and so why do only some shoplift? And how does one explain men's shoplifting which is arguably in conflict with their role?

Lemert drew parallels between prostitutes and other women. He wrote: 'Shopgirls who have sex relations in return for a dinner and a show from their dates are employing sex as a means to certain material goals' (1951: 238). Davis (1971) continued this theme. He viewed prostitution as using the traditional female role in an illegitimate way. He drew parallels between the prostitute selling her favours and a married woman exchanging sexual favours for economic support: 'the prostitute's affront is that she trades promiscuously' (1971: 350). Rosenblum (1975) develops this notion within a labelling rather than a functionalist perspective. She suggests that if women are socialized to regard their sexual favours as marketable and their worth as contingent on their physical attractiveness, then prostitution is a logical consequence. The prostitute, according to Rosenblum, uses the same attributes as other women and she uses them towards the same ends: 'All women, to the degree that they reflect the contemporary female sex role, are primary deviants' (1975: 169). Financial gain and desire for independence may be 'precipitating factors', but more important is the fact that prostitution is a consequence and extension of fundamental aspects of the female role.[22] An obvious question is why more women do not engage in prostitution?

Rosenblum relies on chance incidents in the life of the individual woman, which produce the initiative to act upon the potential for prostitution inherent in all women.

To sustain these arguments, Rosenblum has to make a number of assumptions. She sees the participation of women in crime as primarily participation in prostitution, and prostitutes as almost exclusively female. Hence she is able to generalize from prostitution to all crime and to locate an understanding of women's crime through an understanding of women's role. These assumptions are questionable. To the extent that women are more involved in prostitution, this reflects power structures, economic dependence and labelling processes rather than women's role. Further, the life of the street prostitute is anything but traditionally feminine: she must find customers, sell the service to them, find a place to transact business and collect money. Indeed, prostitution has much in common with the professions and hence with traditionally *male* activities! Moreover, the prostitute's life-style is particularly dangerous. Silbert and Pines (1982) interviewed 200 prostitutes. Three-quarters reported being raped, in most cases by total strangers and involving extensive force. Thus although most women have some insight into prostitution − for example, permitting sexual intercourse when they do not actively wish it − there are many differences which are ignored by Rosenblum and earlier theorists.

Prostitution involves a variety of activities (from the call-girl to the streetwalker) and has a variety of explanations. It is simplistic to focus solely on acting out the female role. In his research on male prostitutes, Allen (1980) found no typical type and pointed to the similarity of backgrounds and motivations among male and female prostitutes.

Women's role is not solely an explanation offered by traditional theorists. Both conventional and feminist writers have depicted conforming *and* criminal women as the products of all-pervasive gender-role conditioning (Naffin, 1985). Carlen, for example, suggests that the autobiographical accounts of women's criminal careers demonstrate how: 'under certain material and ideological conditions . . . law-breaking may indeed comprise rational and coherent responses to women's awareness of the social disabilities imposed on them by discriminatory and exploitative class and gender relations' (1985: 8). She describes the women as rejecting conventional gender roles (as Freud did within a very different theoretical framework) and finding, through crime, roles which 'lift them above the social disabilities imposed on them as women' (1985: 11). Each woman, Carlen claims, 'deliberately engaged in lawbreaking as a way of either achieving satisfaction as a person or of resolving some of the problems facing her as a woman' (1985: 11). Explicitly with reference to two of the women in the book, Chris and Christina, Carlen believes that they have shown that 'criminal activity can provide, at least in the short term, one satisfying alternative to the frustrations of conventional womanhood' (1985: 103).

At the very least, this kind of explanation ignores the fact that most women do not turn to crime. More importantly, it does not fit well with the accounts offered by the women themselves. Admittedly, Christina's history is complex, but Carlen describes her motivation as being the best way of achieving her desire for kicks and a high income. With respect to shoplifting, Christina's own explanation was, in part, the provision of an income for her family: 'I never saw the enormous incompatibility of the situation of being a full-time mother and a full-time thief . . . I thought of it as my worktime' (1985: 78). But later she offers a quite different, less rational, explanation: 'I have since realised that I was overestimating my capacity to control my own weakness. It was the same as when an alcoholic takes that second drink. The stealing just snowballed' (1985: 94). Another of the women, Chris, presents her criminal activities as fulfilling a need for excitement and independence: 'I have broken your law and entered my freedom. I lived the excitement of villainy, the highs, the buzz . . . I was only alive when taking chances along with the others who lived that way as well' (1985: 29–30). And for Jenny it was a way of succeeding as a business woman: 'No great decisions were necessary to become criminal. One could just slip over from legality to illegality without any effort . . . a certain amount of lawbreaking was almost a condition of living in the fast lane' (1985: 113). Presumably Jenny's *male* partner in crime felt much the same. Jenny, Christina and Chris were doing what many men have done and so to explain their crime in terms of the problems facing them as *women* is too crude.

Women's criminality is undoubtedly limited in size and form by limitations in opportunity. Women shoplift because they have opportunities to do so; they do not get much involved in white-collar crime because they do not have access to the opportunities in which they could commit such crimes. Simon (1975) predicted that as opportunities for women increased, so too would their criminality. Other theorists have also taken a predictive step and referred to women's crime rate increasing as gender roles converge (Pollak, 1961; Oakley, 1972). The most well known proponent of this view is Freda Adler (1975 and 1977). Claiming that 'women have entered all categories of crime statistics' and that this is occurring 'throughout the world', she explains that: 'A general social movement is sweeping the world with egalitarian forces to provide women with the opportunity for a more equal footing in the criminal hierarchy . . . this assimilation of sex roles often amounts to an obscuring of boundaries which have traditionally subdued and safeguarded girls' (1977: 101 – 9). The remainder of this section examines the validity of the claims of Adler and Simon. Both, either directly or indirectly, drew links between statistical increases in women's crime and the women's movement.

The 'modern' women's movement (there has been a women's movement since at least the 1890s) dates from the 1960s. It is concerned with equal education and training opportunities, the prohibition of discrimination in employment, the provision of maternity rights and child-care facilities and the right of women to control their reproductive lives. Women's crime appeared to be increasing (and changing) in the mid-1960s and so connections were made.

A major deficiency in the work of Adler and Simon is their use of the criminal statistics. Adler 'demonstrated' her claim by examining the criminal statistics of the United States, England, Brazil, India, East Africa, New Zealand and Germany. There are problems in such an endeavour. Basically, Adler ignored very different codes and legal systems, different cultures and different methods of collecting statistics. But there are problems in relying on the criminal statistics of just one country, as Simon does (the United States). I have already dealt with these in chapter 2. Briefly, there is no doubt that the number of women arrested in recent years has increased and that, for some offences, the rate of increase is higher than that for men. Percentage increases, however, can be misleading. In absolute terms, the number of men arrested continues to far outnumber the number of women arrested.

Further, because of problems associated with the 'dark figure of crime', we cannot say with certainty whether crimes have increased over a given period. Hypothetically, it is quite possible for actual crime to be decreasing while recorded crime is increasing. Nor can we say with certainty that crimes by a particular sex (or class or race for that matter) have actually increased. The criminal statistics are constructed and reflect the assumptions and biases of those who construct them — store detectives, victims, the police and so on.

The conclusion in chapter 2 was that the profile of the typical female offender is much the same as it was 20 years ago — a minor property offender. Further, Steffensmeier and Cobb (1981) concluded that apparent increases in women's crime reflected changes in law-enforcement practices and in the method of collecting statistics, rather than in the criminal behaviour of women. This raises an important point: the extent to which the women's movement or, more generally, social changes in the 1960s led not to changes in criminality among women but to changes *in perceptions* of women and of criminality among women. Gelsthorpe (1986: 130) quotes two police constables she interviewed who demonstrate the strength of these perceptions:

> I think girls are very much more violent now. We see them in here. I'm not surprised by it and I suppose it's mainly due to Women's Lib. and that lot. Much more violent than five to ten years ago, much more assertive.

> It's regrettable that girls now think they've got to be like the boys. Girls were much nicer five or so years ago. I blame the Equal Pay Act myself, it's been a major cause of crime, not only did it lead to more women going out to work and consequently neglecting their children . . . increasing juvenile crime in this way, but women themselves are less satisfied with their lives . . . equal pay forced prices up . . . therefore more women had to go out to work. Career women . . . it's all wrong. If women were content it would solve a lot of problems.

What people believe profoundly affects the way in which they act and, regardless of whether or not women's role changed or the nature of that change, possible changes in the perceptions of victims and criminal justice professionals cannot be ignored. Nor, of course, can changes in women's non-criminal behaviour. Research suggested (De Fleur, 1975) that women who were tearful were likely to be dealt with informally by the police. Women may no longer conform to such stereotyped behaviour.

There are a number of other difficulties in attempting to test Adler's and Simon's predictions: for example, the actual hypotheses are unclear. Is it that more masculine women will commit crime? that feminist women will commit crime? that increased opportunities for women will lead to crime? that the weakening of family and social controls over women will lead to crime? Often in the research papers there is a slippage from one to the other. For example, Adler talks of the convergence of roles — 'as the sex roles merge' (1977: 109) — but she also talks about obscuring 'boundaries which have traditionally subdued and safeguarded girls' (1977: 109), providing women 'with the opportunity for a more equal footing in the criminal hierarchy' (1977: 101), and the masculinization of female roles — 'as the gap narrows, the more similar they look and behave' (1977: 111).

It is also not obvious how to measure 'the women's movement'. Recent researchers (Fox and Hartnagel, 1979; Box and Hale, 1983) have used the following indicators: the rate of women's labour force participation, their educational involvement and the number of single women (increases are seen as indicators of emancipation) and fertility (decreases are seen as indicators of emancipation). These are not clear-cut indicators. The decision to work can arise from need as much as from choice and can reflect oppression (through, for example, additional family responsibilities) as much as emancipation. The indicator 'single' sometimes included the divorced and the widowed; again these do not arise necessarily by choice and most divorced people remarry. Its use as an indicator of freedom from 'patriarchal oppression' (Box and Hale, 1983) is dubious. With respect to women's educational involvement, that has increased but women still end up in different jobs or on different pay scales from men.

Apart from this lack of conceptual clarity, there is evidence to rebut some of Adler's assertions. Female prisoners, for example, score very high on traditional femininity scales. According to Widom (1981), they are more conservative than control groups. They believe that women should be submissive, faithful to their husband and not drink, smoke or commit crime. In a recent article, McCord and Otten (1983) demonstrated that the claim that the rejection of traditional feminine roles leads to crime lacks empirical support. Their study failed to find that women who held feminist opinions were prone to more aggressive attitudes or beliefs than their traditional peers. Nor, on the basis of self-report delinquency data, were feminists more likely to commit crime. McCord and Otten found that women who advocated liberated roles did not seek equality in those illegitimate opportunities offered through crime. Furthermore, feminism seems to have a negative influence on crime. One study (James and Thornton, 1980) found that girls with a high degree of opportunity and social support for delinquency and a low level of parental control — in other words, girls with a high potential for delinquency — were less likely to commit delinquent acts if they held feminist attitudes.[23]

I mentioned earlier that explanations for black women's criminality have focused on the similarity of their socialization to men's. Adler, however, suggested that 'the differences between them (black and white women) are fading, the social forces which mould them are becoming identical, their paths to liberation are converging' (1975: 134); hence she argued that their patterns of criminal behaviour were growing more similar. Young (1980) and Lewis (1981) explored these claims and concluded that they lacked an empirical base. However, Laub and McDermott (1985), in their analysis of crime trends, did find that the crime rates of black women and white women were moving closer together. They explained this, though, as largely due to a decline in the crime rate of black women rather than an increase in white women's crime rate. Their data, therefore, also do not support Adler's claims.

A major assumption underlying the suggestion that increased opportunities lead to increases in women's crime is that women's role has changed, that women now play an equal part in social, economic and political life. It may seem like that, but they do not. In the economic sphere, there has been legislation about equal pay, equal opportunity and equal 'worth'. Yet women's earnings continue to average only about two-thirds of those of men. Overall, the proportion of women's earnings to men's has not changed much from the mid-1960s; also, the implementation of equal pay has not meant equal earnings. This could be explained by differences in the characteristics of male and female employees — for example, differences in education, age, and experience — but Almquist (1977) argues that, at least in the United States, it is due to employers' discrimination: lower earnings are justified on the basis that single women will marry and leave work (in fact, more than half of married women continue to work) and that married women are less productive than male workers. Overall, women make up more than two-thirds of low paid workers (*New Society*, 20–7 December 1984: 477). Even in those areas in which women dominate numerically, their earnings are lower (for example, teaching).

Women now form about 40 per cent of the work force; in 1950 they made up less than 30 per cent. Paradoxically, this expansion has resulted in little widening of job opportunities. It has primarily meant that more women work in the same narrow sections of the economy: as secretaries, nurses, clerical assistants, domestics and primary-school teachers. This is especially so for black women who often end up with jobs others do not want to do (Bryan et al., 1985). They experience both racial and sexual discrimination.

In England, women make up only about 10 per cent of lawyers or doctors and 2 per cent of engineers. (The comparable figures in the United States are higher: about 8 per cent of lawyers, 17 per cent of doctors and 7 per cent of engineers are female.) These figures are undoubtedly higher than they were 20 years ago, and they are likely to increase. But this may be a hollow victory. In professions such as law, medicine, dentistry and college teaching, there is a rapidly developing split in the United States between prestige jobs which involve high pay and autonomy and a new class of more poorly paid jobs with little autonomy. Women are overwhelmingly concentrated in the latter. There is some evidence of this in England and Wales too.

Women also continue to bear the brunt of domestic and child-care responsibilities even when they are in full-time employment. More than half of all children have working mothers. In fact, it can be suggested that women have less freedom now than 40 years ago; they are more commonly expected to contribute to the family's income yet child-care facilities are inadequate for the demands made on them. In addition, the number of single-parent families has increased in recent years, as has the number of women who head such families. One out of every six families is maintained by a woman and these women are much more likely to be living in poverty than married couples with families.

The same dismal picture appears in political life, though again there has been progress: of the 2,579 candidates in the 1983 General Election, 276 were women; this is an increase of 10 per cent over the 1979 figures. However, only 3 per cent of MPs are female, almost the lowest number in Europe. Women are similarly under-represented in trades unions. For example, 72 per cent of the members of the NUT are female, but only 8 (out of 41) of the executive, 2 (out of 19) of the full-time officials and 10 (out of 37) of the TUC delegates are female. Eight of the 50 seats on the TUC General Council are occupied by women and there are only 3 female general secretaries of unions.

Those who link the women's movement and crime are unaware of the kinds of changes which have occurred in women's role over the last 20 years. For some there has certainly been progress. For the majority, however, traditional expectations (for example, marriage and a family) or traditional barriers (for example, type of employment and low wages) have not been discarded or surmounted. But even if we accept the confused notion which proponents of the association have, there remains a paradox: the women's movement has its greatest impact on white, middle-class women; crime and the criminal justice system has its greatest impact on black and working-class women.

Women may be more involved in crime now than 20 years ago. Indeed, there are good reasons why this would be so: unemployment, low wages, poverty, economic marginalization and so on (Box and Hale, 1983). And such factors would explain race and class differences in women's crime rates.[24] The unemployment rate among 16- to 19-year-old black girls, for example, is three times higher than the national average (Bryan et al., 1985). The assumed association between the women's movement and increases in women's crime in any direct causal way is highly suspect. Two events can occur at the same time without them having anything to do with each other (Huff and Geis, 1954). However, women are certainly more involved in the criminal justice system now than 20 years ago and I believe the explanation for this lies not with the women's movement, but with the challenges to the social order which it was seen to represent.

The women's movement gathered momentum in the 1960s alongside student protests, the growth of black power, campaigns for the acceptance of homosexuality, anti-war protests, and so on. The total thrust of such challenges had the effect of sensitizing opinion to the issues raised by the women's movement. The possibility that women might become marginal to the family became a matter of concern, especially at a time when the family was perceived as something solid and dependable amidst these various concerns. The importance of woman's role in the family is unmistakable. Her role in the reproduction and socialization of the young is sufficient to exemplify this. But her role goes beyond this. The family, and it is really *women's* role in the family which people mean when they refer to the family, has been variously described as a form of social control, as a stabilizer and as a form of cement.[25] It is notable that many theories which try to explain delinquency focus on women − working mothers, maternal deprivation, hostile, rejecting mothers, and so on. So, if the family represents an ideal through which harmony can be promoted and conflict dissolved, the mere suggestion that women might be dissatisfied with their position in the family must have a considerable impact. It seems unlikely to be a matter of chance that concern about women's crime increased at a time of moral crises. When crises abound, it becomes natural and inevitable to focus on the family and to re-assert the traditional roles of women (Gelsthorpe, 1981; Morris and Gelsthorpe, 1981; Hutter and Williams, 1981).

The debates surrounding the early women's movement provide a good example of what I mean. Prevalent nineteenth-century views were that women would be degraded by the vote and that education for girls would be a disastrous error because it would aggravate the physiological strains which puberty and ovulation put upon them. Alongside these views were arguments that women's emancipation would create havoc with law and order. Pike, in *A History of Crime in England*, observed that 'every step made by a woman towards her independence is a step towards that precipice at the bottom of which lies a prison' (1876: 527). Educating women and removing from them the constraints of domesticity and maternity would, it was suggested, allow the 'semi-criminal' personality present in all women to emerge. A Home Office memorandum in England, for example, said, concerning suffragettes, that if the *idea* of emancipation encouraged so many women to become obstreperous and hysterical, then the reality of it would be disastrous.

These tactics were part and parcel of an attempt to stem the emancipation of women. Suggestions that women's emancipation leads to the destruction of the family and that the women's movement leads to increases in crime are ideological pretexts for perpetuating the status quo. A clear example of this is the attempt in England to get women out of the labour market, as happened after World War II and during each economic recession since. Superficially, therefore, the debate is about increases in women's crime. But underlying this is the re-assertion of traditional roles for women.[26]

Taking Account of Women

Special theories for women's crime have not been particularly successful. In Carlen's words: 'Any explanations of a taken-for-granted 'female criminality' — whether those explanations be styled feminist, radical, marxist, or whatever — must, by the nature of the project, be as reductionist and essentialising as the much maligned biological ones' (1985: 9). One implication of this (though not one accepted by Carlen) is that we need to reconsider the relevance to women of general criminological theories. This is not to suggest that there is, or will be, *a* general theory of crime. As Walker wrote: 'The quest for a general theory which will account for all instances of crime . . . makes no more sense than would a search for a general theory of disease' (1977: 143). But there is no reason to suppose that explanations for women's crime should be fundamentally different from explanations for men's crime, though gender must play a part in any such explanation. Some theories, as we saw in chapter 1, do not work. There are a number of criminological theories, however, which, though not originally developed for women, do contribute to our understanding of women's crime, especially when combined. Here are three brief examples.

Cloward and Ohlin (1961) agreed with Merton's theory and added that illegitimate means were also unevenly distributed. Their concern was unequal distribution within the class structure;

they did not explicitly discuss female delinquents. But since women do experience unequal opportunities, this is a possible explanation for women's crime. Indeed, logically, one might expect women to have a higher crime rate than men since their opportunities are more limited. Harris (1977) considered this, but suggested that women also have more limited illegitimate opportunities and that this explains their apparently lower crime rate.

There have been a number of explicit attempts to test the validity of Cloward and Ohlin's theory for women. Datesman et al. (1975), for example, found that both black and white female delinquents regarded their opportunities less positively than their non-delinquent counterparts and this perception was more strongly related to girls' involvement in delinquency than boys'. Cernkovich and Giordano's (1979) data also confirmed that perceived absence of opportunities led to delinquency. Thus Cloward and Ohlin's theory seems to have some relevance for the explanation of female criminality. Indeed, Figueira-McDonough (1980) rephrased the original formulation to take account of this: similar levels of frustration will lead to similar behaviour by the two sexes if they have equal knowledge of, and comparable access to, illegitimate means.

The theory of differential association was developed first by Sutherland in the 1930s and was later refined by him and Cressey (1960 and subsequent editions). The basic principles are that criminal behaviour is learned, just like any other behaviour, in interaction with others and particularly in small groups (families and friends). This learning includes not only techniques but also rationalizations, justifications and attitudes and it can vary in frequency, intensity and duration. Sutherland and Cressey believed that an individual became criminal if the definitions favourable to violating the law exceeded those unfavourable to it. Differential association was an attempt to postulate a general theory, explaining all types of crime, but also non-participation in crime.

The theory stemmed from Sutherland's concern with, and as a reaction against, theories which stressed poverty as an explanation for crime. He argued that such explanations ignored the fact that approximately equal numbers of boys and girls were poor yet the majority of those adjudged delinquent were male. Differential association, on the other hand, seemed to explain why men were more delinquent than women. Giordano (1978) tested one aspect of this by examining the role of the peer-group in transmitting definitions favourable to the violation of law. She found that those girls who were part of a regular group were more likely to be delinquent than others and that the more leisure time spent in the group, the more likely a girl was to be delinquent. This provides some support for the relevance of differential association theory in understanding female delinquency.

Hirschi (1969) asked the question 'why do people *not* commit crimes?' rather than why they do. He assumed that all of us are capable of crime and that it is social controls not belief in social values which maintain the law. Without these controls, he argued, crime results. His key concept is social bond and this is divided into four elements: attachment (for example, to one's family), commitment (to, for example, one's reputation), involvement (in, for example, conventional leisure activity), and belief (in, for example, the law). It is the nature of this bond which is important; if people are bonded to society's norms and values, they will remain non-delinquent.

Hirschi conducted a comprehensive examination of his theory and found considerable support for it. Girls, however, were excluded from Hirschi's analysis because few had official records of delinquency,[27] yet it is plausible that low levels of control would lead to delinquent behaviour among both boys and girls. Hindelang (1973) examined the validity of Hirschi's results for a group of rural students, evenly split by sex. Generally, indicators of 'attachment' to parents and the school, 'commitment' to and 'involvement' in conventional activities, and 'belief' in laws were related to reported delinquent involvement among these respondents to about the same extent as Hirschi's urban males.[28]

None of these theories is without criticism. For example, they are difficult to test because of difficulties in operationalizing key concepts. Nor are they the only theories which might contribute to our understanding of women's criminality. Leonard (1982), for example, believes that labelling theory and Marxist discussions of crime would help (see also Box, 1983). My point is simply that criminological theories should be reread and reconsidered in the light of their *potential* for understanding women's crime. Differential opportunity structures, associations, socialization and social bonding can aid our understanding of crimes committed both by men and women and can take account of differences in the nature and extent of their crimes.

Conclusion

Women, like men, commit a variety of crimes for a variety of reasons; there is no single or special theory for their crimes. In Carlen's words 'the essential criminal woman does not exist' (1985: 10). Despite this, conventional criminological conceptions of women's motivations for crime have differed from men's. The importance of these conceptions is that they influence both policy and practice in the criminal justice system towards women. I discuss this further in chapters 4 and 5. Similarly, no single or special theory is necessary to explain why there are comparatively few female criminals. There are also few female judges, police officers and the like. The reasons are remarkably similar. I discuss this further in chapter 6.

4

Women in the Criminal Justice System

Introduction

Feminist writers (for example, Smart and Brophy, 1985) have documented the law's restrictions on women, particularly in the spheres of the family, sexuality and reproduction. But 'law' is not just a collection of legal statutes; it has to be interpreted and although statutes do not differentiate between men and women, practice does. We saw in chapter 3 that legislation designed explicitly to provide equal opportunities in employment — the Equal Pay Act 1970 and the Sex Discrimination Act 1975 — has not achieved this in practice. It is equally clear that the law fails adequately to protect women from sexual assault and domestic violence. This is discussed in chapter 7. In this chapter, I examine whether men and women are dealt with differently in the criminal justice system.

Decisions are made at a variety of points in the criminal justice system: by members of the public, police, prosecutors, juries, judges and so on. There are always choices to be made, and many variables influence these choices. Some of these I discuss in other chapters; for example, the reasons why victims may not report offences to the police and why the police may not record allegations of offences as crimes. The social characteristics of offenders also influence these choices. A considerable body of research has demonstrated the influence of such factors as the race and class of offenders on decision-makers (Piliavin and Briar, 1964; Reiss, 1971). The sex of the offender is also a relevant factor, but its influence is not clear-cut.

The most common assumption is that women are dealt with more leniently than men. They are thought to be less likely to be arrested, convicted or imprisoned. This chapter evaluates the evidence for this at a variety of decision points in the criminal justice system and attempts to identify its underlying rationale. It asks what model of 'woman' informs these decisions and what the wider implications are for women generally.

Initial Responses to Women's Crime

The police play a crucial role in controlling who comes into the criminal justice system. Full enforcement of the law is clearly both impossible and undesirable and so the police have wide discretion in such matters as the allocation of resources and interpretation of the law as well as in encounters with individual suspects. In Bottomley's words: 'The combined effects of this discretion . . . result in only a small minority of all 'offenders' handled by the police proceeding to the next stage of court hearing and judicial decision-making . . . in a very real sense it is a highly selected sample of all police contacts' (1973: 73—4).

It has long been thought that women were dealt with preferentially by the police. The criminal statistics support this at face value, as table 4.1 shows. But the statistics can be explained in other ways. Studies of police discretion (Piliavin and Briar, 1964; Reiss, 1971) stress the importance of demeanour and attitude in interactions with the police. This is relevant for both sexes, but it is plausible that, because of differential socialization processes, women are more likely than men to demonstrate the behaviour which the police take as a sign of lack of 'troublesomeness' (De Fleur, 1975).[1] There is also some evidence (Mawby, 1980) that girls are more favourably disposed to the police than boys. They are more willing than boys to see the police as interested in helping them and are less cynical about police honesty. The police are also less likely to arrest non-serious, non-persistent offenders. Again, women are more likely than men to fall into these categories (Carey, 1979; Baldwin and Bottoms, 1976). Moyer (1981) tested these suggestions by asking police officers in the United States how they would act in certain situations. She found that their decisions were not contingent on the sex of the offender.

TABLE 4.1 OFFENDERS CAUTIONED FOR INDICTABLE AND SUMMARY
OFFENCES, AS PERCENTAGE OF PERSONS FOUND GUILTY OR
CAUTIONED, BY SEX AND AGE, 1985

	Men	*Women*
All ages	20	27
Aged 10 and under 14	80	93
Aged 14 and under 17	52	77
Aged 17 and under 21	9	17
21 and over	10	12

Source: Home Office, 1986a

The major factors influencing the decisions were the nature of the offence and the offender's demeanour. Carey (1979) interviewed a sample of police officers in England and they too all maintained that the sex of the accused had no bearing at all on the decision whether or not to prosecute. Cautions were given for routine rather than idiosyncratic or discriminatory reasons.[2] (See also studies by Landau, 1981 and Landau and Nathan, 1983 in the metropolitan area of London, and Fisher and Mawby's (1982) study in Bradford.)[3]

Evidence for the preferential treatment of women by the police *because they are women* is weak. In contrast, there is some clear evidence of women experiencing a very different kind of treatment. Prostitutes, for example, complain of harrassment and that allegations of crimes against them are not treated seriously. The police have also been criticized for not acting urgently enough when the victims of homicide appear to be prostitutes. It is impossible to establish this but police did seem to make distinctions between prostitutes and other women in the hunt for the so-called Yorkshire Ripper (Peter Sutcliffe). Initially, Sutcliffe killed prostitutes. After the death of an apparently 'respectable' woman, an Assistant Chief Constable was quoted in a newspaper as saying 'All women are now in danger. The next Ripper victim could be anyone's wife, daughter or girlfriend' (The *Daily Mirror*, 7 April 1979). Further, the Bradford police published a poster with the words: 'the next victim may be innocent' (Dumaresq, 1981).

Rape victims are another exception. They have complained of aggressive questioning and disbelief by police officers. I will discuss this in chapter 7. Neither do black and working-class women experience leniency; both race and class influence police attitudes and decisions (Landau, 1981; Landau and Nathan, 1983; Visher 1983). Their demeanour, both in police and subsequent interactions, may not reflect the approved 'feminine' traits of passivity and remorse. There is also considerable evidence that female status offenders are dealt with differently, and more harshly, by the police than their delinquent sisters and brothers (Chesney-Lind, 1973; Terry, 1970). I will return to this later in the chapter. Women involved in peace campaigns also provide many examples of police intimidation and harassment.

The question which these findings raise is whether, to the extent that women are dealt with leniently by the police (and this is still unclear), this depends on conformity to traditional role stereotypes. That is, lenient dispositions may be reserved for passive, unaggressive, remorseful, white, middle-class women. This is a recurrent theme in research on the influence of gender in the criminal justice system and I will explore it further later.

Women and the Courts

Bail consideration is one of the earliest and most important decision points in the criminal justice system. Refusal of bail may have an effect on both the likelihood of conviction and the nature of the sentence imposed (Friedland, 1965; Bottomley, 1970; Roberts and Palermo, 1958). Also, of course, the consequence of a refusal of bail is a period of imprisonment before trial and this can disrupt the personal, social and family life of the alleged offender. The counter-argument is that it is a matter of concern if a person granted bail either absconds or commits further offences while on bail. The main issue in bail, at least in theory, is reconciling these concerns with the interests of the individual.

The official statistics do not give information on bail decisions according to the sex of the person, and potential sex differences in the decision whether or not to grant bail have not been much examined. In Edwards's (1984) study in Manchester, women were refused bail particularly in those offences viewed as 'untypical' of female offenders: burglary and robbery. These offences, however, were the more serious and male offenders in these categories probably also have a high likelihood of remand in custody. (Edwards provides no comparative information.) Edwards also suggested that a high proportion of her sample of women were remanded in custody for their own protection, but this was mentioned only 12 times out of 171 factors cited. Failure to surrender to custody and the commission of further offences[4] were cited much more frequently as grounds for refusal of bail.

According to Edwards (1984: 16), women are more likely than men to be remanded for medical or psychiatric reports. She cites figures from Gibbens, Soothill and Pope's (1977) survey in the inner-London area that 18 per cent of men were remanded for medical reports, compared with 32 per cent of women. The figures quoted, however, refer only to offences committed in 'schools, shops and hospitals', and create quite the wrong impression. The percentage of men remanded for medical reports overall in the inner-London magistrates' courts was 9.3 per cent compared with 7.1 per cent for women. In Edwards's study, only 2 per cent of women were remanded for medical reports and she provides no comparable data for men.

On the other hand, Megan Bull, former governor of Holloway prison, asserted in her evidence to the Parliamentary subcommittee on *Women in the Penal System* that many remands of women in custody for reports were 'negative':

> We have a very large proportion of women remanded for medical reports and a high proportion are negative in the sense that there is no medical recommendation, and I think sometimes this is simply a device to put a woman in prison for three weeks with the supposition that a medical report might do something, or perhaps just as a punitive way, because a very high proportion are negative. (quoted in Matthews, 1981: 10 – 11)[5]

Some support for the punitive nature of remands in custody is found in the fact that women remanded in custody are less likely than men to receive custodial sentences (Home Office, 1986c: tables 2.1, 2.2, 2(e) and 2(f). Almost 18,000 men (that is, 29 per cent of those remanded in custody) and just over 1,600 women (that is, 47 per cent of those remanded in custody) subsequently received non-custodial sentences in 1985.[6] Of course, this does not necessarily mean that the remand in custody was punitive or negative. Considerations taken into account in determining the question of bail are different from those taken into account in sentencing. And sentences are likely to reflect the fact that offenders have spent some time in custody. Nevertheless, this marked disparity in the treatment of men and women requires explanation. It is at least plausible to speculate that giving women 'a taste of imprisonment' by remanding them in custody serves the deterrent or retributive aspects of sentencing without breaching for long women's domestic or child-care responsibilities.

Plea bargaining is a critical stage in the criminal justice system.[7] Again, the influence of sex has not been much investigated. In the United States, Bernstein et al. (1977) found that men did better in the negotiation process than women. An Alabama study (Alabama Law Review, 1975) found the opposite. Almost three times as many female defendants as males had their charges reduced. A more recent study by Bishop et al. (1983) supports neither view: women were treated neither more leniently nor more punitively than men.[8] There is no comparable English research, but one disturbing factor which has emerged here is the existence of people who plead guilty but maintain their innocence (Dell, 1971; Edwards, 1984). The reasons cited for this are police pressure or advice, a belief that there is no point in defending the case (where, for example, a woman is charged with soliciting or offences relating to drunkenness), a desire to avoid remands in custody and fear of a harsher sentence. It is not known whether this practice is more common among women than men. Baldwin and McConville's (1977) sample included both men and women (the numbers are unspecified) but they present no evidence on whether sex was an important variable in this claim of innocence.

It is often stated that juries are sympathetic towards female defendants and are, therefore, likely to acquit them. Kalvan and Zeisel (1966), however, on the basis of experimental data, argued that it was not easy to isolate the fact that the defendant was a woman from circumstances of attractiveness, sympathy and remorse which benefited both sexes. In Baldwin and McConville's (1979) study of actual jury trials in Birmingham and London, the sex of the defendant was not presented as a factor which influenced acquittals. The most important factors were 'some weakness in the prosecution case' and 'the strength of the defence case' (1979: 49). The factor 'jury swayed by sympathy with defendant or antipathy to victim' was identified as important by judges, prosecutors and the police in between a quarter and a third of the acquittals, but there was no evidence that this was linked to the sex of the victim or the offender.

The bulk of the research on the effect of sex on decisions has been carried out in the field of sentencing.[9] Published statistics suggest that women are more likely to receive discharges and probation orders and are less likely to receive custodial penalties than men. This holds good for offences which women are commonly sentenced for. They are also more likely to receive shorter sentences of imprisonment. Tables 4.2 to 4.6 demonstrate this.

Traditional criminologists frequently referred to such statistics in support of their thesis that female defendants were dealt with leniently (Mannheim, 1965; Walker, 1965; Reckless and Kay, 1967; Pollak, 1961), and much of the early research confirmed this preferential treatment model (Nagel and Weitzman, 1971; Green, 1961; Alabama Law Review, 1975). Sometimes, when controls were added (for example, the seriousness of the offence or previous convictions), such differences disappeared, but other researchers have concluded that the pattern of lenient treatment for women in the courts is 'pervasive' (Moulds, 1980).

The issue, however, is more complex than this. Nagel's (1981)

TABLE 4.2   PERCENTAGE OF OFFENDERS AGED 21 AND OVER, SENTENCED FOR INDICTABLE OFFENCES, BY SEX AND TYPE OF SENTENCE OR ORDER, 1985 (ENGLAND AND WALES)

	Men	*Women*
Absolute or conditional discharge	9	23
Probation order	7	18
Fine	43	41
Community service order	7	3
Imprisonment		
Fully suspended	12	8
Partly suspended	2	1
Unsuspended	19	6
Otherwise dealt with	1	1

Source: Home Office, 1986a

TABLE 4.3   PERSONS AGED 21 AND OVER, SENTENCED AT
MAGISTRATES' COURTS, BY SEX AND RESULT (INDICTABLE OFFENCES
ONLY, AND EXCLUDING MOTORING OFFENCES), [a] 1985 (ENGLAND AND
WALES)

	Men	*Women*
Absolute or conditional discharge	12	26
Probation order	8	18
Fine	54	46
Community service order	7	2
Imprisonment		
Fully suspended	8	5
Partly suspended	1	1
Unsuspended	9	3
Otherwise dealt with	1	1

[a]   For summary offences, 97 per cent of men and 96 per cent of women were fined.
Source: Home Office, 1986a

TABLE 4.4   PERCENTAGE OF OFFENDERS AGED 21 AND OVER,
SENTENCED AT MAGISTRATES' [a] COURTS FOR SHOPLIFTING, BY SEX
AND TYPE OF SENTENCE, 1985 (ENGLAND AND WALES)

	Men	*Women*
Absolute or conditional discharge	14	23
Probation order	9	16
Fine	59	53
Community service order	4	2
Imprisonment		
Fully suspended	6	4
Partly suspended	1	1
Unsuspended	7	2
Otherwise dealt with	1	1

[a]   Only 2,746 men and 1,374 women were sentenced at the Crown Courts.
Source: Home Office, 1986b

TABLE 4.5 PERCENTAGE OF OFFENDERS AGED 21 AND OVER,
SENTENCED AT MAGISTRATES' COURTS TO IMMEDIATE
IMPRISONMENT, FOR ALL TYPES OF OFFENCE, BY SEX AND LENGTH OF
SENTENCE, 1985 (ENGLAND AND WALES)

	Men	*Women*
14 days and under	8	10
Over 14 days and up to 1 month	21	30
Over 1 month and up to 2 months	12	10
Over 2 months and up to 3 months	30	30
Over 3 months and up to 6 months	29	20
Over 6 months	—	—

Source: Home Office, 1986a

TABLE 4.6 PERCENTAGE OF OFFENDERS SENTENCED AT THE CROWN
COURTS TO IMMEDIATE IMPRISONMENT, FOR ALL TYPES OF OFFENCE,
BY SEX AND LENGTH OF SENTENCE, 1985 (ENGLAND AND WALES)

	Men	*Women*
6 months and under	30	41
Over 6 months up to and including 12 months	29	28
Over 12 months up to and including 2 years	24	23
Over 2 years up to and including 4 years	12	7
Over 4 years	5	2

Source: Home Office, 1986a

findings generally indicated more lenient sentences for women, but there were exceptions. She found that a whole range of variables which traditionally affected sentencing decisions for men — for example, the severity of the offence and the number of previous convictions — did not significantly affect the severity of sentences for women. Conversely, marital status, a variable not significant for men, had a strong effect on a woman's likelihood of being sent to prison. The type of offence was also relevant for women, but not for men. Thus female violent offenders were punished more harshly than female property offenders. Nagel explains this as punishment for a breach of role expectations in addition to the breach of the criminal law.[10] The same point has been made to explain the over-representation of black women in prisons in the United States. Black women may not conform to traditional role expectations; for example, they are more likely to commit violent offences and to be heads of households than white women. Lewis suggests that their over-representation reflects 'the extent to which sexism exacerbates existing disadvantages of racism' (1981: 100).

Farrington and Morris's (1983) research in Cambridge supports Nagel's conclusions. They found that women appeared to be more leniently dealt with than men, as table 4.7 demonstrates. But we know that minor offenders and non-persistent offenders

TABLE 4.7   NUMBER AND PERCENTAGE OF OFFENDERS SENTENCED FOR THEFT IN CAMBRIDGE (JANUARY TO JULY 1979) BY SEX AND TYPE OF SENTENCE

	Men		*Women*	
	Number	*Percentage*	*Number*	*Percentage*
Discharge	22	7.7	15	13.9
Fine (£25 or less)	43	15.0	27	25.0
Fine (£26 – £75)	116	40.4	49	45.4
Probation	14	4.9	12	11.1
Fine (£26 or more)	31	10.8	2	1.9
Community service order	18	6.3	0	0.0
Suspended sentence	9	3.1	1	0.9
Imprisonment (less than 3 months)	21	7.3	0	0.0
Imprisonment (more than 3 months) or committed to Crown Court	13	4.5	2	1.9
TOTAL	287	100.0	108	100.0

Source: Farrington and Morris, 1983

are likely to be dealt with leniently and when these factors were taken into account, Farrington and Morris found that the two sexes were dealt with in the same way: sex was not related to sentencing severity independent of other factors.[11] However, they also found that certain factors influenced sentences for women which did not influence the sentences given to men, namely marital status,[12] family background, the sexual composition of the bench and the involvement of other offenders. Table 4.8 gives full details of the ranking of factors which influenced the severity of sentences for men and women. The factors which were independently important for women but not for men are interesting. Women convicted with one or more other offenders were more likely to receive severe sentences than those convicted alone. Divorced and separated women received relatively severe sentences, as did women coming from a deviant family back-

TABLE 4.8   FACTORS INFLUENCING SENTENCE SEVERITY, IN ORDER OF IMPORTANCE

Total sample	*Men*	*Women*
Type of offence	Type of offence	Current problems
Current problems	Current problems	Convicted in the previous 2 years
Number of previous convictions	Number of previous convictions	Other offenders involved
Legal representation[a]	Legal representation	Number of Theft Act offences
Convicted in the previous 2 years	Number of Theft Act offences	Marital status[c]
Age	Age	Family background
Plea[b]	Plea	Sexual composition of the bench[d]

[a]   Those represented received the more severe sentences.
[b]   Pleading guilty led to more severe sentences.
[c]   Divorced and separated women were given more severe sentences.
[d]   Women appearing before a bench containing two female magistrates were sentenced more severely than those appearing before a bench containing two male magistrates.

ground. These may be the kind of women whom magistrates, especially female magistrates, disapprove of: they are women who do not conform to notions of 'respectable' women. (See also Dominelli, 1984; Eaton, 1983, 1985 and 1986.)

The importance of 'respectability' was also identified by Kruttschnitt (1982a). From a statistical analysis of more than a thousand cases involving female offenders, she found that the more 'respectable' a woman was, the more lenient her sentence. 'Respectability' referred to a good employment record, no alcohol or drug use and no psychiatric history. Kruttschnitt found that, regardless of the offence, the lower a woman's respectability the greater the likelihood that she would receive a severe sentence and that women with previous convictions who were respectable were given more lenient sentences than women viewed as disreputable who had no criminal record. Kruttschnitt (1982b) also found that the more economically dependent a woman was, the less severe her disposition. She linked both of these factors to the social control of women. Men, she argues, are less economically dependent than women and reputation is both less important and less easily damaged for men than women.

The research referred to so far has been based on statistical analysis of sentencing patterns. Observational research and interviews with sentencers attempt to look beyond these patterns and to explain them. A number of interesting case studies have been carried out in different parts of Great Britain which link sentencing patterns to conventional explanations of women's crimes. A woman who enters the criminal justice system is 'incongruous' (Worrall, 1981); a man is not. Hence, explanations for her presence are sought: menstruation, mental illness, poor socialization and so on. These explanations influence women's subsequent processing through the system. Pearson (1976), for example, from a small study of the magistrates' court in Cardiff, argued that women were responded to in the way in which we normally respond to juveniles — that is, they were viewed as not fully responsible for their actions. Responsibility was lessened in two ways: women were seen as social casualties or as mentally ill. By 'social casualties' Pearson meant women living on welfare, often heads of one-parent families with dependent children. Poverty was the basic problem and responsibility was lessened by this. The magistrates tended to respond to these women by remanding them for social inquiry reports and then subsequently imposing a nominal penalty such as a fine or a discharge. Responsibility was also lessened by reference to changes in behaviour, for example, by tacit references to the menopause. In these cases, there was also a tendency to remand the women for reports; the behaviour was seen as non-rational and as requiring an explanation. Pearson gives the example of a woman who pleaded guilty to stealing a cheque-book. The magistrates asked her why she did it. She replied, 'because I was broke'. She was remanded for reports despite the apparently rational explanation.

Worrall examined the processing of adult offenders in another magistrates' court. She found that the majority of offenders of either sex were charged with theft of a relatively minor nature and that the majority were eventually fined. This apparently simple conclusion concealed, however, a process which was both complex and sexually related. The most important consideration in sentencing men was the offence; for women, personal circumstances were significantly more important. According to Worrall, provided the woman acts her part (is modest, humble, remorseful) and references can be made to her previous good character or competence in the home, she is not seen as 'criminal'. References to domestic pressures or evidence of 'feminine conditions' also confirm that she cannot really be 'a criminal'. But once a woman has a criminal record or does not conform to these expectations, she is not viewed as a woman at all; she can no longer claim to be 'out of place'.

Eaton's (1983) case study was carried out in a court on the outskirts of London. Magistrates frequently told Eaton that they responded to the case itself and not to the sex of the offender. Observation seemed to confirm this; as in Worrall's study, most cases were dealt with on a routine basis by fining the defendants. In less routine matters, family circumstances were considered important in deciding the sentence for both sexes, along with the nature of the offence and the offender's previous record. The family was viewed by magistrates as a site of both social responsibility and social control and it was central to pleas in mitigation offered by counsel on behalf of both men and women. Magistrates were concerned with the domestic responsibilities of defendants and, in the interviews, many magistrates said that they would be influenced by the presence of children if the defendant was responsible for child care. According to Eaton, this concern was present whether the defendant was male or female.[13] But responsibility for children is more likely to arise in cases involving women than men and so Eaton concludes that the differential treatment of women results from differential family roles. This emphasis on family considerations for defendants of both sexes appears impartial but, in Eaton's words, 'actually perpetuates inequality'. Court-room practice both reveals and reinforces prevailing patriarchal ideologies. Thus it is women's role within the family, not her sex *per se* which is influential in sentencing.[14] (See also Thomas, 1979; Eaton, 1985 and 1986.)

This theme is reiterated in Carlen's (1983) interviews with sheriffs (judges) in Scotland. They all claimed that when sentencing women to prison, they took into account the same factors as in sentencing men, that is, the seriousness of the offence and the likely response of the public to the offence. But it gradually emerged in the interviews that the sheriffs were not prepared to satisfy public opinion at the expense of the women's children. The women sent to prison were those who, in the eyes of the sheriffs, *had failed as mothers.*[15] Thus sheriffs not only wanted to know whether a woman was a mother, but whether she was a *good* mother.[16] In the words of one sheriff:

> If she's a good mother, we don't want to take her away. If she's not a good mother, it doesn't matter (1983: 67).

Also, if the children were in care, the woman was more likely to be sent to prison than if the children were living at home. Again, to quote a sheriff:

> If . . . a woman has no children then it clears the way to send her to prison. If . . . they are in care . . . I treat her as a single women (1983: 67).

Sheriffs also viewed husbands and families as good disciplinary controls:

> If she has a husband, he may just tell her to stop it (1983: 67).

> Not many women with steady husbands or cohabitees commit crime. They're kept occupied (1983: 67).

The importance of considering women's domestic responsibilities is also stressed by the Home Office. As early as 1959, the provision of social enquiry reports before sentencing women was recommended by the Home Office because of the social consequences of imprisoning women. This was repeated in a 1968 circular which advised the use of social inquiry reports before imposing 'any sentence of imprisonment on a woman',[17] and this recommendation was expanded further in a 1971 circular to include 'any other woman defendant'.[18] The rationale was made explicit in 1977:

> To send a woman to prison, or indeed to any residential institution
> — even a hospital — is to take her away from her family; her
> children, in particular, may suffer from this deprivation, which can
> lead to the break-up of the home even where there is a stable
> marriage. When a man is absent from home, it can be kept going
> by his wife if she is provided with sufficient money and support.
> But when it is the woman who is absent, the husband is often
> unable to cope . . . the home may have to be broken up and the
> children scattered either into the care of the local authority, or to
> different relatives. (Home Office, 1977: para. 185)

The extent to which these recommendations are followed in practice is not known. Edwards (1984) argues that social enquiry reports are more likely to be requested 'in the non-typical female crimes of burglary and violence than in the more typical female offences of theft, or DHSS deception' (1984: 191). Her data do not support this, however. Social inquiry reports were requested in about a third of the cases involving violent offences. But they were also requested in about a third of the cases involving prostitution. However, social enquiry reports do have a major effect on sentencers (Hardiker, 1977). In Edwards's (1984) study of magistrates' courts, magistrates agreed with probation officers' recommendations in more than half of the cases. Research in the United States (Frazier et al., 1983) suggested that, independent of other potential influences (for example, the number of previous convictions or the nature of the offence), being female greatly increased the likelihood of probation officers recommending a non-custodial sentence. The reasons for this were much the same as those which seem to influence sentencers. Probation officers held traditional ideas about roles, believed that the motives for criminal behaviour were different for men and women and believed that imprisonment was not, for that reason, appropriate for women.[19] The most common explanations for women's crimes were mental-health problems and unsatisfactory family relationships. Men's crimes were seen as related to irresponsible behaviour and men were viewed as more culpable and dangerous than women.[20]

Girls in the Juvenile Justice System

So far this discussion has focused on adult offenders. Girls are also dealt with differently from boys in the juvenile justice system. Paternalism is a theme throughout debates on juvenile justice but it has a greater impact on girls than boys because of different perceptions of their respective needs. In practice, it means that girls may be referred to the juvenile court for different reasons from boys,[21] and experience different types of dispositions. A major reason for these differences is the preoccupation in the juvenile justice system[22] with the sexuality of teenage girls.[23] Bryan et al. (1985) argue that prevailing stereotypes of black women as 'immoral' or 'promiscuous' make social workers hypersensitive to the possibility of moral danger among young black women who are sexually active.

Girls are more likely than boys to come into the juvenile justice system for status or moral danger offences[24] (Sarri, 1983). In Casburn's (1979) three-month period of observation in a juvenile court in London, over half the girls were before the court for non-criminal matters compared with one boy (out of 168 boys and he was a 6-month-old baby, the subject of proceedings on the ground of parental neglect). Chesney-Lind (1973) cites examples of referrals to the juvenile court for refusing to bathe, lying, refusing to do chores, lack of chastity and being an invertebrate (*sic*) liar. There is also some evidence that non-sex offences committed by girls are overlooked by such agencies as the police and that the girls' behaviour is redefined as sexual. Shacklady-Smith cites the example of 'Kathy' who said:

> It's funny because once when I was down the cop shop for fighting, this woman saw the swastika on my arm and forgot all about what she was looking for. They never did nothing — just told me to stop fighting. But the woman cop, she kept on about the swastika and Hell's Angels. What a bad lot they were for a girl to go around with, and how I had better stop going around with the Angels or else I'd get a really bad name for myself. Then she kept asking me if I'd had sex with any of 'em or taken drugs. (1978: 83)

Kathy was only subsequently taken to the juvenile court when her father complained that she stayed out most nights and was beyond his control.

Self-report studies consistently show that boys are as involved in status offences as girls and that girls are over-represented in such referrals to the juvenile court (Teilmann and Landry, 1981). Thus the difference is not in the behaviour of the sexes, but in society's response to that behaviour. This is sharply brought out in the case in 1985 involving Victoria Gillick, a mother of ten children, who sought to prohibit doctors prescribing contraceptives to girls under 16 without their parents' consent. Her concern was to control girls' sexuality rather than to prevent pregnancy, and was with parental authority rather than personal autonomy. Thus it was a concern about life-styles. The debate was about 'appropriate behaviour' for 'nice girls' and the construction of femininity.

Research by Morris and Wilkinson (1983) on the reasons why girls were placed in a secure assessment facility in England demonstrates further this preoccupation with 'appropriate' behaviour. Over a period of one year, 32 girls were placed in this particular institution. Only eight were there because of delinquent behaviour. The remainder were truants, beyond parental control, neglected, in moral danger or had been voluntarily placed in care by their parents. By far the most frequent reason for the secure placement was absconding. Morris and Wilkinson asked the social workers concerned why they had sought the secure placement. What emerged clearly from this was that it was rarely a response to perceived danger to others. In most cases, the reasons were phrased in protective terms:

> She was so vulnerable . . . we didn't know where she was, who she was with.
>
> It was for her own safety.
>
> She was going to kill herself; it was real, not attention-seeking.
>
> Really it was to get the glue out of her system.

The consequence of that 'protection', however, was secure detention. What these examples demonstrate is that repression of any transgression from sexual passivity or 'appropriate' behaviour underlies the 'protection' of girls.

The first major decision point within the juvenile justice system is whether or not to refer the juvenile to the juvenile court. Nationally about half of all cases referred to the police are diverted by them from the juvenile courts, but official statistics show that female delinquents are more likely to be diverted than male delinquents: in England and Wales in 1985, 93 per cent of girls aged between 10 and 14 were cautioned by the police compared with 80 per cent of boys in this age-group. I discussed possible explanations for this earlier in the chapter. To recap briefly: such differences may merely indicate that girls commit less serious offences than boys and commit them less frequently.

Specific programmes, involving counselling or some similar intervention, are less well developed in England and Wales than elsewhere. The major example here is intermediate treatment (IT) though this takes many forms (Bottoms, 1986). About 20 per cent of those currently involved in IT are girls. But it is clear that there are important differences between the girls receiving IT and the boys. Whereas 80 per cent of the boys are offenders, under a quarter of girls are (Bottoms and Pratt, 1985).[25] The girls in this research project were also primarily involved in IT on a voluntary basis: 69 per cent compared with 22 per cent of the boys. Bottoms and Pratt do not elaborate on the characteristics of these girls, but it is likely that they would correspond broadly to 'status offenders'. There is an interesting paradox here. Many of the women running these groups would describe themselves as feminists and would be critical of state intervention with female sexuality yet they are encouraging the referral of non-delinquent girls to these groups. This may lead to increased intervention at a later stage if the girl is referred to a juvenile court (Adler and Polk, 1982).

Bottoms and Pratt also noted differences in the content of the programmes for boys and girls (see also Bambridge, 1979). A prominent discussion topic in the groups for girls was the range of discriminatory assumptions made of them simply on account of their sex. Bottoms and Pratt argue from this that what begins as an attempt to make problematic perceived ideas about female sexuality, 'in practice becomes a focus on the supposed sexual problems of girls'. They go on to suggest that the female group-workers in this way are 'pathologising female sexuality'. This seems to me to reflect a male perspective. Female sexuality or, at least, our response to it *is* a problem for young girls, and discussions in a supportive situation are very different from placing girls in an institution in order to 'protect' them.

At the disposition stage, there are two broad suggestions in the American literature: girls are given harsher dispositions than boys for status offences and girls are given less severe dispositions than boys for delinquent behaviour (Chesney-Lind, 1973; Terry, 1970). Often, however, adequate controls were lacking in research which purported to test these suggestions. In a more careful study, Datesman and Scarpitti (1980) found that, for status offences, girls were given more severe dispositions, and that this was especially so for repeat offenders. With respect to criminal offences, on the other hand, boys were given more severe sanctions.[26] Datesman and Scarpitti suggested that these decisions reflect stereotypic notions about 'appropriate' behaviour for girls. Delinquent girls were viewed as less responsible and less dangerous than delinquent boys and female status offenders were viewed with more concern than male status offenders. These discrepancies, however, were less apparent for black girls, that is, they received more severe sanctions for criminal offences and less severe dispositions for status offences than white girls. Datesman and Scarpitti explain this by suggesting that black girls are more likely to depart from stereotypic expectations of proper female behaviour than white girls — hence they are punished more severely for delinquent acts — but that judges view black girls as less wedded to the female role and thus in less need of protection than white girls, hence their status offences are not viewed severely.

The situation in England is more complex. Sentencing patterns in the juvenile courts show some disparities in the sentences of boys and girls, as tables 4.9 and 4.10 demonstrate. It appears from these tables that, for example, girls are more likely to be given discharges than boys. But interpretation is difficult because the same measures are not available in the juvenile courts for both boys and girls. This in itself is, of course, worthy of comment.

In 1968, the Advisory Council on the Penal System (1968a) recommended to the government that the only detention centre (short-term residential institution in which the emphasis is on discipline) for girls should be closed without replacement.[27] In its words: 'We are sure that the detention centre concept is not appropriate for girls . . . The needs of delinquent boys and girls

TABLE 4.9   PERCENTAGE OF PERSONS AGED 10 AND UNDER 14
SENTENCED FOR INDICTABLE OFFENCES, BY SEX AND TYPE OF
SENTENCE OR ORDER, 1985

	Males	*Females*
Absolute or conditional discharge	39	55
Supervision order	18	18
Fine	16	18
Attendance centre order	22	5
Care order	4	3
Otherwise dealt with	1	Less than ½ per cent

Source: Home Office, 1986a

TABLE 4.10   PERCENTAGE OF PERSONS AGED 14 AND UNDER 17
SENTENCED FOR INDICTABLE OFFENCES, BY SEX AND TYPE OF
SENTENCE OR ORDER, 1985

	Males	*Females*
Absolute or conditional discharge	22	39
Supervision order	17	20
Fine	25	28
Community service order	4	1
Attendance centre order	16	7
Detention centre order	8	—
Care order	2	3
Youth custody	4	2
Otherwise dealt with	1	1

Source: home Office, 1986a

are so dissimilar that there is no reason why disposals open to the courts should be the same for both'.[28] The Council viewed female delinquents as 'usually unhappy and disturbed, often sexually promiscuous and often rejected by their families. They are usually in great need of help and understanding'. Whether or not this is so is, in fact, irrelevant, for it is how girls are perceived which profoundly effects the dispositions available for them. The detention centre for girls was subsequently closed. Attendance centres — the deprivation of leisure time for two hours on Saturday afternoons for a maximum of 12 weeks — were also, until recently, not available for girls and are now available only in certain areas.

How girls are perceived also affects the choice of dispositions for them. The majority of girls in Casburn's (1979) sample were given care or supervision orders (none of the boys were given care orders, compared with nine girls). The majority of boys, on the other hand, were fined; those sent to institutions had long records of previous convictions. The cases of a sister and brother in Casburn's sample demonstrate this differential response. Sharon, aged 14, was before the juvenile court for truancy. She was made the subject of a care order. Half an hour later, her 13-year-old brother appeared in court. He was charged with a serious offence of theft and malicious damage, and was given a conditional discharge. For both, the decisions were made with reference to an unhappy home background. Casburn describes the juvenile court's decisions for girls as the 'surveillance' of girls: 'The juvenile court provides for the regulation and continued surveillance of behaviour deemed an unacceptable part of the female role . . . [it] functions as a management tool, equipped to correct and survey female behaviour which . . . flaunts normative expectations' (1979: 21).

Cawson (1981) also found evidence of earlier and more incursive intervention into the lives of girls and, more recently, Webb (1984) showed that girls recommended for, and made the subject of, supervision orders included a high proportion of girls who had committed minor offences and who had no criminal history. For example, about half of the boys but three-quarters of the girls were first-offenders. Walker (1985) has questioned Webb's conclusion because a greater proportion of all girls appearing in the juvenile court are minor- or first-offenders. Hence, she argues, discriminatory practices cannot be determined on the basis of supervision order figures alone. However, if sex is not a relevant variable in the decision-making of report writers and juvenile court magistrates, one would expect female minor- and first-offenders to receive discharges or low fines.

Parker et al. (1981) provide evidence that magistrates look at girls somewhat differently from boys even where charged with similar offences, and that the level of intervention for girls is higher than for boys: girls are more likely to be placed on supervision; and boys are more likely to be fined or discharged. In part, this is due to the fact that the dispositions available for girls are more limited. In addition, however, magistrates show certain attitudes towards girls which lead to modifications of the normal tariff towards more severe penalties. Offences of violence, for example, are regarded with a mixture of horror and amazement. There is also more focus on non-school attendance and behaviour at school for girls than for boys, what Parker et al. call 'hidden offences'. The case of Sandy demonstrates this. Sandy was charged with the theft of a doll from a shop. She pled not guilty; her co-accused pled guilty and gave evidence that Sandy played no part in the offence. The magistrates, however, found her guilty and it was clear, in sentencing Sandy, that her school behaviour was the magistrates' main concern. In the chairman's words: 'She was out that day and she should have been at school. This is what I'm concerned about.' Sandy was placed on supervision. Perhaps not surprisingly, Parker et al. found that this upward modification of dispositions added to girls' sense of injustice (1981: 100, 104).

So far I have concentrated on dispositional patterns within the juvenile justice system. Schwartz et al. (1984) note a trend occurring in the United States: the existence of a *private* correctional system for juveniles. Using the records of mental-health and drug-treatment agencies, they identified what they call a 'hidden population' of juveniles who are incarcerated. Girls are over-represented in this population. Thus, for example, although the admission of girls to training schools has decreased over recent years, the admission of girls to private institutions has increased. De-institutionalization has not occurred, but, rather, transfer of girls from one kind of institution to another. The extent to which a similar phenomenon exists in England and Wales is unknown, but is currently being investigated.

Conclusion

The treatment of women and girls in the criminal justice system has been described as sexist (Heidensohn, 1985). But it is more complex than this. First, such factors as race, home circumstances, type of offence, demeanour and family commitments all clearly mediate the treatment of female *and* male defendants. Research also suggests that sexist beliefs, where they exist, are mediated by administrative and organizational factors. Gelsthorpe writes: '"Sexist ideology" is not a discrete phenomenon, but a mixture of personal views, professional policies and practices which are continually "shaped" by the exigencies of practice and organisational constraints' (1986: 142). She argues that simply to dismiss the criminal justice system and allied agencies as sexist obscures our understanding of the processing of offenders. What we need to know more precisely is how sexism works in practice. Thus, in making sense of work in a police juvenile bureau, Gelsthorpe found that the need for officers to be seen to be 'busy' and to be doing 'real police work' had to be considered alongside any notion of sexism.

Secondly, the allegation of sexism ignores the fact that a considerable body of research indicates that women are dealt with in much the same way as men: routine cases are routinely processed.[29] On the other hand, there is some evidence that *certain* women and girls — for example those who are divorced, aggressive, sexual or black — are dealt with differently. In essence, those viewed as 'ladies' or 'nice girls' are likely to receive different sentences from those who breach these expectations. Decision-makers (police, social workers, magistrates and so on) have limited understanding of, and insight into, the lives of women with different cultural values or who experience different family structures. Stereotypical assumptions about 'appropriate' behaviour are, therefore, relied on. For this reason, Moulds (1980) argues that we should use the word 'paternalism' rather than 'leniency' as this more accurately describes the underlying process. The common thread is that lenient, paternalistic and harsh dispositions are all linked to the perpetuation of traditional role stereotypes. Lenient treatment is presented as conditional on the acceptance of stereotypical behaviour; paternalistic and harsh treatment as punishment for the breach of that behaviour in addition to the breach of the criminal law.[30]

The criminal justice system overtly controls both male and female offenders, but it seems to control female offenders more subtly by distinguishing among that population. To this extent, processing in the criminal justice system can be viewed as a way of patrolling and controlling the boundaries of the female role. The juvenile justice system, for example, seems more concerned with protection of the status quo than with protection of the girls themselves. Morris and Wilkinson (1983) suggest that the growth in secure facilities (the increase in the number of places for girls is greater than that for boys) reflects an easy answer to social workers' concerns about girls rather than a solution to the girls' problems. Indeed, they suggest that secure placement exacerbated the difficulties that many of the girls in their sample had.

According to Reckless (1961), responding to female offenders differently represents male-dominated society's deference to the symbol of women. De Crow (1975), however, describes this process as a two-edged sword: putting women on a pedestal helps keep them in their place. Steffensmeier (1980) points to the wider implications of the differential treatment of women: the possibility that beliefs about the special nature and treatment of female offenders are intertwined with the exclusion of women from economic and political processes. Moulds (1980) views the lenient treatment of some female offenders as too high a price for women to pay. She describes it as involving a basic denial of self-determination and calls for a sex-fair criminal justice system and for equal treatment of male and female offenders.[31] This is not as simple as it sounds. Such an endeavour would involve deciding such questions as whether to legalize prostitution or to penalize prostitutes' clients, and whether to decriminalize status offences or to refer male status offenders more frequently to the juvenile courts.[32]

Equal treatment, however, is not necessarily the right objective. There may well be differences between men and women which *justify* differential dispositions. Walker, in the discussion at the Cropwood Conference on Women and Crime (Morris and Gelsthorpe, 1981), distinguished between paper and real justice. 'Paper justice' involves giving like penalties to women and men for like offences,[33] but 'real justice' involves taking into account the impact of a penalty: for example, the fact that, at least in this culture and at this time, child-rearing *is* primarily the responsibility of women and that women earn less than men, or the possibility that imprisonment *is* a greater punishment for women than for men. If research showed that men and women do respond differently to different sentences, this would provide a *rational* rather than a prejudicial basis for differential sentencing. Smart and Brophy (1985: 3) make a similar but more general point: 'The idea of a complete legal equality and even equal treatment is not a sufficient goal for feminists where, structurally, women are in a disadvantaged place *vis-à-vis* men.' Legal equality does not necessarily provide substantive equality.

5

Women in Prison

Introduction

Historically, the penal system in England did not differentiate much between male and female offenders. Women were whipped, hanged, transported and imprisoned. Gradually some notice was taken of the defendant's sex. For example, from the seventeenth century women could be granted stays of execution if they were pregnant and statutes in the early nineteenth century abolished the whipping of women, first in public and later in private. Now there exist dispositions for male offenders which are either not available or are not much used for female offenders. In part, this reflects stereotypical conceptions of the women and men who commit offences. But it is also more complex than this. Female offenders remain offenders and responses to them cannot ignore considerations of punishment and deterrence.

Not much is known about women's responses to non-custodial options although it is apparent from the information presented in the previous chapter that women are more likely than men to be dealt with in this way. We do not know, for example, whether the content of a probation order differs for men and women[1] or whether men and women respond differently to probation. Policy documents have also ignored female prisoners. The May Committee's inquiry into the British prison system (Home Office, 1979) contained nothing about women in prison in its 347 pages. In 1978 the House of Commons Expenditure Committee did embark on a survey, *Women and the Penal System* (Expenditure Committee, 1978–9). Evidence was heard, but in April 1979 an election was called and no report has been published.[2] More recently, the Control Review Committee produced a report (Home

Office, 1984a) on regimes for long-term prisoners. It explicitly excluded the female prison system from consideration on the grounds that it had characteristics and problems of its own (1984a: 1). These have not subsequently been explored. This chapter seeks to redress the balance and to consider the experiences of female prisoners.

The Development of Women's Prisons

Until the nineteenth century,[3] women were imprisoned in the same institutions as men, although in some they were housed in separate rooms (Pugh, 1968). The policy towards both men and women was one of uniformity; no particular account was taken of the prisoner's sex (or age). In the words of Webb, 'a prisoner was a prisoner and practically nothing else' (quoted in Prochaska, 1980: 173). John Howard (1780) argued for special facilities for women as part of his overall proposals to reform prison conditions,[4] and Elizabeth Fry promoted the view that the needs of female prisoners were different from those of male prisoners. She established the Ladies Committee[5] for visiting female prisoners and introduced work and bible-reading classes for them. Indeed, they devised an elaborate timetable for the women in Newgate: reading classes, sewing, knitting. Swearing, quarrelling, card playing and reading novels were all forbidden. In Prochaska's words (1980: 145): 'Within the framework of cleanliness, godliness and needlework, the visiting scheme sought to prepare prisoners for a return to society.'

Fry also gave evidence before a variety of committees investigating prison conditions. She suggested, amongst other recommendations, separate buildings and female officers for female prisoners. Little attention, however, was paid to her and, in fact, many of her immediate changes were later stopped by prison inspectors. For example, they closed the shop she introduced in Newgate and abolished the female monitors she had chosen from amongst the inmates. Those reforms allowed were often no more than palliatives. Fox (1952: 29) sums up nicely the progress of Fry's reforms: everything she asked of Parliament for her women in 1818 was granted by Parliament — in 1948.

In the model prisons built from the 1840s onwards, female prisoners were segregated from male prisoners though the regime differed only slightly — female wardresses were introduced and women were relieved from hard labour. The dominant models of imprisonment — the separate and silent systems — were imposed on men and women alike. Those reforms which were made, for example, the introduction by Webb of the three-stage system by which women progressed through three different prisons on their way to release, were simply part of a general move to reform prisons and did not reflect any special consideration of female prisoners.[6]

The Gladstone Committee (1895), in its report, shifted the emphasis in penal theory: reformation through classification. Particularly for women, it recommended work in association and improved work facilities (for example, the installation of knitting machines). Such differences led McConville to conclude: 'The contrast between male and female convict management in these decades is pronounced: on the one hand, harsh regimentation, on the other, a strict regime, but with considerable toleration of refractory episodes and even a degree of individualisation' (1981: 427). Heidensohn (1985: 65), however, argues that McConville misses the point: 'the purpose of penal systems was clearly to deal with *male* delinquency and crime' (emphasis in the original). Women convicts, she argues, had fewer previous convictions than their male counterparts, received very short sentences and were primarily imprisoned for offences of drunkenness or prostitution. Therefore, one would *expect* differences in the regimes. In the main, though, developments in women's institutions continued to parallel those in men's.

Accounts by suffragettes, imprisoned between 1905 and 1914, provide graphic evidence of the conditions in women's prisons (Lytton, 1914; Blagg and Wilson, 1912)[7] and the interviews they gave on release led to some improvement in prison conditions. The appointment of Dr Mary Gordon as the first inspector of women's prisons in 1907 also led to some improvements. Her appointment was described as bringing 'a much needed feminine view to the matter of women in prison' (Camp, 1974: 75). Gordon was very critical of the system for dealing with female prisoners and compared it unfavourably with the French:

French prisoners are, therefore, in several important respects, under much less stress than ours, whose penal discipline includes a severe, unappetising and uniform diet, a very limited amount of communication with friends at long intervals and a general condition of reduction of material comforts to a minimum. Our prisons are also more crowded, prisoners are more closely herded and space and room to be comfortable is much less generously provided. (1922: 209)

A number of other women, for example, Mary Size, Lillian Barker[8] and Selina Fox, began to work in women's prisons. Together, they worked to improve conditions: redecoration, the planting of flower beds, pictures in the rooms and tuition in nursing, hygiene and handicrafts. What emerged was a gradual awareness that conditions *should* be different for male and female prisoners. Ruggles-Brise, chairman of the Prison Commission in the early 1920s, pointed to the 'inhumanity of treating men and women in prison in exactly the same way' (quoted in Camp, 1974: 77). He stressed the physiological and emotional differences between men and women in their reaction to prison life and how women suffered much more, mentally, than men. Also underlying his thinking was the belief that there were differences between the sexes in their motives for criminal behaviour.

In the United States, the first women's prisons were also part of men's prisons and then they too gradually grew separate. According to Rafter (1985), the early institutions were characterized by the neglect of inmates and inferior conditions: for example, overcrowding and the lack of exercise yards. By the late nineteenth century, they had become independent of their male counterparts and from 1860 the creation of reformatories for women (modelled on institutions for juveniles) was urged. The purpose of the reformatories was: 'to reform the character (of the inmates), preserve the health, secure fixed habits of industry and morality, to the end that the inmates shall be rendered intelligent, industrious and useful citizens' (Lekkerkerker, 1931: 162). These early institutions had systems of parole and classification, and reflected the individualization of treatment derived from positivist criminology. Women were seen much more as erring human beings needing help than dangerous criminals against whom society needed protection. Female prisoners then were primarily guilty of drunkenness or sexual delinquency. (See Rafter, 1985 for further information.)

Women also influenced the early development of institutions in the United States. Mary Harris, the first superintendent of the Federal Institution for Women at Alderson wrote of the need to 'abandon . . . the outworn prison structures' and 'old prison traditions, customs, habits of thought, vocabulary, attitudes' (1936: 395). To this end, there were few bars in the institution and it was built as a series of cottages, each of which had its own kitchen and dining room. Each prisoner had her own room. The atmosphere was described as informal and domestic. There were also committees of women who handled infractions in the cottages. Indeed, the American model was quoted as the ideal by English penal administrators. Alexander Paterson (quoted in Ruck, 1951: 72), for example, wrote: 'America is teaching the world that a woman's prison is an anomaly, that it is unnecessary and misplaced. If she is to learn a lesson, she can do so in the home life of a cottage more readily than in an amorphous mass behind a wall too high for low skirts.'

The dominant model of training in both countries was domestic: the socialization of women to her traditionally accepted role. The emphasis, therefore, was on gardening and housework, and instruction was provided in needlework, cookery, child care and dressmaking. Rafter (1985: 174) makes an interesting point in this context. She refers to the work of such writers as Foucault (1977) who argue that imprisonment was economically useful to capitalism. But whereas imprisoned men did provide a source of cheap labour, the institutions for women functioned to keep women *out* of the industrial labour force. Where training was given to women it paralleled as nearly as possible the work which the women would do on release: namely domestic work. The prison commissioners, in their report for 1945, sum up this objective well. Training should be directed towards: 'better housewives rather than better housemaids. Every aspect of domestic work, whether in shops or in the service of prison, should be made to serve one idea — that of instilling into the women the ideas of a good home and how they may best be achieved' (Commissioners of Prisons, 1947: 73). The objective was to turn female inmates into decent housewives and good mothers. This emphasis continues today.

A basic issue runs through early discussions on women's prisons: the extent to which imprisonment affects women differently from men. Those minor modifications which occurred were premised on the belief that prison was more stressful for women. This issue remains current and unresolved: policy statements and research findings are unclear. In the 1960s, however, the answer did seem clear: most women in custody were mentally disturbed and the appropriate response was a psychiatric one.

The Psychiatric Influence on the Development of Women's Prisons

The major women's prison in England is Holloway prison in London which has an average population of around 300. The old Holloway[9] was erected in early Victorian times and the traditional design based on segregation and silence clearly affected the type of training possible. The discussions surrounding the development of the new Holloway provide an excellent example of the way in which female prisoners are distinguished from male prisoners.[10]

In 1968, James Callaghan, then Home Secretary, announced that the government had decided to embark on a programme to reshape the system of penal establishments for women in England and Wales. In the course of announcing in Parliament the redevelopment of Holloway, the Home Secretary stated that 'most women and girls in custody require some form of medical, psychiatric or remedial treatment'. Even at the time, the evidence for this claim was not strong (I discuss this further in the next section), but the Home Secretary continued: '[Holloway] will be basically a secure hospital to act as the hub of the female system. Its medical and psychiatric facilities will be its central feature and normal custodial facilities will comprise a relatively small part of the establishment'. Holloway was to be redeveloped as a psychiatrically oriented institution. Faulkner (1971), then Assistant Secretary in the Prison Department and chairman of the Holloway Development Group, elaborated this theme. Since most of the women in custody were inadequate and many were highly disturbed, they were to be classified not so much in terms of their sentence or offence, but rather in terms of the treatment which they required. The objective was to make Holloway look as unlike a prison as possible. The entry point was to be made informal and reassuring and, according to Faulkner, the buildings were to be centred on a green 'to give an open aspect and an appearance of freedom while preserving a high degree of supervision' (1971: 132). The underlying rationale was that women 'are generally more sensitive to their surroundings and less able to conform to institutional patterns of behaviour' (1971: 122—3). Holloway was to be designed in a series of self-contained units each with a 'family centre'.[11] Kelley (1970: 5), a former governor of Holloway, echoes these images: the design of the units was to establish a pattern of 'home' and 'the neighbours'. Training was to focus on the development of relationships within the units, family life, home management, cooking, and the education and training of children. Thus the ethos was to remain domestic. Industrial activity was not intended to be productive. Rather it was viewed, in Faulkner's words, as having a 'therapeutic rather than an industrial purpose' (1971: 130). He went on: 'there will be no attempt to reproduce industrial conditions or to set industrial targets of production. This was primarily because the *home* was seen as the centre for the whole-time employment of the majority of the women after their release. This is nicely summed up by Kelley: 'It must be claimed to be greatly to the credit of this country that it is the mothers and future mothers whose retraining has been given priority' (1970: 3).

Cornton Vale, the only prison for women in Scotland, was also built in the 1970s and it, too, is based on the family unit/psychiatric model.[12] A pamphlet published by the Scottish Information Office described it as follows: 'Inmates live in small units . . . One woman in each unit is given the role of 'homemaker'. She acts as a 'mother', supplies meals for the unit and is responsible for keeping the place tidy while other members of the unit are at work.'[13] In preparation for the opening of Cornton Vale, a working party was set up to make recommendations for the training of the women. It, too, referred to the high incidence of psychiatric disorder among the women and proposed a regime geared to respond to their psychiatric needs. (See Dobash, Dobash and Gutteridge, 1986 for a detailed discussion.)

The first of the new buildings at Holloway were occupied in 1977 and rebuilding was completed at the end of 1987. Practice, however, has not met the ideals set out in the early 1970s. In

January 1986 around 60 per cent of Holloway's population was on remand, either unconvicted or unsentenced. Only around 11 per cent of those sentenced were serving sentences of four years and over and a further 4 per cent were serving life sentences. It is, therefore, a highly transient population. The image of the 'typical' female prisoner has changed too. The redevelopment was based on the belief that most female prisoners required psychiatric treatment. By 1980, they were viewed by the Prison Department in much the same terms as male prisoners.

There has been considerable public (Moorehead, 1985) and Parliamentary disquiet about the regime in Holloway generally and in the psychiatric wing in particular, especially over incidents of self-mutilation among the prisoners.[14] It is widely recognized now that one of the effects of the Mental Health (Amendment) Act 1982 has been to make it difficult to find hospital places for disturbed offenders, male and female alike. One consequence of this is that the prisons must hold some disturbed individuals who, on other grounds, should not be in prison. But a further problem in Holloway's psychiatric unit was that it held not only mentally disturbed women but those whose behaviour in the ordinary prison was viewed as persistently disruptive: the mad and the bad were held together. Stewart and Shine (1984) have also shown that the majority of referrals to the unit were remands for medical assessments. Thus it was not operating as a long-stay therapeutic unit.

Recent Increases

Women are a minority among prisoners. In England, only about 3 per cent of prisoners are female.[15] However, there is concern about increases in the number of female prisoners. Between 1938 and 1973 the number of women in prison varied only between 800 and 1,000, whereas the number of men in custody trebled. But there was an increase of 55 per cent in the number of female prisoners between 1975 and 1980; the rate of increase in the male prison population over the same period was 12 per cent.[16] There are now twice as many women in prison in England as there were in the early 1970s and the projected figures, as table 5.1 indicates, show a continued increase.

TABLE 5.1   AVERAGE FEMALE PRISON POPULATION, 1972, 1977, 1980 AND
1983, AND HOME OFFICE POPULATION PROJECTIONS, 1985 – 92

Year	Population
1972	1,000
1977	1,400
1980	1,500
1983	1,400
1985	1,400
1986	1,400
1987	1,500
1988	1,500
1989	1,500
1990	1,600
1991	1,600
1992	1,600

Source: Home Office 1984b

Numbers are, of course, still relatively small: the average
population in men's establishments in 1985 was 44,701 compared
with an average population of 1,532 in women's establishments
(Home Office, 1986c, table 1.2).[17] It is also commonly forgotten
that in the nineteenth century far more women were imprisoned
than now. In 1899, 49,000 women were sentenced to prison.
Then they made up about 20 per cent of the prison population.
Furthermore, because the number of women in prison is small,
we must be cautious about interpreting percentage increases. On
the other hand, the imprisonment rate for women has increased
faster than the crime rate for women (Seear and Player, 1986).
This contrasts markedly with the statement of the Home Office
as recently as 1970 that:

> It may well be that as the end of the century draws nearer,
> penological progress will result in even fewer or no women at all
> being given prison sentences. Other forms of penalty will be
> devised which will reduce the number of women unnecessarily
> taken from their homes, which so often ends in permanent disaster
> and breakdown in family life. (Home Office, 1970)

There are a number of possible explanations for this increase. There may have been changes in the nature of women's criminality. It was certainly *believed* that this had occurred (Adler, 1975), but, as I discussed in chapter 2, the empirical basis for this is suspect. Such beliefs, however, may have profoundly influenced the actions of criminal justice professionals. Magistrates and judges, for example, may now be more willing to send women to prison. There is some indirect (and inconclusive) support for this in the fact that although more women are being sentenced to imprisonment now than ten years ago, they are being sentenced for shorter periods. Sixty per cent of women received into prison in 1985 were sentenced to less than six months, compared with about half of those in 1975 (Home Office, 1986c, table 5.4).

There are now in England five closed prisons for women, three open prisons and three remand centres (these take women pre-trial and pre-sentence and are attached to remand centres for men).[18] A list of these institutions is given in table 5.2. Table 5.3 details the types of custody of women in prison.

Women in Prison

The vast majority of women in English prisons have been convicted of offences of fraud, forgery, theft and handling;[19] that is, they are mainly petty property offenders (Home Office, 1986c).[20] Few have been convicted of robbery and more women have been convicted of offences relating to prostitution[21] than offences of burglary. The number of women convicted of drug offences, however, has increased markedly in recent years (from 56 in 1975 to 316 in 1985). More than a quarter of the women in Holloway in January 1986 were there for drug offences. (The overall picture is similar for those women imprisoned in Scotland; see Carlen, 1983.) Comparisons of the male and female prison population indicate that women have committed less serious offences.[22] On the other hand, women seem to be committing more serious offences now than 30 years ago; this is especially so for young women.

A common assumption about women in prison, and one with a long history, is that they are hard-core offenders. However, only just over a quarter of the women in English prisons have had previous custodial sentences:[23] 27 per cent in 1981 compared with 78 per cent of men (Home Office, 1982).[24] A significant minority of women in prison have no previous convictions at all: 11 per cent of the population under sentence on 30 June 1985. The equivalent figure for men was 4 per cent (Home Office, 1986c, tables 5.10 and 4.10).[25] For a surprisingly large number of women, no information on previous convictions was available: 37 per cent compared with 16 per cent for men. Although 26 per cent of adult women serving sentences on 30 June 1985 were known to have six or more previous convictions, this was much lower than the figure of 57 per cent for men. Those serving sentences for theft,

TABLE 5.2   FEMALE PRISON DEPARTMENT ESTABLISHMENTS: ACCOMMODATION AND POPULATION ON 21 MAY 1985

Establishment	Certified normal accommodation	Population
Closed		
Holloway (prison)	303	343
Styal (prison and youth custody centre)	237	255
Bullwood Hall (prison and youth custody centre)	120	118
Cookham Wood (prison)	119	117
Pucklechurch (remand centre)	56	89
'H' wing, Durham (prison)	39	37
Low Newton (remand centre)	35	53
Risley (remand centre)	84	127
Open		
Askham Grange (prison)	132	125
Drake Hall (prison and youth custody centre)	250	253
East Sutton Park (prison and youth custody centre)	74	66
TOTALS	1449	1581

Source: Holloway Project Committee, 1985

TABLE 5.3 FEMALES IN PRISON CUSTODY: TYPE OF CUSTODY AS
PERCENTAGE OF AVERAGE DAILY POPULATION, 1950–84

	1950	1955	1960	1965	1970	1975	1980	1982	1983	1984
Untried remand	7.4	4.2	4.9	5.9	9.9	10.7	11.1	13.2	14.82	15.88
Convicted remand	3.2	6.6	7.0	10.7	13.3	13.8	9.0	9.9	7.69	7.60
Sentenced	89.3	88.2	86.9	82.6	75.8	74.8	79.0	75.6	75.46	75.28
Civil	0.2	0.9	1.2	0.7	1.0	0.7	0.8	1.4	1.94	1.22

Source: Holloway Project Committee, 1985

handling, fraud and forgery and for burglary or robbery were
particularly likely to have an extensive criminal history.[26]

Recent social background information on the whole of the
female prison population is not available. A survey of a sample of
women in Holloway in 1967 found that the women, like most
male prisoners, tended to come from the manual and unskilled
social classes, many had young children already in the care of the
local authority, and a significant minority had serious marital
problems (Gibbens, 1971; Gibbs, 1971). More recently, the Home
Office, in a statistical bulletin (1986b), stated that on 30 June
1985, more than 75 per cent of the female prison population were
white and 12 per cent were of West Indian or African origin. This
is a higher figure than expected from the proportion of ethnic
minorities in the population; it is also much higher than 12 per
cent in some prisons. Bryan et al. (1985) put the current Holloway
figure at 40 per cent. The bulletin also stated that male prisoners
of West Indian or African origin had fewer previous convictions
than white prisoners. It did not include a similar breakdown for
female prisoners, but the point is probably equally valid for them.

A much more comprehensive description of female prisoners is
available in the United States from Glick and Neto's (1977)
survey of 14 states.[27] The majority were young (two-thirds were
under 30); minority groups were over-represented (over half were
black);[28] three-quarters had children and half had responsibility
for them at the time of their incarceration; the majority were

single heads of households and living on welfare; and, of those employed, the employment was mainly in low-skill positions and either temporary or part-time. Sarri (1981), in contrasting women incarcerated in 1968 and 1978, found that the latter were socially and economically more disadvantaged than their counterparts in 1968. The picture for male prisoners in the United States is broadly similar to that of female prisoners but the profile of jail inmates collected in 1978 suggests that women may be an even more disadvantaged group.

The Experience of Imprisonment[29]

On the surface, most women's prisons are more attractive than men's. Some have been converted from country mansions or children's homes and the obvious aspects of security (such as gun towers in the United States) are often lacking. Indeed, the Prison Department has recognized that for women security considerations do not loom so large because there is less public anxiety and fear when women escape from custody. Women can also wear their own clothes[30] and decorate their rooms. But facades are deceptive. In many ways female prisoners are worse off than their male counterparts.[31]

Women's institutions are often in remote, inaccessible locations and, consequently, women are often far from their homes. (Because of overcrowding at Holloway, which serves the whole of the south of England, on 26 June 1985 there were 89 women in Styal prison and 25 in 'H' wing at Durham who had been transferred from Holloway.) This makes visiting difficult, given the additional fact that many of their families are poor. Visits are in any case restricted in number and time: one every 14 days for up to one and a half hours. In England, unlike the United States, there is little access to telephones other than for emergency use, except in open prisons, or as an alternative to a visit. Not surprisingly, many women receive no visits. In 1979, out of 186 girls discharged from Bullwood Hall borstal, almost a quarter had received no visits and 20 per cent had had only one visit[32] (Matthews, 1981). Proposals to introduce family visits in portacabins at one women's prison, including staying the night if necessary, were opposed by the Prison Officers' Association. This makes mail all the more important, but there are restrictions on the numbers of letters which can be sent and received. Mail is subject to censorship except in open institutions, and often women are not allowed to correspond with men who are not members of their family.

These difficulties are particularly acute for women with children. Ward and Kassebaum argue that the prison experience is more severe for women because of their close links with the care and upbringing of their children: 'The confined mother's concern is not only with separation from her children but also with how they will be cared for while the husband works' (1965: 15). The 1982 prison census for England found that of the 1,288 women then in prison, 719 were mothers with a total of 1,649 children. Two hundred and nine of these were under the age of three (NACRO, 1985).[33] At one time, some institutions made no provision for visits by children and in others, where visits were permitted, partitions prevented physical contact. Since the 1970s this has changed and there have been more efforts to allow contact between prison mothers and their children, including granting mothers leave from open prisons to visit them.[34]

When a mother is sentenced to imprisonment, an obvious problem is the provision of substitute child care. In 1979, the psychology unit at Holloway undertook a survey to establish how many women there had children aged under five, what kind of arrangements had been made for them and how satisfactory these arrangements were (Posen, 1979). They found that 65 women (almost a quarter of the total sample) had children under the age of five. As many women as possible were interviewed. Two-thirds were single parents and the majority of the children were being looked after by the inmate's mother or relatives during the prison sentence. Just over one-third of the children were in care or fostered (one-quarter had been in care or fostered prior to the prison sentence).[35] Most of the women were happy with the arrangements made for their children; 14 were not. Areas of concern focused on difficulties in maintaining contact with the child, retaining care of the child on release and the observation of distress in the children on visits. (See also Dobash, Dobash and Gutteridge, 1986.)

'Babies in prison' is a controversial and complex issue. In England, currently, there are places for 77 women in mother-

and-baby units (at Askham Grange, Styal and Holloway).[36] Thirty-four of these are for women with babies; the remainder are for pregnant women. In January 1981, 23 children were in prison with their mothers. Between 1 January 1984 and 31 March 1985, 71 prisoners gave birth to babies. In its report for 1983 (Prison Department, 1984: para. 121), the Prison Department makes it clear that decisions about placement are reached with the interests of the infant paramount. Current practice seems to be to remove the child as soon as possible after birth (usually within four weeks) where the mother is a long-term prisoner.[37] Priority in the units is given to women who will give birth during their sentence rather than to those coming in with babies. Babies can remain until the age of 9 months in closed institutions and to about 18 months in open conditions.[38] (For further information, see Matthews, 1981; NACRO, 1985.)

A critical question is whether prison is a good environment for a baby. In the early months, physical surroundings are to a large extent unimportant. The quality of the child's life depends mainly on the quality of the relationship and care he or she experiences. Psychologists stress also the importance of bonding in early childhood in terms of future healthy personality development and a recent report by a child psychiatrist, Stewart Britten (reported in *Guardian*, 18 September 1986) claims that psychological problems are experienced by adolescents whose mothers were in prison during their formative years. Whether this is due to the absence of the mother or the poor quality of substitute care is unclear, but Britten advocates keeping mothers and children together up to one year before school age and, thereafter, provision for daily visiting.[39] The opposite view was expressed by James Anderson while governor of Styal prison; in his opinion women with young babies should not be given custodial sentences other than in exceptional circumstances. The reasons for this are the effect on the child (and on the mother) of removing the child after 9 or 18 months, and the effect on other prisoners who are not allowed to have their children with them. The expense of keeping babies in prison has also been pointed to, but this is not an excessive sum when one considers the total cost of imprisonment and the provision of alternative care. The issue is also complicated by confusion about the objectives of sentencing:

deterrence, rehabilitation, punishment or incapacitation.[40] Whether or not babies and young children should be with their mothers in prison must depend on which of these objectives one gives priority to.

Many of these issues were raised recently in an English case in which an 8-month-old baby was removed from her mother (who was serving a 12-month youth custody sentence) because of the mother's transfer to a youth custody centre with no facilities for babies, due to her disruptive behaviour. She had arrived late for work, left the workshop early to feed her baby and taken raspberries from the prison garden (*Guardian*, 9 August 1985). There were also subsequent allegations of neglect and verbal abuse of the child (*Guardian*, 21 August 1985). The court held that in this case the prison's needs took priority over the child's (*Guardian*, 12 October 1985). The National Council for Civil Liberties has referred this case to the European Court of Human Rights.

A related issue is whether prisoners are fit parents. Should a woman lose her right to be a parent when sent to prison? Neglect and abandonment are common reasons for the termination of parental rights and in some American states imprisonment *per se* has been used as a reason for such termination.[41] In England, female prisoners certainly express concern that they may not be able to retain custody of their children on their release. On the other hand, some women are in prison precisely because they *are* mothers and resort to stealing or prostitution in order to provide for their children.

Since there are so few women's prisons, women of all ages[42] and all crimes are thrown together. The population is also much more heterogeneous than in men's prisons where there is the opportunity for some degree of classification. Classification systems serve two purposes: to provide the type of security arrangements necessary to protect society and to consider the personal characteristics of the individual insofar as these may reflect possibilities for training. But most jurisdictions have few institutions for women and so in effect women remain unclass-ified.[43] In contrast, an effort is made to separate experienced male offenders from the less dangerous. Consequently, though only about 5 per cent of female offenders are estimated to be dangerous, most women in prison are in closed conditions.[44] Hence the majority of women experience the rules and restrictions necessary only for the minority.

There is one maximum-security prison for women in England. A wing of Durham prison (primarily a men's prison) was opened for this use in October 1974 and contains 39 cells. Previously it had been used as a special security and punishment unit for male prisoners. Throughout the 1960s, there were a series of hunger strikes and internal disturbances in the unit. Two successive reports criticized the effects of keeping prisoners in such conditions — the Mountbatten Report (Home Office, 1966) and the Radzinowicz Report (Advisory Council on the Penal System, 1968b). Indeed, the Radzinowicz Report went as far as to say that the 'containment of prisoners in such small confined units can be no more than a temporary and most undesirable expedient' (1968: para 200). The unit was closed three years later. A further three years on, the wing was re-opened for female offenders.[45] Women can spend three or four years there, and at least one woman has been in Durham for 11 years. Jenny Hicks describes her experience there:

> At Durham a prisoner's every movement is monitored and controlled. You have to be very quiet and you can get told off for laughing. The regime is totally oppressive. Even when you're locked in your cell someone will look through the Judas-hole every hour, on the hour. There is an electronic lock on the door and once you're locked in you cannot get taken out of your room unless the Governor is called out of his bed. They can't even push a sanitary towel or a pill through to you if you get taken ill. You move about in very small spaces and only three women can talk together at one time — though never behind a closed door. You always have to leave the door open. Tension builds up. I met some interesting women in Durham and I took two Open University courses there but I changed physically, emotionally and mentally. My skin became grey and I looked much harder. I began to walk differently — much more aggressively — and I learned to hate. (Carlen (ed.) 1985: 133)

In general, little has changed in terms of security since the men were there. The experience has been described by former inmates as 'claustrophobic' and 'as physically restrictive as it is mentally and psychologically oppressive' (Hicks and Boyle, 1983: 8—9). There is said to be a high level of depression amongst the prisoners. Recently there have been hunger strikes as a protest about conditions. The Chief Inspector of Prisons (1982) also described the atmosphere there as claustrophobic. He particularly noted that half of the female inmates at Durham were from the south of England. Although long-term prisoners who are not category A can be transferred elsewhere for visits, category A prisoners cannot. Contact with their children, relatives and friends, therefore, is especially difficult to maintain.

There is in women's prisons little provision for work or education, primarily because of the domestic ideology which permeates the regimes.[46] In the words of Dobash, Dobash and Gutteridge, 'the emphasis which predominates implies that the failure of women prisoners is their failure as wives, mothers and housekeepers' (1986: 182). In practice, work is geared to the maintenance of the institution and seems to have little positive purpose. Tansy and Sear (1985), two prisoners at Styal, claimed that windows were cleaned inside and out on a daily basis and cite an incident in which floors were scrubbed six times in one day. Women are offered few training schemes other than in the use of sewing machines. This is not to say that work is good in men's prisons, but there are clear differences in emphasis. At the date of writing, the workshops in Holloway are open for about five hours a week and the well-equipped education department rarely operates at full capacity. Indeed, the Prison Statistics for 1985 did not produce a breakdown of the type of work done in women's prisons.

Women's prisons in England are, somewhat paradoxically, described as notoriously difficult to run. They are characterized by tension, hysteria and assaults. As early as 1862, Mayhew and Binny recorded that female prisoners 'destroyed their clothes, tore up their bedding and smashed their windows and frequently threatened the officers with violence' (1862: 180−2). And Quinton, referring to Millbank, wrote that the governors were able to manage 600 military prisoners and 500 male convicts but that difficulties were experienced in managing the 250 female convicts: 'too often the female pentagon was in a pandemonium' (1910: 42). Currently the incidence of violence in women's establishments is two and a half times higher than in men's[47] and the number of offences against prison discipline generally is high.[48] The rate per 100 population for all female establishments in 1985 was 335; for male establishments it was 160. The majority of these 'offences', however, are disobedience and disrespect.

There are a number of possible explanations for the higher 'offence' rate in women's prisons. Women may be less able to cope with institutional life than men. There is early impressionistic support for this view. A medical officer is quoted by Mayhew and Binny as saying: 'My experience of the past year has convinced me that the female prisoners, as a body, do not bear imprisonment so well as the male prisoners; they get anxious, restless, more irritable in temper, and are more readily excited' (1862: 180). Alternatively, the difference may have something to do with the characteristics of female prisoners. There is a clear division of opinion on this. The official view is that female prisoners are now similar in terms of crimes, circumstances and personalities to male prisoners (Prison Department, 1980). On the other hand, some prison officers and prisoners in their evidence to the House of Commons Sub-Committee on *Women in the Penal System* (Expenditure Committee, 1978–9) presented a very different picture of abnormality and subnormality among female prisoners.[49] Yet a third view was offered to the Sub-Committee by the Prison Officers' Association who viewed female prisoners as sophisticated, callous and cunning. The truth is probably somewhere in between. Professor Gibbens, in his evidence to the Sub-Committee, however, introduced a different perspective: 'They look as mad as can be but they are really reacting to prison life' (Expenditure Committee, 1978–9: 61–viii, 154, 594).

Women's accounts of why they mutilate themselves provide some support for this view.[50] Toynbee (*Guardian*, 15 October 1984) quotes women saying '[it] makes me feel better . . . relieves the tension.' 'It calms me down. It's the only way I can get to sleep.' Moorehead (1985, 40) quotes another woman: 'It's sheer desperation. As if you've become a non-entity. You're nothing. Then you do anything to get feeling . . . You want to feel pain, anything to feel some experience.' She also quotes a psychiatrist, Dr Rollin: 'there is a direct correlation between boredom and inactivity and the degree to which people mutilate themselves'. Paradoxically, incidents of self-mutilation are reportable offences, categorized as assault (Dobash, Dobash and Gutteridge, 1986).

According to Carlen (1985), high standards of behaviour are required of women in prison, and women are closely regulated.

She writes that: 'hundreds of petty rules, violation of any of them possibly resulting in loss of pay and privileges, ensured that the women never forgot that they were in prison' (1985: 134). Mawby's (1982) research in Askham Grange supports this view. The women criticized the staff for the restrictive rules imposed on them. A majority of the women felt that the rules were stricter there than in closed prisons. Jenny Hicks, a former inmate, writes:

> I hated the pettiness of it all, the kind of things you were put on report for. I'd managed to get that far without getting a report but at Askham I lost two weeks' pay just for picking a handful of blackberries. Someone else lost two days' remission for having a piece of bread in her room. You could be put on report for running up the stairs. (Carlen, 1985: 134)

Dobash, Dobash and Gutteridge (1986) assert that women are put on report for behaviour which would be tolerated in a men's prison.

A further explanation may lie in the characteristics of female prison officers. Kozuba-Kozubska and Turrell (1978) raised this possibility when they suggested that difficulties experienced in dealing with borstal girls were due to management problems, staffing difficulties and an inadequate response to the girls' behaviour. Certainly, female prison officers have little training in dealing with women, are relatively inexperienced, and there is a high staff turnover. There is also said to be a high level of absence through sickness among female prison officers. Marsh et al.'s (1985) research on prison officers found some differences between male and female officers. This is explored further in chapter 6.

Mandaraka-Sheppard (1986) tested these various explanations. She collected data within six women's prisons (three open and three closed) and produced convincing evidence that it is the organization of the prisons themselves which is the key factor in understanding women's misbehaviour. This is not to say that individual factors are irrelevant. Mandaraka-Sheppard found that younger women (that is, women aged under 30) were more involved in prison offences than older women. So, too, were single women and women without children. Perhaps surprisingly, neither a current violent offence nor previous violence in the criminal record distinguished the 'offenders' from 'non-offenders'. However, institutional variables were identified by Mandaraka-Sheppard as the more important: for example, almost two-thirds of the explained variance in physical violence was attributed to institutional characteristics. These included methods of punishment within the prisons, a lack of autonomy as perceived by the prisoners, few incentives for good behaviour, the quality of inmate/staff relations and the staff's age and experience. She concludes that 'to a very large extent serious misbehaviour of women in prison is directly a function of their response to the particular negative aspects of institutions' (1986: 189).

Mandaraka-Sheppard identifies much to be concerned about: the triviality of some of the behaviour recorded as offences against prison discipline, the vagueness of many of the rules and the wide discretion which prison officers have about whether or not to report incidents (which results in inconsistency). A most damning indictment is laid against Styal prison in particular. What such responses ignore, according to Mandaraka-Sheppard, is the potentially *positive* functions of rule-breaking, not just for inmates but for the prison too. She argues, for example, that the use of bad language and 'squabbling' offers outlets to the women for aggression which accumulates due to frustrations caused by the prison environment.

Concern has been expressed about the level of prescription of tranquilizers and psychotropic drugs to female prisoners. It is not easy to make direct comparisons because individual institutions are not always identifiable and because of differences in inmate populations, but, between January 1984 and March 1985, there were 32,990 prescriptions for psychotropic drugs in Holloway. The average population was 335. Grendon prison for men prescribed only 3,599; it had an average population of 176 (Prison Department, 1985).[51] Glick and Neto (1977) suggested that the underlying rationale for drug use is to control female prisoners. (This issue has also been raised in relation to male prisoners (Fitzgerald and Sim, 1982).) But it is more complex than this. There may well be differences in the characteristics of female and male prisoners. For example, mental illness is a common explanation for women's criminality. The evidence for this is not strong (see the discussion in chapter 3), but the proportion of mentally ill women in prison may be greater than the proportion of such men in prison. In June 1981 there were 38 women in English prisons considered to be suffering from mental disorders, compared with 282 male prisoners. This is relatively high when one considers the ratio of men to women in prison. The Prison Department report for 1979 explained the high dosage rates in women's prisons as being:

> an indirect result of the efforts made by the courts to avoid custodial sentences for women wherever possible: by the time that the courts decide upon a custodial sentence the typical female offender is more likely to have a history of emotional disturbance than the typical male offender received for the first time into prison. It is also the impression of prison medical officers and others that female prisoners are more likely than male prisoners to seek help from doctors for anxieties and psychological sufferings. (Prison Department, 1980: para. 74)

But there are other possible explanations: women may experience the rigours of imprisonment more severely than men, or drugs may be sought to ease the pain of separation from their children. Drug use in prison, however, may merely be an extension of women's greater use of drugs in the community.

Coping with Imprisonment

Sykes (1958) described the pains of imprisonment for men as the deprivation of liberty, the deprivation of goods and services, the deprivation of heterosexual relationships, the deprivation of autonomy and the deprivation of security. All these deprivations apply equally to female prisoners,[52] and some may be more severe for women. Separation from one's family is an obvious example of this. Women may also suffer from receiving fewer leisure, work and educational opportunities and closer surveillance than men.

Common themes in research on women's prisons in the United States (Ward and Kassebaum, 1965; Giallombardo, 1966; Heffernan, 1972) is that women repeat the family structure of the outside community and hence prisoners play the roles of 'husband', 'wife', 'child', 'grandparent' and so on. This is primarily seen as a response to loneliness and the deprivations of prison life, and fulfils support, economic, socialization and protective purposes. Thus the recreated 'family' permits a sense of belonging, relieves loneliness and tension, provides a sense of security and emotional support, teaches the rules and roles of being an inmate, shares goods and services and protects women from violence. It may involve homosexuality.

There has been little research on inmate subcultures in England. The deputy governor of Bullwood Hall (then a borstal), in her evidence to the House of Commons Sub-Committee on *Women and the Penal System* (Expenditure Committee, 1978– 9), did say that the strength of the subculture there was very great and that the girls very quickly got involved in it (Expenditure Committee, 1978– 9: 61– xi, 215– 16). The Prison Officers Association in its evidence stated that homosexuality was 'one of the most dominant features of women prisoners' subculture' (Expenditure Committee, 1978– 9: 61– vi, 130) and Professor Gibbens suggested that 'homosexuality runs through the whole female criminal population' (Expenditure Committee, 1978– 9: 61– vii, 154 and 591). Research, however, does not confirm this. Mawby (1982) at Askham Grange, Ward (1982) at Styal, and Genders and Player (1986) in a range of women's penal institutions found little evidence of lesbianism or pseudo-families. Ward found rather a lack of solidarity among prisoners and that what subculture there was was based on providing information to the staff.

It is likely that the shorter periods spent in prison in England inhibit the development of inmate subcultures. (They do not seem to exist in men's prisons, either, to the same extent as in the United States; see Morris and Morris, 1963.) For longer-term prisoners, Carlen (1985: 167– 73) identifies a range of 'losing modes', that is, consequences of the failure to survive the pains of imprisonment. They are death, institutionalization, self-mutilation and madness. The main means of survival were the formation of relationships with other prisoners. Dobash, Dobash and Gutteridge, however, document that in Cornton Vale strong relationships between inmates could not exist. They go on: 'Indeed, it would take extraordinary strength to resist the degree of control, surveillance and manipulation directed at preventing the foundation of such bonds or at breaking them once formed' (1986: 186).

In sum, women's prisons increase women's dependency, stress women's domestic rather than employment role, aggravate women's emotional and physical isolation, can destroy family and other relationships, engender a sense of injustice (because they are denied many of the opportunities available to male prisoners) and may indirectly intensify the pains of imprisonment.

Towards Change

Changes in women's prisons are more apparent in the United States than in England and Wales. In 1964, the Supreme Court ruled that state prisoners could sue state officials in federal courts for the denial of their constitutional rights. Since then, the courts have upheld prisoners' rights in such areas as the need to maintain a law library, limits on censorship of mail and procedural fairness in prison discipline. Women in prison did not initially benefit from many of these rulings because court decisions have generally been limited to conditions in specific prisons and in response to suits from male prisoners. In the 1970s, however, female prisoners took a more active role (for a more detailed discussion, see Leonard, 1983). Most of the litigation has been based on two constitutional amendments: the fourteenth which guarantees equal protection of the law and the eighth which prohibits cruel and unusual punishment. For example, the court held that prisoners in a women's jail in San Francisco must be allowed to participate in a work furlough programme from which they had been excluded. Other cases have given reasonable parity with male prisoners in vocational training, apprenticeship programmes, medical care, educational programmes, work-release opportunities and access to legal materials. A class action suit by women in a New York county jail resulted in a judgement that it was unconstitutional for the conditions of imprisonment for women to be inferior to those of male prisoners.

An interesting case arose in Kentucky in 1980. Female prisoners had fewer resources than male prisoners but, in addition, certain rules applied to them which did not apply to men (for example, they were not allowed photographs in their cell and had to go to bed earlier). The Department of Corrections denied discrimination and argued that the constitution did not require exact equality for men and women but simply parity in terms of percentages. (There were only 164 female prisoners compared with 4,000 male prisoners.) In July 1982, however, the judge held that female prisoners must be granted the same institutional privileges as men. The Department of Corrections appealed against this decision but the case was settled out of court in 1983.

It is questionable, however, that achieving parity with men's prisons is the best solution. These institutions are themselves in considerable need of reform. Nor would complete equality be entirely beneficial for women. To attempt to eradicate gender differences within prison while they persist in the outside world makes little sense. For example, the fact that women continue to be responsible for child care means that prison programmes should be designed to take this into account. (See Baunach, 1985 for examples of programmes which are geared towards female prisoners increasing contact with their children.)

An alternative approach in the United States was the establishment of co-correctional institutions. In the mid-1970s, there were over 20 co-correctional state and federal institutions but, since then, over half have reverted to one-sex institutions. Co-correctional institutions have a variety of objectives: to reduce the dehumanizing and destructive aspects of confinement, to reduce institutional control problems (that is, to reduce assaultive homosexuality and violent behaviour), to provide a more normal atmosphere, to aid the prisoner's adjustment on release, to obtain economies in staffing and in the provision of training programmes, to relieve overcrowding, to provide more equal access to training programmes for both male and female prisoners and to expand the career opportunities for female correctional officers (Smykla, 1979 and 1980).

Much of the research points to positive results (Arditi et al., 1973). There were fewer incidents of violence, more attention was paid to appearance and grooming, staff and inmate morale was better and the environment was described as more humane. Recidivism rates, however, were, not surprisingly, much the same as from other institutions. (See also Follet, *The Times*, 12 January 1981 for a description of a Danish co-correctional prison.)

Co-correctional institutions are not without their critics. Crawford (1980), for example, draws attention to the fact that they still have a disproportionately male population. This has two consequences: it destroys any separate programming for women and forces the women into programmes designed to meet the needs of male prisoners, and the atmosphere in co-correctional prisons continues the exploitation by men which many of the women in institutions previously experienced in the outside world. According to Crawford, the real reasons behind the move to co-corrections are money, overcrowding and the need to smooth out the operation of *men's* institutions. They do not meet the unique and special needs of female offenders. Instead, she proposes mother−child institutions. Another critic (SchWeber, 1984) makes much the same point. She believes that men continue to dominate higher status positions and occupational courses in the institutions and proposes instead what she calls the 'co-ordinate' prison. This means that the women's prison is separate but shares programmes and services with a nearby male facility.

This is similar to the strategy in England suggested to the House of Commons Expenditure Committee by the Prison Governors' Association:

> A promising strategy for increasing accommodation for women in the most beneficial way would be to open up a number of small units scattered throughout the country and linked to male establishments, either as separate wings or units within existing accommodation or as satellites nearby. Both staff and inmates would then share many of the resources at present available to their male counterparts. There is no reason why suitable female inmates should not be able to mix with male inmates in the context of supervised work, educational classes, some recreational activities, etc. Staff would be able to share training resources and other facilities. Many female inmates would be able to be located nearer to their home areas with all the consequential advantages that would follow. They would be in relatively small groups in which they could feel personally known and understood and could receive individual attention . . . Staff would have more choice of geographical location in which to serve, and hence could be expected to be readier to seek promotion. (quoted in Matthews, 1981)

The Howard League, in a recent report (Seear and Player, 1986), also came out in favour of co-correctional institutions.[53] It felt that the most practical solution was to 'abandon the women only prison system and to substitute a system in which men and women shared resources'. The recommendations, however, took a different form from those of the prison governors. Seear and Player write: 'We would not be in favour of moving small numbers of women into special wings of men's prisons . . . On the other hand, if a small proportion of selected male prisoners were transferred to existing women's prisons . . . the needs of both men and women could be met' (1986: 14). They take no account of the issues raised by Crawford and Schweber with respect to the disadvantages to women of co-corrections and the special needs of female prisoners.

Heidensohn (1985) has argued that the prison system was designed to deal with men, but discussions of, for example, the merits of the silent versus the separate system, were not geared towards one particular sex. Rather, their adoption resulted from beliefs about the best way to mould the *human* spirit. Also the domestic and psychiatric ideologies which have permeated the regimes of women's prisons indicate that special account was taken of female prisoners. The real difficulty is that stereotypical assumptions have been made about the characteristics of female prisoners and hence about their 'needs'. We clearly need to know much more about who these women are. Only then can we design a coherent policy for dealing with them.

Seear and Player, on the other hand, are right to call for the removal from prisons of some of those currently detained there: for example, many of those remanded, the mentally ill, drunks and so on. Female prisoners are primarily petty offenders, offenders for whom the cost (economic and human) of imprisonment has to be questioned.

6

Women as Criminal Justice Professionals

Women's Work

Historically, professions which offered economic and political power to their members were male domains generally closed to women. Sachs and Wilson (1978), for example, document the various devices used both in the United States and Britain to exclude women from the legal and medical professions. The main argument was that women were incapacitated solely on the grounds of gender from participating in professional and political life. They were too 'delicate' or 'refined' for such participation; or, alternatively, their maternal and domestic responsibilities were viewed as their most important activities. Myra Bradwell's case provides a good example of this reasoning. She wanted to practise law and in 1873 she took her attempt to the Supreme Court of the United States. The words of Justice Bradley demonstrate how society viewed women's role at that time:

> Man is, or should be, woman's protector and defender. The natural and proper timidity and delicacy which belongs to the female sex evidently unfits it for many of the occupations of civil life. The constitution of the family organisation, which is founded in the divine ordinance, as well as in the nature of things, indicates the domestic sphere as that which properly belongs to the domain and functions of womanhood. The harmony . . . of interests and views which belong . . . to the family institution is repugnant to the idea of a woman adopting a distinct and independent career from that of her husband . . . It is true that many women are unmarried . . . but these are exceptions to the general rule. The paramount destiny

and mission of women are to fulfil the noble and benign offices of wife and mother. This is the law of the Creator. (*Bradwell* v. *Illinois*, 1873)

These sentiments are substantially echoed by Lord Neaves in rejecting Sophia Jex-Blake's attempt to enter Edinburgh University as a medical student:

> It is a belief, widely entertained, that there is a great difference in the mental constitution of the two sexes, just as there is in their physical conformation. The powers and susceptibilities of women are as noble as those of men; but they are thought to be different, and, in particular, it is considered that they have not the same power of intense labour as men are endowed with . . . Add to this the special acquirements and accomplishments at which women must aim, but from which men may easily remain exempt. Much time must, or ought to be, given by women to the acquisition of a knowledge of household affairs and family duties, as well as to those ornamental parts of education which tend so much to social refinement and domestic happiness, and the study necessary for mastering these must always form a serious distraction from severer pursuits, while there is little doubt that, in public estimation, the want of these feminine arts and attractions in a woman would be ill supplied by such branches of knowledge as a University could bestow. (quoted in Sachs and Wilson, 1978: 18)

Women, however, were not thought unsuitable for all work, only for the more lucrative and prestigious professions. Working-class women were fit enough for factory work, at least initially. In 1850, more than half the labour force were women and children and there was hardly any job which was not performed by both men and women. Although in the course of the nineteenth century the hours and working conditions of working-class women gradually improved in the larger industrial concerns[1] (especially in the textile factories), the women who were employed in the small craft or sweat-shops worked at all hours and under unhealthy conditions. Working-class women served as a cheap source of labour.

Subsequently, similar statements to those of Justice Bradley's and Lord Neave's are found in the attempts to restrict the working lives of working-class women. In 1908, the American Supreme Court accepted that a woman's 'physical structure and a proper discharge of her maternal functions — having in view not merely her own health but the well-being of the race — justify legislation to protect her from the greed as well as the passion of man'

(*Muller* v. *Oregon*, 1908). Commentators in England also stressed the effect of work on women's maternal role and on her moral and religious character (Hewitt, 1958). Such concerns led to a series of 'protective' labour laws in both countries. Jobs were scarce and this led to the closure of certain jobs to women. The motivations for these laws are complex but they are early indications of the belief that women's work *ought* to be different from men's.

They certainly had a profound effect on the shape of women's employment. There is a clear sexual division of labour; women were, and are not, excluded from work which is seen as an extension of their domestic role and hence as 'women's work'. Thus almost three-quarters of all working women are employed in clerical work, sales, teaching, nursing and service-related jobs. These jobs tend to pay considerably less than 'men's work'. Even in fields in which women dominate — elementary teaching and social work — they earn less, and the key posts are predominantly held by men (Popplestone, 1980; Richardson, 1981).[2] Working conditions are often poorer for women, and women experience greater employment insecurity. They are seen as residual labour, necessary in times of economic expansion and labour shortages (for example, during World War II) but redundant in periods of recession.

Women's careers are also affected by the shortage of child-care provisions, the lack of facilities for part-time work, especially at higher levels, and the inflexibility of working hours. Thus women's employment is structured by beliefs that a woman's place is in the home and that any paid work she takes on has to be consistent with her family and domestic responsibilities. Traditionally, a woman's career is secondary to her husband's. This too has implications for women's promotion prospects since geographic mobility is often a prerequisite. It has also been suggested that the sexual division of labour is a product of women's values and attitudes, but these are shaped from birth by society's attitudes to and expectations of women. Though there are few differences in ability between boys and girls at school, there are considerable differences in attainment. For example, girls do better than boys in A-level exams in England, but fewer go on to further education. They experience a conflict between their motivation to achieve and stereotypical expectations of them. Horner (1970) described this in female college students as 'fear of success'.[3]

Education and the educational process influence both academic achievement and career patterns. Hence school curricula have traditionally channelled girls in one direction (for example, towards biology and domestic sciences) and boys in another (for example, towards physics and chemistry, and metal and wood work). Government committees in Britain (for example, the Crowther Committee, 1959 and the Newsom Committee, 1963) consistently and persistently presented education as a preparation for occupational roles for boys and for domestic roles for girls. By establishing this dichotomy between work (men) and home/ marriage (women), the reports provided an ideological basis for the perpetuation of an education system which did not open up new possibilities for the majority of girls. The influence of hidden curricula may be even more pervasive. Teachers, for example, give boys more attention and see boys as more interesting to teach (ILEA Inspectorate, 1982).

The sexual division of labour is apparent in the criminal justice system: judges, lawyers, police and prison officers are, in the main, male. Women are employed primarily as secretaries or perform stereotypical tasks. For example, until recently, female police officers dealt mainly with women and children and until 1967, female probation officers could only supervise women and juveniles. The 1960s and 1970s did produce some changes, in part as a result of the women's movement, but primarily as a result of a wider civil rights movement, and now legislation prohibits discrimination on the ground of sex.[4] All jobs must be open to both men and women unless it can be proved that belonging to a particular sex is necessary to the normal operation of that job.[5] This means that jobs can be restricted to members of one sex for reasons of authenticity (for example, an actor or actress), decency or privacy (for example, a toilet attendant) and entertainment. A job cannot be restricted to one sex because customers or co-workers would prefer a certain sex; because some or most of one sex are unable or unwilling to perform the job, because the job was traditionally restricted to one sex; because of assumed characteristics of the sexes (for example, the assumption that the turnover rate among women is higher than among men); or because of stereotypical characteristics of the sexes (for example, the assumption that men are more aggressive than women or that women are more dexterous than men).

In most criminal justice professions — police, probation, law, teaching, research and prisons[6] — such exceptions do not apply yet the statistics present a dismal picture. In England, about 10 per cent of basic-grade police officers and 2 per cent of sergeants are female though about a quarter of recruits are.[7] The prison service is predominantly male — only 14 per cent of its staff are female — and female staff are concentrated in particular jobs and grades within it. Most of the women are clerical officers and assistants. Only 19 per cent of all women working in the prison service are disciplinary officers; the comparable figure for men is 52 per cent (Marsh et al., 1985). Women make up about 35 per cent of all grades of probation officers, but only 16 per cent of senior probation officers and 9 per cent of chief probation officers. About 15 per cent of solicitors and 11 per cent of barristers are female. Currently there are only 3 female High Court judges (all sit in the Family Division) and 15 female circuit judges (out of 386). On the other hand, about half of all magistrates (who are unpaid volunteers) are female. In the academic world, women are over-represented in the lower grades (for example, in short-term research posts) and under-represented in the higher grades (for example, heads of department or representatives on grant-giving bodies).

Why, overall, do women remain a minority among criminal justice professionals? I will present first some general considerations and then explore these further in two case studies: women as police officers and women as prison officers. These have been chosen because there is research material available. Much of the research referred to, however, is from the United States. These issues have been discussed in more detail there but the material is relevant to developments in England and Wales and to attempts to increase the representation of women in the criminal justice professions.

'Masculinity' and Criminal Justice

Criminal justice professions are seen quite simply as male professions; it is man's work requiring the characteristics of men. I have contrasted commonly attributed gender differences in previous chapters. In brief, men are viewed as active, self-reliant, aggressive, assertive, strong, tough, analytical and cool. This fits in with the dominant organizational model in the criminal justice system: crime control.[8] 'Maleness' was thus converted into one of the attributes desired among criminal justice professionals; it became part of their 'character'. The attributes of the ideal woman contradict these characteristics and their admission is often seen as threatening to the identity of the criminal justice system itself. Hence women in general are viewed as unsuitable for work in the criminal justice system (Koser Wilson, 1982).

Female criminal justice professionals have to deal with perceptions of themselves as inadequate or incompetent, simply because they are statistically rare. An example of the strength of this is provided by Hodgson and Pryor (reported in *New Society*, 25 April 1985: 135) who presented the closing remarks of a defence lawyer, after a mock trial for breaking and entering, to three groups of students. One group heard the remarks spoken by a man, another group heard the same remarks spoken by a woman and a third group simply read the arguments. The client was found guilty by over half of the respondents where a woman was defending, but by only just over a third where the lawyer was a man. Women, in particular, judged the female attorney more harshly, considering her to be less intelligent, less capable, less expert and less experienced than the male lawyer. Sexual divisions may also create a self-perpetuating defeatist attitude among women. Golden (1982), for example, questioned a sample of almost 300 criminal justice students about their career plans. The women expressed more interest in probation and youth work than in law enforcement; they preferred not to enter non-traditional areas.

The attitudes of male criminal justice professionals is one of the major difficulties identified by women entering this area; the occupational culture is masculine and emphasizes male comaraderie. This means women experience both exclusion and testing. Hunt (1984) refers to the difficulties she experienced in doing fieldwork with the police. They tested her in a variety of ways, for example, taking her to topless bars. Her response was to exhibit her toughness through the use of guns and her skill at judo. Thus she was accepted by the police officers by aligning herself with *male* values. This strategy may not be available or acceptable to all women.

However, it is more than sexism or prejudice amongst individual professionals that creates difficulties for women; the system itself is deeply rooted in favour of men. Sexism is institutionalized through organizational structures (Jurik, 1985). Female entrants to the criminal justice professions, for example, often have to have better qualifications than male entrants. In England, one in five male and one in eight female applicants are selected for the police though female entrants are recognized to be better qualified at the outset. According to a survey by the American Bar Association (1983), female lawyers were better qualified and worked harder than their male colleagues, but earned less. Formerly, in the United States, candidates for entry to the police had to meet certain physical requirements (with respect to height and/or weight). These have now been successfully challenged as they were not proved to be job-related[9] but certain criteria, for example, strength and agility, still continue to be applied to candidates at the *entry* point to the profession. This discriminates against women. Since few women also have direct military experience, the veteran's preference system also discriminates against women in the United States (see Flynn, 1982, for an elaboration of this), as do rules specifying a certain number of years legal practice for qualification to the bench. In England, a female police officer who leaves to marry and raise a family and who later wishes to return must start again as a probationer. Many professions prohibit part-time work, for example, the police in England, and this again imposes difficulties on women seeking to combine such a career with family commitments. These practices take no account of the interruptions which are part of many women's career patterns. Men's career pattern is taken as the norm. Women also find it difficult to penetrate the 'old boy' network (Martin, 1980). This has always provided an arena for patronage and hence promotion, but it also means that women can miss out on essential information-sharing. The woman who attempts to penetrate this network may have to cope with sexual overtures (Baunach and Rafter, 1982).

Women's Entry into Criminal Justice

Women started their work in the criminal justice system as

volunteers. The social history of the nineteenth century is full of female pioneers in social reform: Mary Carpenter, Elizabeth Fry, Octavia Hill and Josephine Butler, to name but a few. Middle-class Victorian women were freed from many of their domestic duties, but there were few alternatives to a life of refined idleness, and very little employment suited to them besides writing and being governesses. Philanthropy was an obvious direction to move in; it was their outlet for self-expression. After all, they traditionally cared for the young, the sick, the elderly and the poor. Since indigence was seen as the result of moral failing, the religious and domestic skills of women were ideally suited to remedy this — through moral reformation. Thus, whereas women were prohibited from public service 'by reason and decorum' (Priscilla Wakefield, writing in 1798, and quoted by Prochaska, 1980: 140), they were not excluded from promoting the welfare of society by means 'better adapted to their powers and attainments'. Visiting workhouses, schools, refuges and prisons[10] was viewed as a fit and proper concern for women and they soon became powerful figures in the charitable societies which dealt with women and children (for example, the British Society of Ladies for Promoting the Reformation of Female Prisoners, founded by Elizabeth Fry in 1821, and the Children's Aid Society, founded in 1856). A reformatory without a woman, it was said, was 'like a home without a mother — a place of desolation' (Sichels in the Proceedings of the National Conference of Charities and Correction, 1884, quoted in Platt, 1978: 79). Women, therefore, lobbied for protective legislation for juveniles, particularly for statutes creating juvenile courts, and actually served as probation officers or assistants in institutions, or participated in the selection of such persons.

Not everyone agreed that such interventions were beneficial. Prochaska (1980: 140) quotes one commentator who complained of women wandering around the country visiting prisons when they ought to have been at home disciplining their children. Such objections were overcome by women attending only to female inmates and by making connections between institutions and the home; they focused on the domestic arrangements of the institutions and drew parallels between their role as the mistress of a house instructing their maids and the prison visitor instructing inmates. Their work was presented as an extension of their mothering and family duties.

The women who were subsequently first admitted to the criminal justice professions were admitted as women and not as professionals. Hence they carried out special tasks (as in the police). This sexual stereotyping has continued but the emphasis on the unique or special qualities of women which allowed women's entry into these professions in the first place is now being used to keep them in their specialized areas: police work and working within men's prisons are often presented as too dangerous for women. Thus myths about women are perpetuated: they need to be protected; they are too emotional to make decisions; they cannot supervise men and so on. These will be examined further in the two case studies but there are two further points to make about the relative absence of women among criminal justice professionals: first, women themselves may not be interested in joining these fields because of the way in which they are presented; secondly, though this is rarely explicitly stated, men have a direct economic reason for excluding women from such jobs; the presence of women diminishes *their* job opportunities.

Women in the Police

There is a long history of female police officers (Higgins, 1951; Owings, 1969).[11] In England, during World War I,[12] voluntary women patrols were set up which did preventive work with women.[13] Between 4,000 and 5,000 women were trained for this and these formed the nucleus from which 100 policewomen were recruited by the Metropolitan Police Commissioner in 1918. There also existed a privately organized Women's Police Service which paid women to patrol the streets of London in uniforms resembling a police officer's.

However, Critchley documents the history of women in the police in England as 'a depressing one of apathy and prejudice' (1967: 215). Although a variety of committees during the years 1919–39 had emphasized their value, most police authorities regarded them as 'an unnecessarily extravagant luxury'. For example, in 1920, the Baird Committee reviewed the question of the employment of policewomen in peace time. It recognized that during the War women had successfully carried out duties previously carried out solely by male police officers, and recommended that women should form an integral part of the police force (see also the recommendations of the Bridgeman Committee (1924)). These had little effect and few women were recruited; indeed, because of financial pressures many female officers lost their employment.[14] In 1924, the *total* strength of police women was 110.[15]

The Royal Commission on Police Powers and Procedure (1929) again concluded that 'the time is ripe for a substantial increase in their [women's] numbers, more particularly in cities for patrol work in uniform' (paras 256−7). But again, nothing much changed. However, in 1930 the Home Secretary laid down what the main duties of policewomen were to be: they included patrolling, dealing with missing, homeless or destitute women, taking statements from women and children and taking statements from female prisoners. It was not until World War II that women were incorporated as a part of every police force in England and Wales.

Women's employment in the police was closely linked to traditional stereotypes of women (Sulton and Townsey, 1981). In England, before the integration of men and women in the police (1975), there existed separate women's police departments and separate promotional opportunities for female officers.[16] Though training was identical, what men and women actually did on their return to the police was different. Policewomen's work primarily involved dealing with female and juvenile offenders and female victims. This was justified on the basis of women's 'natural' aptitudes; the female officer was assigned these tasks not because of individual talents but because she was a woman. In addition, women did not work night shifts, worked half an hour a week less and were paid 90 per cent of male officers' salaries. Since integration, women are expected to be involved in all branches of police work, including working at nights.

Integrating the Police

The police are now required to recruit and deploy women and men on an equal basis. Police representatives in England and Wales had argued very strongly that the police should be excluded from the Sex Discrimination Act and, indeed, according to Sullivan (1979) many of those in favour of such exclusion were female police officers. They argued that they had joined the police to deal particularly with women and children, that their talents and expertise would thus be lost, and that they did not wish to work the full three-shift system. The arguments presented by male police officers were different: women should not be expected to patrol at night, women were a liability if there was trouble, and the service would be overwhelmed by women because it was generally agreed that the educational qualifications of female applicants were higher than those of males. So what has happened since 1975?

Southgate (1981) undertook a survey of policewomen's views on integration at the end of 1977. Six hundred and eighty policewomen from five police forces were sent questionnaires. Sixty per cent had joined the police before integration and so were able to compare their present with their previous tasks. A wide range of effects were reported, with no single good or bad effect characterized by the majority. For example, just over a quarter mentioned that integration had led to a greater variety of work, but just over a quarter did not mention any good effect on their work. A few mentioned bad effects on work. Nine per cent mentioned male prejudice and rudeness, 7 per cent exposure to danger and violence and 9 per cent less interest, satisfaction and involvement. Almost a quarter mentioned the disruption to personal life caused by shift work. Overall, just under a third were in favour of the integrated role, though almost a half preferred a more modified role, that is, that policewomen should take on similar duties to men except where violence is anticipated. Less than a quarter thought that women should specialize in the work traditionally done by them.

Respondents were asked to make judgements about their capability in various tasks and situations in comparison with a male officer. Table 6.1 presents this data in full. From this it is clear that in only one situation — dealing with a crowd of 4—6 male drunks — did the majority believe that they would cope worse than a man.

One of the purposes of the research was to assess what effect integration might have on the apparent reluctance of policewomen to remain in the job as a long-term career and to try for promotion. Southgate found that more than one-third of the women had considered resigning at some time and that this was twice as common among those who had joined before integration than those who had joined since. This was not wholly explained by age, or length of service, so that the experience of integration itself did seem to be a factor. Shift work was cited by one in four

TABLE 6.1 RESPONDENTS' JUDGEMENT OF THEIR OWN CAPABILITY IN VARIOUS TASKS AND SITUATIONS, IN COMPARISON WITH A MALE OFFICER (n=660[a])

Task/situation	Own capability (%) [b]		
	Better	*Same*	*Worse*
Questioning victims of rape/indecency offences	94	5	1
Child-abuse cases	80	19	0
Interviewing female suspects	73	26	2
Clerical work	50	50	0
Juvenile offenders	26	73	1
Writing reports	22	78	1
Domestic disputes	15	75	10
Observation work	14	85	2
A crowd of 4—6 male drunks	7	31	62
Getting information at crime scenes	6	89	6
Threatening situations where someone has a knife or gun	6	56	38
Motoring offences	5	80	15
Foot patrol	4	88	8
Traffic accidents	4	88	9
Interviewing male suspects	4	58	39
General-purpose motor patrol	3	87	10

[a] Constables and sergeants only.
[b] Percentages are rounded figures and may not add up to 100.
Source: Southgate, 1981

of those who considered resigning. However, as Southgate acknowledges, the proportion of predominantly male officers in Reiner's (1978) sample who considered resigning was similar: just over a quarter. Shift work was also cited by them as one of the most common reasons.

Comparison of Southgate's results with those of Reiner on the issue of promotion does suggest that policewomen are less ambitious than policemen: just over half of the women compared with four out of five men had applied for promotion. Importantly, 30 per cent of the women felt that their promotion chances were now worse because of integration. Amongst those believing this, three out of ten blamed male prejudice and six out of ten the new structure. Certainly, very few women occupy supervisory ranks. The proportion of women constables rose from 4 per cent in 1974 to almost 10 per cent in 1979, but the proportion of sergeants was less than 2 per cent in both years. Sullivan (1979: 341) presents information (table 6.2) on the number of officers in post which indicates that the 1975 legislation had little immediate impact. The number of female probationers, on the other hand, has increased; in the Metropolitan Police it rose from 11 per cent in 1974 to 22 per cent in 1977 and in 1986 was about a quarter. There is some concern about this. The Commissioner of the Metropolitan Police, Sir David McNee, wrote in his 1977 annual report: 'If this striking change in the balance of the sexes in the Force continues at the same rate in future, it will affect

TABLE 6.2   NUMBERS OF WOMEN IN VARIOUS POSTS IN THE POLICE FORCE, 1975 AND 1978

	31 December 1975	31 December 1978	Variation
Chief Superintendent	4	6	+ 2
Superintendent	34	28	− 6
Chief Inspector	43	41	− 2
Inspector	132	107	− 25
Sergeant	396	330	− 66
Constable	4,288	6,399	+211

Source: Sullivan, 1979

significantly the ability of the Force to meet its physical commitments . . . it would be out of the question in my opinion deliberately to employ women officers on duties which they would be exposed to physical violence' (1978: 2).

Policing as a Masculine Pursuit

Policemen's perception of policing is that it involves strength, danger and action (Vega and Silverman, 1982); it is a masculine pursuit. The imagery, reinforced by the media,[17] is of the armed man of action fighting crime and criminals.[18] The prevailing attitudes and norms in the police were described by Smith as those of an all-male institution. He summarized them as follows:

> Remaining dominant in any encounter and not losing face, the emphasis placed on masculine solidarity and on backing-up other men in the group especially when they are in the wrong, the stress on drinking as a test of manliness and a basis for good fellowship, the importance given to physical courage and the glamour attached to violence (1983: 91).

Women, of course, are easily excluded from this, but, more importantly, by far the greatest part of police work is non-violent. Between 80 and 90 per cent is described as peaceful, non-physical and dull (Reiss, 1971; Wilson, 1968), and the majority of police calls are service calls.

A recent study conducted by the Home Office Research and Planning Unit, *Contacts between the Police and the Public* (Southgate and Ekblom, 1984), found that almost a quarter of all contacts were requests for directions and 11 per cent were requests for help or advice. Only 14 per cent involved reporting a crime. Ekblom and Heal (1982) previously suggested that many such requests were, in effect, seeking help in coping with the emotional and economic consequences of the crime rather than expecting the police to catch the offender. Furthermore, Jones (1983) found that the public evaluated the police primarily in terms of their performance in providing help and comfort to them. Women can clearly play this role as effectively as men.

In dangerous situations, the ability to think quickly and clearly is more important than physical strength. (The single highest cause of police fatalities is ambush and so there is little one can do in advance.) Underground mining and construction work are also considered dangerous work and both of these are now open to women in the United States. Moreover, while women generally are not as strong as men, they can train themselves to a level of fitness well within the demands of the profession (Charles, 1982). Nevertheless, it is women's assumed inability to cope with violence that runs through many of the arguments for restricting women's role in the police. Avery (1981: 81), for example, wrote that there are important reasons why it was advantageous that the great majority of police officers should be men, 'muscular, fit and intelligent men at that', but he did not actually specify them other than saying, incidentally, that in violent confrontations 'muscularity is a necessary asset' (1981: 82).

Excluding Women

There has been tremendous grassroots resistance to women as patrol or beat officers (Bell, 1982; Remington, 1981; Horne, 1980). Sir Robert Mark, for example, in his autobiography, admitted to being:

> a bit worried at the prospect of 120 young women at Hendon where the cadet school houses 500 young men, healthy, energetic and full of go. I enquired . . . if . . . a professional abortionist [was] to be assigned, or was it that recruiting was so bad that we now had to breed our own, as we had already attempted to do with dogs and horses. (1978: 219)

Male officers' responses to women in policing are based on cultural stereotypes of male and female attributes and on an understanding of police work which centres round traits culturally viewed as male: physical strength and aggressiveness, for example. Thus women can be formally, but not necessarily culturally or professionally, integrated into police work.

This is demonstrated in Remington's (1981) research on the interaction of male and female police officers. In the sexually mixed detective units, the women adopted a subservient style when partnered with men: the men always drove, dominated calls and dictated activities; the women handled the paper work and, sometimes, merely recorded the responses to questions asked by the male partner.[19] The men coped with the presence of female officers by dealing with them as subordinates and as not bona-fide police officers.

Female police officers refer to problems of obstruction masquerading as concern, overprotectiveness, and verbal and physical abuse from their male colleagues.[20] Wexler and Logan (1983) interviewed 25 female patrol officers. Five main sources of stress were mentioned. Table 6.3 demonstrates the number of women mentioning each. The most common ones centred round their being female.[21] Within this last category, the highest source of individual stress, mentioned by 20 women, was 'the negative attitudes of male officers'. Within this, the most frequent manifestation was 'questions about sexual orientation'. Thirteen women mentioned this. In the words of one respondent 'if you are sleeping with someone you are a slut; if you are not, you are a dyke'. Nine women mentioned their colleagues' refusal to talk to them.

There is some support for 'negative attitudes among male workers' in research published by the Policy Studies Institute on the Metropolitan Police in London. That report refers to prejudice, sexism and the cult of masculinity within the police service and Smith (1983: 163) concludes quite simply that 'women face substantial prejudice' within the police force. He argues that

TABLE 6.3   SOURCES OF STRESS EXPERIENCED BY WOMEN POLICE OFFICERS (25 IN SAMPLE)

Type of stress	*Number of women mentioning it*
External stress (e.g. negative public or media attitudes)	18
Organizational stress (e.g. lack of training and promotional opportunities)	24
Task-related stress (e.g. exposure to trouble or danger)	17
Personal stress (e.g. health or marital problems)	13
Female-related stress (e.g. negative attitudes of other officers or other men)	23

Source: Wexler and Logan, 1983

there is discrimination against female applicants,[22] that women achieve promotion more slowly than men, that women have made few inroads into the specialist units and jobs considered attractive and that there is a strong body of opinion that equality of work is neither pacticable nor desirable. He also speculates on the existence of considerable tension between men and women in the police. As evidence, he cites his finding that a majority of the policemen interviewed, but only a quarter of the policewomen, believed that women were allocated less demanding jobs than men. Respondents were also asked about the place of women in the force. A majority of the policemen, but less than a quarter of the policewomen, were in favour of a return to the pre-1975 position. Very few of the policemen, but more than 40 per cent of the policewomen, thought that policewomen should take all the duties of a policeman, without exception. A further third of policewomen (and a quarter of policemen) thought that the duties should be the same except where violence is anticipated. Taken together, these figures indicate that a majority of the policemen in Smith's sample opposed the integration of women into the police force. This seems primarily based on male officers' views that women are physically incapable of dealing with certain situations, especially threats or violence. (See Smith, 1983: table ix. 5, 168.) Policemen's attitudes to women are nicely summarized by Sullivan (1979), at the time of writing, a police inspector in Kent: '"How soon might it be before I can think of being an Assistant Chief Constable?" "Never!" "But why not?" "Because you're a woman."'[23]

Can Women do Police Work?

There is now a considerable body of research from the United States which has evaluated the effectiveness of women as fully operational police officers. Bloch and Anderson (1974) concluded with respect to newly hired men and women in Washington DC that they performed police work in generally similar manners. There were no reported incidents which cast serious doubt on the ability of women to perform their work satisfactorily. Among their other findings were: the public had positive attitudes towards female patrol officers, female officers were more effective in defusing potentially violent situations and they generally fostered a less aggressive style of policing. Male patrol officers, however, preferred not to work with them.

Sherman's study in St Louis, Missouri (1975) supports the Washington findings: female officers had a less aggressive style, made fewer arrests and the public response was good. So too do studies in Denver (Bartlett and Rosenblum, 1977) and in New York (Sichel et al., 1978). One negative note was raised by a Philadelphia study. The researchers (Bartell Associates, 1978), who were hired by the police department, compared 100 patrolmen and 100 patrolwomen. There was no difference in the number of arrests made and female officers were rated higher than male officers in dealing with a man with a gun, family disturbances and car stops. Male officers were only rated higher than females in handling searches of buildings. Nevertheless, the researchers concluded that female officers did not project an image of strength and power to the same degree as male officers. It is questionable whether power and strength are the essential ingredients of a good police service and, interestingly, the court did not accept the researchers' conclusions. It ordered the Philadelphia police department to cease its discrimination against women. Overall, the research shows that women can perform as well as men as police officers. The data are consistent in different geographic areas and in different police departments. (See also Snortum and Beyers, 1983; Southgate, 1981.)

Some police administrators, however, have urged a return to specialization for female police officers (and some female officers would prefer this). Indeed, in certain areas in England (for example, Kent, Avon and Somerset) specialized women's units dealing mainly with women and children have already been re-established. The argument is that expansion to a generalist role led to a loss of status and a loss of identity among policewomen. This view is summed up in the Report of the Committee of Inquiry on the Police, chaired by Lord Edmund-Davies. It stated:

> We found great force in the argument that the abolition of separate women's departments and the assimilation of women officers into the full range of police work had resulted in a serious loss of expertise in dealing with juveniles, women, missing persons and certain offences such as rape. There has also been a more indefinable loss in relation to what might be called the social service role of women police officers . . . Much of the community involvement

has gone. The expertise built up by women officers in these aspects of police work is in danger of being lost for ever as experienced women officers leave the service. (Committee of Inquiry on the Police, 1978: para. 384)

This kind of argument is insidious because it is based on a belief that women share special natural aptitudes and attributes. There is no such thing as 'separate but equal'; segregation means 'separate but unequal'. This is obvious from the English experience where women did different tasks prior to 1975 but were not readily accepted as 'real' police officers. Specialization is to be encouraged but it should be on the basis of individual talents not sex. An example of this is the response by the police to public disquiet about the questioning of rape victims. Police officers are now increasingly being given special training in order to deal with this sensitively. However, it is not exclusively female officers who are being given such training but, rather, specially selected officers. Indeed, the Edmund Davies report took this point. It recommended the establishment of specialist departments staffed by suitable women *and* men to undertake the range of work previously done by women. Female and male officers would then have the choice of serving in these departments or in general police work. Such suggestions have considerable ground support. May (1981), for example, quotes a variety of police officers from different regions who believe that the loss of expertise in dealing with women and children has resulted in the public receiving an inferior service.

A different view is presented by Van Wormer (described in *New Society*, 19 February 1981: 317). She reversed the usual question and asked: are men suited to police work? She accepted the usual advantages cited (strength and relevant prior job experience) but she raised six potential disadvantages: male officers are more likely to provoke violence, are less likely to get public co-operation, are more likely to smash up police cars, are overprotective towards female colleagues, are less well educated and are less sympathetic in handling domestic violence and rape than female officers. Underlying this is an important issue. From the research it appears that policewomen are not aggressive police officers. Should non-aggressive policing serve as the model policing strategy for both men and women? Hilton (1976) suggests that female officers may soften and humanize the image of the police service. An interesting example of this is Mansfield's (1979) idea that female police officers should increasingly be deployed in immigrant areas because immigrants feel that they get a fairer deal from policewomen. James, a recently retired female superintendent (interviewed by Jespersen, 1986), also felt that female officers policed industrial disputes better than did male officers. According to Sherman (1975), the question of whether women could perform general police duties was primarily political, rather than scientific, from the very beginning. The research served as a diversion from the most important question: what kind of *person* makes a good police officer? Gender is not a relevant characteristic of that person. What is necessary is a consideration of the nature, goals and organization of policing.[24] It is not accidental that we primarily refer to the police *force* rather than the police *service*.

This issue was raised recently in a case brought before the European Court of Justice in Luxembourg by a woman who joined the Royal Ulster Constabulary full-time reserve in 1974 on a three-year contract. Her contract was extended for a further three years in 1977. In 1980, although it was accepted that she was an efficient police officer, the Chief Constable refused to offer her a further contract of full-time employment. She would have been offered this is she had been a man, but she was not appointed because of a policy that female officers should not carry firearms or be trained in their use. The Chief Constable gave his reasons for this:

> If they were armed it would increase the risk that they might become targets for assassination by IRA terrorists and . . . their firearms could be stolen . . . [giving women firearms would be] a much greater departure from . . . the ideal of an unarmed force carrying out its duties among the community . . . and [it would] reduce their effectiveness [in other police work such as welfare activities] which they can frequently carry out more effectively than male officers.

The Secretary of State for Northern Ireland confirmed that the reasons for refusing to allow female officers to carry guns were safeguarding national security and protecting public safety and public order. Underlying these statements are stereotyped assumptions about the different abilities and characteristics of men and women to do police work. The European Court held that the Chief Constable was within his rights to deny female officers the right to carry guns, but that he could not then legally sack the woman.

It is possible, however, that women, rather than changing or improving the police service, could be changed by it. That is, women might be forced to sacrifice some of their qualities in order to gain acceptance from their male colleagues. A recently retired police superintendent, Rachael James, expressed her concern that policewomen were beginning to 'ape the men' (Jespersen, 1986: 1394). In so doing, she felt that women were in danger of losing what she regards as their two main qualities: understanding and a healthy lack of aggression. Martin (1980), in her research in Washington DC, identified two patterns of coping with this potential conflict between sex- and occupational-role norms. *Police*women conformed primarily to occupational norms, showed high commitment to the job and wanted patrol assignments. Police*women*, on the other hand, conformed primarily to sex-role norms, had a lack of occupational commitment and did not seek patrol assignments. Martin summed up the dilemma for women working in law enforcement as follows: they must 'think like men, work like dogs and act like ladies' (1980: 219).

Women Working in Prisons

In total, women make up 14 per cent of all those employed in the Prison Service and 5 per cent of prison officers.[25] Though there are female clerical assistants and there may be female probation officers in men's prisons, there are very few female prison officers. Indeed, until recently it was thought that they were excluded from working in men's prisons because sex was a genuine occupational qualification (section 7, the Sex Discrimination Act 1975). It now seems, as a result of a case brought before an industrial tribunal by the Equal Opportunities Commission, that such a defence depends on the precise nature of the job. It has to be shown in relation to any particular job that the character of the institution requires that that job be held by a man (or a woman). I will discuss the detail of this case later.

Moreover, in September 1986 the Home Office announced that up to 16 senior male prisoner officers were to be drafted into

Holloway prison as part of a new policy to put male officers into jobs that will bring them into direct line with female prisoners (reported in *Guardian*, 22 September 1986). The Home Office also said that female officers would have the chance to work in male establishments. Certainly, a number of women working in the Prison Service interviewed by Marsh et al. (1985) felt that there should be more female staff in male prisons; some felt this because it would aid career development, others because it would improve the prison atmosphere:

> I'd like to see more female officers in male establishments — recognizing the qualities that women would bring to these dreadful places.

> [There should be] greater interchange of staff between male and female side of service.

> [Female Specialist Officers] are trained to have the same qualifications as the men and are quite capable of doing the job. Therefore they should have the opportunity of variety in their work by being able to work in different establishments regardless of male or female inmates. Should stop thinking of females as being a security risk in male establishments.

Integration of the men's and women's prison services has already occurred at the governor grade, with the effect that of the current women's institutions all but one are headed by men. Currently, five female governors run men's prisons.[26]

In the United States, the National Advisory Commission on Criminal Justice Standards and Goals (1973) encouraged the recruitment and hiring of women for all types of positions in prisons. However, less than a third of those employed there in the correctional field are female and they are concentrated in clerical and support staff positions. Overall, 12 per cent of prison officers in the United States are female (Hunter, 1986). To the extent that women work in direct contact with offenders, it is primarily with females and juveniles. The majority of women work in sexually segregated institutions. According to Zimmer (1986), nationwide, women constitute only about 6 per cent of the officers working in men's prisons.[27]

Restricting Women from Men's Prisons

The thinking behind this exclusion of women in law or practice is demonstrated in the American decision of *Dothard* v. *Rawlinson* (97 US Supreme Court (1977)). Rawlinson failed to meet the minimum 120 pound weight and 5 feet 2 inches height requirements to be a prison officer in Alabama. She brought a class action suit against the Alabama Department of Corrections challenging these requirements and a regulation establishing gender criteria for assigning officers to contact positions as a violation of Title VII of the Civil Rights Act 1964. The Alabama Department of Corrections claimed that the presence of female guards in an all-male maximum-security prison had a disruptive influence on the institution and posed great danger to the women. It suggested that sex should be a bona-fide occupational qualification for such a job.

The Alabama height-and-weight requirements excluded over 40 per cent of the female population but less than 1 per cent of the male population and so the District Court held that there was a prima-facie case made out of unlawful sexual discrimination. The District Court also held that the regulation establishing gender criteria for assigning officers to contact positions was impermissible as it was based on stereotyped characterizations of the sexes. The Supreme Court agreed with respect to the height-and-weight requirements, but held that sex was a necessary qualification for contact positions. The Court based its decision on evidence that there was considerable violence in the Alabama prison system, that inmate access to guards was facilitated by dormitory living arrangements, that every correctional institution was understaffed, and that a substantial proportion of the inmate population was composed of sex offenders mixed at random with other prisoners. The Court maintained that the use of female guards would pose a substantial security problem which was directly linked to their sex. The Court asserted that there was 'a basis in fact' for expecting sex offenders to assault women if they had access to them and that there was 'a real risk' that other inmates would assault female guards because they were women. The Court continued: 'The employee's very womanhood would thus directly undermine her capacity to provide the security that is the essence of a correctional counsellor's responsibility.'[28]

Mr Justice Marshall dissented. In his view, the Court 'should not accept [these conditions] as justifying conduct that would otherwise violate a statute intended to remedy age-old discrimination'. According to him, all the dangers outlined by the court were dangers inherent in a prison setting, whatever the sex of the guards, and that common sense, fairness and mental and emotional stability were the qualities which a guard needed to cope with the danger of the job. He went on: 'Well qualified and properly trained women, no less than men, have these psychological weapons at their disposal.' Mr Justice Marshall saw the Court's decision as lacking an empirical base (it had discounted *amicus curiae* briefs filed by the states of Washington and California which attested to the success of using female guards in all-male institutions) and as perpetuating stereotypical portrayals of women.

The decision in *Dothard* v. *Rawlinson*, however, was limited to the 'barbaric and inhumane' conditions in the Alabama prisons, for the Supreme Court rejected the argument that the job *per se* was too dangerous. The purpose of the Civil Rights Act was to allow individual women to make such choices themselves and thus, in the usual case, the Act mandates the hiring of qualified women in maximum-security institutions. This mandate was described by Zimmer as 'among the most dramatic and all-encompassing changes forced upon the prisons' (1982: 144).

Very similar issues were raised in England, in 1983, in a case brought to an industrial tribunal by the Equal Opportunities Commission. It involved the transfer of a female catering officer to a senior male detention centre (case number 18054/83). The prison officers there took industrial action in an attempt to induce the Home Office to move the woman to a female institution. In the words of the branch chairman of the Prison Officers' Association, 'our objection to her was as a woman'.

The industrial tribunal held that the genuine occupational qualification defence did not apply in this case as the catering officer had already been appointed to the post. It was, therefore, not strictly necessary for the tribunal to consider this issue further, but it went on to analyze in detail the job requirements of a catering officer and to deal with the matters raised by the respondents (the Prison Officers' Association) relating to genuine occupational qualification. First, they had raised the question of search. Inmates must be searched by an officer of the same sex and prisoners should be given a rub-down search on leaving their place of work. A female catering officer could not do this. The tribunal held that searching inmates was not an essential ingredient of her job. She could easily request a male officer to do this. Also, alternative security devices could be used, for example, tools and knives displayed on a shadow board. Secondly, the respondents had raised the matter of access to sensitive areas by a female officer and the consequent problems of decency and privacy. Again, the tribunal felt this was not an insurmountable problem; 'modesty walls' could be used. The respondents finally questioned a woman's ability to be a disciplinary officer in a men's prison. The tribunal accepted that certain duties − unlocking dormitories, supervising dressing and showers, and reception duties − could not be carried out by a woman, but decided that these were not of themselves sufficient to reduce her value significantly as part of the disciplinary team. The genuine occupational qualification defence, therefore, *on the facts of the particular case*, was not available to the respondents. In 1986 there were no more than a handful of female disciplinary officers in male prisons. It remains to be seen whether an increased number, as proposed by the Home Office, will be accepted by their male colleagues.

Women in Men's Prisons

Various assumptions, based on stereotypical beliefs about women, have been made about the presence of women in men's institutions: it would be stimulating to inmates who would be unable to control their behaviour; women would be too weak to defend themselves in a physical confrontation; the risk of hostage-taking would increase as inmates would believe that a female hostage would increase their bargaining power; women would be easily manipulated by inmates to bring in contraband and aid escapes; and women would be unable to handle the physical and emotional stress.

Research findings from the United States dispute these claims. A study of federal prisons (Ingram, 1980) showed that the performance of female staff was as good as that of male staff. Questionnaires were given to female and male staff and inmates in Boulder jail, in 1976 and 1977, about the employment of women there (Kissel and Katsampes, 1980). Women were seen as an asset to the functioning of the institution. They had a softening influence on the institution which reduced tension and lessened the likelihood of violent confrontations between inmates and the staff. Table 6.4 presents some of the specific findings from inmates.

Analysis of inmates' questionnaire returns in Wisconsin (Bowser Petersen, 1982) also indicate a moderately positive attitude towards female correctional officers though there was a significant number of neutral responses (see also Holland et al., 1979). As one respondent wrote: 'a screw is a screw whether it's a male or a female'. Interestingly, while none of the female officers interviewed expressed concern about assaults on them, all of the male officers did. Male officers also saw the sexual attractiveness of female officers as a serious problem. Just over a third of the inmates thought that female staff would have difficulties with inmates making improper advances.

The contrast between inmates' and male officers' views is repeated in Holman and Krepps-Hess's (1983) study in the California Department of Corrections. A substantial majority of the prisoners did not feel that female officers invaded their privacy and two-thirds felt that female officers improved the

TABLE 6.4   ATTITUDES OF PRISON INMATES TOWARDS FEMALE STAFF
(BOULDER, COLORADO, USA)

Questions asked to inmates (n=35)	% Yes	% No
Would you be less likely to be physically aggressive toward female staff?	54	46
Are females easier to manipulate or intimidate than males on the staff?	11	89
Would you take a protective role in regard to female staff?	43	57

Source: Kissel and Katsampes, 1980

prison environment. A majority of the male officers disagreed. Most of the prisoners did not feel that female officers were less effective than male officers on any of the principal assignments; a majority of male officers did.

Female prison officers are also probably as physically competent as many of the male staff. As in the discussion on law enforcement, physical strength *per se* is not as important as male professionals believe. Women can use their verbal skills to talk to inmates. Further, women can be trained to cope with physical confrontation. The prediction about taking women as hostages has not occurred, probably because female officers are seen as officers rather than as women. The incidence of male staff bringing in contraband and becoming involved with inmates is said to be significantly higher than the incidence of these events among female staff. Overall, the presence of female officers in men's institutions seems to have normalized the environment, relaxed tension, and led to improvements in the inmates' behaviour, dress and language.[29] The underlying reason for these effects remains unclear, however, and requires further exploration. It could mean that inmates are responding to female officers as women or that female officers use different styles of management from male officers. Crouch and Alpert (1982) provide some support for this second suggestion. They report that male guards became more punitive and aggressive over their first six months on the job whereas female guards became less so.

The attitudes of male colleagues are presented as a major problem by female prison officers (Jurik and Halemba, 1984; Zimmer, 1986). This can take the form of hostility and resentment, sexual harassment or over-protection. Bowersox (1981) found that male prison officers tended to shield female prison officers from possible assault and that the female officers resented this. Further, such over-protection is self-defeating and potentially dangerous. If a woman is never given the chance to handle an assault, she will not learn how to handle it. In the Boulder jail study already cited (Kissel and Katsampes, 1980), the 13 women employed there were asked whether they ever felt vulnerable because they were female. More than three-quarters said that they sometimes did. On the other hand, almost the same number felt that they were capable of handling most crisis situations. Moreover, in this study, the inmates were aware of the male prison officers' hostility to female prison officers. This, together with female prison officers' exclusion from the occupational subculture, may well have made female officers' jobs more difficult. Women do not experience the usual camaraderie and support offered to male officers by their colleagues (Horne, 1985). The industrial action taken against the appointment of the female catering officer discussed previously effectively demonstrates this.

The most recent justification for sex as a necessary occupational qualification in prisons in the United States is inmates' right to privacy, somewhat paradoxical in jurisdictions where such rights are generally ignored. (It was also raised in the English case discussed earlier.) In the Maryland case of *Hudson* v. *Goodlander* (1980 494 F Supp. 890), for example, Hudson alleged that his constitutional rights to privacy were violated when female prison officers viewed him undressing, showering and in the toilet. The court decided his rights were violated but this has been described elsewhere as a 'feeble excuse for discrimination' (Mr Justice Marshall in *Dothard* v. *Rawlinson*). It would be possible, through the use of screens in toilets and showers, to balance inmates' rights to privacy and women's equal employment rights. Further, exact equality of assignment between male and female prison officers is not necessary. Thus body searches could be conducted only by someone of the same sex as the inmate.

This question arose in Cynthia Gunther's attempt to achieve promotion. The duties of a correctional officer II included responsibility for riot control, patrol of cell blocks and super-intending inmates in baths and showers. Gunther was denied promotion. The state trial court ordered her promotion but held that she should be excluded from the performance of duties which violated prisoners' rights of privacy. The Supreme Court of Iowa reversed this on the grounds that the duties which Gunther could not perform were the core of the correctional officer II classification. Before this decision was announced, Gunther filed a complaint in the federal District Court under the Civil Rights Act 1964. The Court then ordered the defendants to promote Gunther and the state was ordered to make adjustments to protect the plaintiff's interest in equal employment opportunity, the state's interest in prison security and prisoners' interest in preserving privacy.

In practice, in many states, although female prison officers do work in men's institutions, their assignments are limited to the control room, and visiting and clerical areas. Without further assignments it is, therefore, difficult, if not impossible, for women to obtain promotion. This 'special treatment' also fuels the resentment of male officers. The answer to this lies in training female officers to cope with all assignments, for example, through self-defence programmes. Improvement of prison conditions might also protect both male and female prison officers from assault.

Conclusion

The California Supreme Court summarized well the impact of current restrictions on women's employment, whether direct or indirect:

> Laws and customs which disable women from full participation in the political business and economic areas are often characterised as 'protective' and 'beneficial'. Those same laws and customs applied to racial and ethnic minorities would readily be recognised as invidious and impermissible. The pedestal upon which women have been placed has all too often, upon closer inspection, been revealed as a cage. We conclude that sexual classifications are properly treated as suspect, particularly when these classifications are made with respect to a fundamental interest such as employment. (*Sail'er Inn, Inc* v. *Kirby*, 5 Cal. 3d 1, 485 p. 2d 529, 1971)

All criminal justice positions should be fully available to *qualified* women, just as they should be *restricted* to qualified men.

7

Women as Victims

Introduction

Women are more afraid of crime than men. A recent crime survey in England and Wales (Hough and Mayhew, 1985) asked respondents how safe they felt walking out alone after dark. Almost half the female respondents reported feeling 'a bit' or 'very' unsafe. Less than a sixth of male respondents felt this way. An earlier but similar study in Britain found much the same (Hough and Mayhew, 1983), as did the National Crime Survey in the United States (US Department of Justice, 1986). Research consistently shows that those who feel least safe are women, the elderly and those living in inner cities. Table 7.1 demonstrates this.

This level of fear has obvious consequences. For women,[1] it restricts their activities, including work and social opportunities; and it affects the quality of their lives. Riger and Gordon (1981) asked men and women whether fear prevented them from doing things they wanted to, like going to movies or visiting friends. More than two-thirds of the women responded that it did, compared with only a quarter of the men. The figures were similar with respect to questions about necessary activities, for example, shopping. Hough and Mayhew (1983) found that a third of the women in their sample, but very few men, said that they sometimes avoided going out after dark. The proportion was even higher for young, middle-aged and old women in inner cities.[2] Maxfield (1984) reports that a fifth of women living in inner-city areas mentioned crime when asked why they never went out at night. (See also Radford, 1983; Hall, 1985; Jones et al., 1986.)

TABLE 7.1 FEARS FOR PERSONAL SAFETY BY AGE, SEX AND AREA:
PERCENTAGE FEELING 'VERY UNSAFE' WALKING ALONE IN THIS AREA
AFTER DARK

Sex/age	*Inner cities*	*Other large city areas*	*Other areas*
Men			
16 – 30	3	1	1
31 – 60	11	3	1
61 and over	27	12	6
Women			
16 – 30	28	18	11
31 – 60	38	21	13
61 and over	60	41	29

Source: Hough and Mayhew, 1983

There is an apparent paradox in these different levels of fear
for men and women, for women constitute a minority of the
victims of crime: those who feel most unsafe are those least often
victims. Table 7.2 compares, by age and sex, the fear of crime and
the extent to which people fall victim to street crime. According
to the British Crime Survey (Hough and Mayhew, 1983 and 1985)
the 'typical' victim is male, under 30 years old, single, spends
several evenings a week out, drinks heavily and assaults others.
They go on to suggest that women's fears may be excessive and
irrational though they acknowledge that fear of victimization may
make potential victims take increased precautions. Hough and
Mayhew, however, miss the point; the fear of crime extends well
beyond the women who have themselves been victimized. As one
respondent in Hall's (1985: 37) study said: 'fear of assault is a
constant consideration in day-to-day living and increases feelings
of dependence'. Furthermore, Maxfield (1984: 13), also using
British Crime Survey data, showed that when it comes to street
crime (that is robbery, sex offences and thefts from the person),
women *are* more often victimized than men. He refers to a rate of
1.2 per 100 for men and 2.0 for women. This is also true in the
United States. The victimization rate for personal larceny with

contact (primarily purse snatching) is higher for women than for men. The victimization rate for black women is especially high. Hall (1985) also notes in her London sample that black women had higher victimization rates than white women.

Thus women are not worrying about nothing; their fears, especially black women's fears, do have a real basis. That is, women *know* that they are quite likely to be victimized at some point in their lives. Hall (1985) noted, for example, that out of more than 1,200 women, over a third said that they had been raped or sexually assaulted. More than three-quarters had been physically grabbed or touched against their will. In Russell's (1982) random sample of almost 1,000 women, just under half said they had been the victims of rape or attempted rape. The FBI's view is that one in four women will be sexually assaulted in their lifetime and Johnson (1980) estimated that almost a third of girls now aged 12 will suffer a violent sexual attack during their life. It is similar to their likelihood of getting divorced. Violence by men to women in the home is equally prevalent. Crime surveys, because they are geared to discover unrecorded crime 'outside', miss the bulk of crime which affects women: crimes inside the home committed by those known to them (for a more detailed discussion of this point, see Worrall and Pease, 1986).

Furthermore, it is not simply rates of victimization which

TABLE 7.2   FEARS FOR PERSONAL SAFETY AFTER DARK AND RISKS OF 'STREET CRIME'

Sex/age	% feeling 'very unsafe'	% victims of 'street crime'
Men		
16 – 30	1	7.7
31 – 60	2	1.6
61 and over	9	0.6
Women		
16 – 30	15	2.8
31 – 60	17	1.4
61 and over	34	1.2

Source: Hough and Mayhew, 1983

generate women's fear, it is the nature of that victimization. Many crimes against women have certain distinctive features. In brief, they are:

> Most women are victimized by men.
>
> Women are more likely than men to know their attacker.
>
> Women are more likely than men to be attacked in their home.
>
> Women are more likely than men to experience long-term emotional distress after victimization.
>
> Women are more likely than men to experience some blame for their victimization.

This chapter focuses on three crimes committed primarily against women: rape, domestic assault and the sexual abuse of children.[3] These crimes cannot be discussed exhaustively within a single chapter, but I will attempt to critically examine themes which run through conventional thinking about these offences.

Rape

Introduction

Rape is not often discussed in criminological texts. In Wisan's (1979) review of criminal justice texts published between 1970 and 1977 (13 in all), four had no discussion of rape and five only dealt with it briefly. Where there was some discussion, it tended to perpetuate stereotypical views about rape. For example, Bloch and Geis (1970: 249) wrote that: 'It can never be determined accurately how many forcible rape cases involve real resistance to the attack and how many involve mere token resistance in which the criminal charge is an afterthought.' They also suggested that many rapes reported to the police were in reality not offences but were rather charges levelled to save the reputation of the woman or for the purposes of blackmail. Gibbons (1977), throughout his discussion of rape, placed quotation marks round the word victim and referred to the rapist as an 'uneducated, opportunistic, and basically goodhearted soul who takes his pleasure where he finds it' (1977: 383−4). In the sociology of deviance, the researchers' commitment was to empathize with the offender, to see his world as he sees it. But, as Rodmell writes: 'It is only possible to empathize with the heterosexual sex offender . . . if one is able to, and prepared to, ignore the third party' (1981: 150).

This section challenges assumptions about rape and demonstrates further how these assumptions have become part of our mechanisms for the social control of women.

Although rape makes up only about half a per cent of recorded serious crime in both England and Wales and the United States, the number of recorded rapes is now considerably higher than 15 years ago. For example, in England and Wales, there were 893 recorded rapes in 1972 and 1,842 in 1985. Victimization data, however, put the figures much higher. In the United States, the National Crime Survey indicated that less than half had been reported by the victims to the police and recorded by them. In Hall's (1985) London sample, about a third said that they had been raped or sexually assaulted. Only 8 per cent of alleged rapes and 18 per cent of alleged sexual assaults had been reported by the women to the police. The Criminal Statistics for England and Wales (Home Office, 1984c) contrasted British Crime Survey figures with the number of notifiable offences recorded by the police for 1981. There were 12,000 rapes and indecent assaults notified to the police that year; adjusted for comparison this became 8,000. The British Crime Survey estimate of sexual offences was 30,000 which means that only about a quarter were reported to, or recorded by, the police.

However, reliability of these estimates depends on the reliability of victimization data generally, and the reasons why a victim did not report the offence to the police might equally prevent her from telling her family or a researcher.[4] The major reasons cited by victims in American crime surveys for not reporting rapes to the police were that it was a private matter, nothing could be done about it, and fear of reprisal. Hall (1985), on the other hand, found that nearly half the respondents did not report the incident to the police because they thought the police would be unsympathetic. Black women in particular express feelings that the police will not take their allegations seriously (Bryan et al., 1985). Williams (1984) found that the key factor which determined whether or not a rape was reported was the circumstances of the rape itself. The rape victim had to feel confident that others, especially the police, would perceive her as being a genuine victim. Consequently it was the 'classic' rape — a sudden, violent attack by a stranger, where the victim resisted physically and verbally — which was most likely to be reported to the police. Ageton's (1983b) findings support this. Very few of the assaults experienced by her respondents were reported to the police and these usually involved unknown or multiple assailants. The majority of the other incidents occurred on dates, primarily in the respondents' own, or their boyfriend's, home or in a vehicle.

In addition to the fact that many, perhaps most, rape victims do not report their victimization to the police, few cases go to trial and even fewer result in convictions or incarceration (Feldman-Summers and Lindner, 1976; Robin, 1977; LaFree, 1980; Chandler and Torney, 1981; Galvin and Polk, 1983; Wright, 1984). Galvin and Polk argue that rape is not unique in this respect (see also Polk, 1985).[5] They compared the loss of rape cases at key points in the criminal justice system with other serious offences (homicide, robbery, assault and burglary). They found that rape generally fell in the middle of the five offences with regard to either further processing or disposition at each point examined.[6]

Such a statistical analysis, however, begs an important question: why did the attrition take place? It is likely that this was for different reasons in each of the offences. The reasons why rape victims do not report alleged rapes to the police (for example, shame, embarrassment, guilt and self-blame) are very different from the reasons for non-reporting by the victims of robbery, assault, and burglary (Shapland et al., 1985). Furthermore, police, prosecutors, juries and judges are often sceptical about the credibility of rape victims; this rarely arises in these other offences. Landau (1974) sums this up nicely by pointing to two competing emotions in rape cases: revulsion for the crime of rape and distrust of those women who accuse a man of having committed it.

Most of us believe we know what rape is, but our knowledge is derived from social not legal definitions.[7] 'True' rape in popular imagination involves the use of weapons, the infliction of serious injury and occurs in a lonely place late at night. The 'true' rapist is over-sexed, sexually frustrated or mentally ill, and is a stranger. The 'true' rape victim is a virgin (or has had no extra-marital affairs), was not voluntarily in the place where the act took place, fought to the end and has bruises to show for it.[8] These notions are perpetuated by media accounts of rape (Smart and Smart,

1978; Brownmiller, 1975; Voumvakis and Erikson, 1984) which act as cautionary tales for women and which have certain implications for determining whether or not rape has occurred:

> Men who do not fit the stereotype are probably not rapists.
>
> Women who do not fit the stereotype are probably not victims.
>
> Rapes which do not fit the stereotype are difficult to establish and easy to dismiss.

Schultz and De Savage (1975), for example, asked students to select on a scale of increasing sexual violence that point at which, in their judgement, a legal rape took place while on a date. About half of them incorrectly defined legal rape. They were also asked if legal rape took place when consent was given and then withdrawn, after which non-voluntary intercourse took place. Almost three-quarters of the male students described this as forcible rape compared with just over half of the female students.[9] (See also Koss and Oros, 1982.) Finkelhor and Yllo (1982) present the following case history: a man who was drunk started to have intercourse with his girlfriend. He decided he wanted anal intercourse. She refused and screamed. He became very violent, held her down so that she could not move and forced her to submit. When the woman was asked by the researchers whether she had ever been forced to have sex, she replied 'no'.

The reason why these kinds of situations are not seen as rape is the strength of the assumptions we hold about rape. These traditional attitudes reveal themselves particularly in 'greyer' forms of rapes: rapes which do not fit stereotypical conceptions. I will now examine some of these assumptions. (See also Schwendinger and Schwendinger, 1974; Mills (1982) explores the role of the medical profession in the origin of many of these assumptions.)

'Rape is impossible'

Mapes (1917: 430) provides an example of this thinking: 'No adult female can be forcibly compelled to acquiesce, since for anatomic and physiologic reasons the male is incapable of successfully "fighting and copulating" at the same time.' More recently, Mendelsohn argued that rape was impossible because of the position of the sexual organs. He believed that 'authentic' rape occurred in only two situations: where the 'volcanic temperament of the victim' had obscured her reasoning faculty and as a result of 'the libertine social surroundings of the victim' (1974: 4).

Other criminologists (for example, Glaser, 1972: 61) have argued that to force a woman into intercourse is an impossible task in most cases if the woman is conscious and extreme pain is not inflicted. These beliefs have become part of rape folklore ('you can't thread a moving needle'; 'a woman with her skirt up can run faster than a man with his trousers down' and the like) and embedded in the practice of criminal justice professionals. Robin (1977: 141), for example, quotes a judge who stated that, unless there was extensive physical trauma, 'a hostile vagina will not admit a penis'.

What these beliefs ignore is that often things are not equal. Brownmiller (1975) quotes a study in Washington by Hayman in which the age of the victim ranged from 15 months to 82 years. The London Rape Crisis Centre (1984) reported that it has been contacted by or on behalf of women and girls of all ages — from 3 to 90. Such beliefs also ignore the effect of fear and threats on women. Brownmiller demonstrates this in the story of a man who asked a girl in a bar to move a beer glass around while he tried to insert a truncheon. She avoided his attempts easily. 'You try it', he said. The girl smashed his arm with the truncheon; he dropped the glass and looked surprised.

These beliefs also ignore the impact of socialization on women. Women have been discouraged from asserting themselves and encouraged to be submissive and deferential. Weis and Borges (1973) see differential socialization patterns as producing both the rape victim and the rapist.

'Women want to be raped'

This assumption has its roots in Freudian beliefs about the masochistic nature of female sexuality. Helen Deutsch, for example, saw masochistic traits as part of the ideal and healthy female personality. She wrote that 'the masochistic tendency now betrays itself only in the painful longing and wish to suffer for her lover (often unknown)' (1944: 225) and described rape as the archetypal sexual experience for women. (See also Bromberg, 1965.) These writers have ignored the impact of culture on women and on their sexuality. (See, for example, Horney, 1926, 1932 and 1937.)

Nevertheless, rape is believed to dominate women's sexual fantasies for it is said to satisfy their masochistic, self-destructive needs. Kanin (1982) asked a sample of university women to fill in questionnaires on their fantasies and she found that more than half did report experiencing rape fantasies. However, on analysis, about half of these were in fact seduction fantasies. Just over a quarter of the women had had rape fantasies and these were essentially non-erotic. That is, they led to fear rather than sexual arousal. Crepault and Couture's (1980) data are not directly comparable but provide some information on men's fantasies. They interviewed married men. All admitted erotic fantasies and there were three main themes: confirmation of sexual power, aggressiveness and masochism. One of the themes which emerged from Beneke's (1982) book on men and rape was the frequency with which *men* referred to rape fantasies. Beliefs about women's fantasies may well, therefore, reflect men's fantasies about women's fantasies. Faust (1982: 122) writes: 'Men's proclivity for sexual fantasy leads them to project their own hopes, needs and wants on to women: women do not want it, but men want to imagine that they do. Men and women see rape differently because they see sex differently.' Furthermore, even if women do have rape fantasies, as fantasies they are controllable and thus very different from rape. Faust (1982: 142) demonstrates this by reference to differences in the sexual and erotic styles of men and women: 'Masculine pornography is concerned with behaviour: fucking. Female pornography is concerned with rape, fucking, compassionate intercourse, nurturing intercourse, seduction by the man, seduction by the woman, shared carnal desire, and shared passionate love.'

Wright (1980), from his analysis of recorded rapes in six areas of England, suggests that it is difficult to imagine that a woman could enjoy being raped since in the majority of his sample there was some form of physical violence, though few were severely beaten or seriously injured. Given also that most of the victims resisted their attackers, it is illogical to suppose that they enjoyed what occurred.

'"No" means "yes"'

Nineteenth-century women – or, at least, ladies – were seen as asexual and presumed not to enjoy sex. Whereas they were passive and submitted (rather than consented) to the sex act, men were viewed as the aggressors and the initiators, and as having sexual needs. These beliefs have resonances today. Dating is a ritual in which women possess the prize which men attempt to win. Women are thus the sexual gatekeepers. Men are expected to make advances (otherwise the woman thinks she is unattractive) and women are expected to be sexually attractive and, at the same time, both coy and flirtatious. They are expected to play hard to get, to need to be seduced. Gebhard et al. (1965: 177), for example, wrote: 'Any reasonably experienced male has learned to disregard [the] minor protestations of the female . . . a male is supposed to be physically forceful in his sexual behaviour.' Such thinking is also reflected in judicial pronouncements. A judge in a recent rape trial in Cambridge told the jury that women sometimes said 'no' to sex when they meant 'yes' and to remember the expression 'Stop it. I like it.' He continued: 'It is not just a question of saying 'no'. It is a question of how she says it, how she shows and makes it clear. If she does not want it, she has only to keep her legs shut and he would not get it without force, and there would be marks of force being used.' The defendant in this case was acquitted.

In dates, the actors are placed in an ambiguous situation with maximum privacy. It is not surprising that rapes can result. According to Herman (1979: 43): 'Our culture can be characterized as a rape culture because the image of heterosexual intercourse is based on a rape model of sexuality.' This type of assertion goes too far. Sexual intercourse can be an act of love between two equal parties. But equality is rare in the real world and important elements underlie such assertions. Rape is, in part, the horror show of our sexual socialization and this produces in turn both victims and offenders (Weis and Borges, 1973); rape and seduction are part of the same continuum of taking.

'"Yes" to one, then "yes" to all'

Consent is a major issue in rape trials; consequently, the victim's moral character becomes a public issue. A commonplace event in a rape trial was, until recently, questioning the victim about her prior sexual experiences (Edwards, 1981). Such information was seen as relevant by criminal justice agencies and undoubtedly influenced juries to acquit (Kalvan and Zeisel, 1966; Pugh, 1983). Mills (1982: 48) quotes a male gynaecologist as saying 'there is one type of woman I would have a hard time believing was raped: a woman between 16 and 25, on the pill and no longer a virgin'. Katz and Mazur (1979) in their book on rape devote a chapter to the sexual history of rape victims. A parallel chapter on the purchasing history of property victims is difficult to imagine.[10]

Prior sexual experience is presented as in some way bearing on the victim's credibility,[11] but there is no evidence that women who engage in sexual behaviour lie more frequently than those who do not. Indeed, women who answer such questions freely may be more honest than those who refuse to answer such questions. Yet Catton's (1975) findings suggest that admissions of prior sexual experience serve to indicate consent to the alleged intercourse and to diminish the guilt of the accused in the eyes of the jury. Catton also found that even where the judge instructed the rape victim not to answer a question regarding her sexual history, the mere fact of having heard the question led mock jurors to perceive the accused as less guilty. According to Sealy and Wain (1980), the perception of the victim as untrustworthy was the single best predictor of verdicts even where there was a strong case against the defendant. Impressions of the *defendant's* credibility were either unrelated or minimally related to verdicts. What underlies the issue of credibility is the moral character of the victim: the jurors ask themselves 'is she the *type* of woman who would consent to intercourse?' The answer, of course, reflects preconceived prejudices about rape.

There have in many jurisdictions been recent legislative changes to preclude questions about prior sexual activity. Instances of prior consensual activity with the defendant usually remain admissible but instances of prior sexual activity with any other person are generally not admitted in evidence, unless the consent of the victim is at issue and such activity tends to establish a pattern of conduct which is relevant to the issue of consent. As consent usually *is* at issue, however, prior sexual experience continues to be admitted.

This is certainly what happened in England where previous sexual experience can now only be introduced where a prior relationship existed between the victim and the offender or with the permission of the judge (Sexual Offences (Amendment) Act 1976, section 2). Adler (1982) analyzed a sample of rape trials which were heard at the Old Bailey in London. A standard line of defence in the trials was consent and, in more than half of the cases, formal application was made to introduce evidence of the complainant's prior sexual experience. Three-quarters of these applications were successful. The criterion to be used in determining such applications is whether the jury would take a different view of the evidence if the information was included. Given the kinds of assumptions made about rape victims, the answer to this will almost certainly be 'yes'. Judges also interpreted the section very widely. In the words of one, quoted by Adler: 'This wretched section overturns many of our habits in criminal trials. I am very troubled about this. It goes against the grain to deny the defence latitude and to give it to the complainant. I'll take a bold course and allow the question to be asked.' Adler also found that counsel, without leave, briefly asked a few, brief questions like 'are you on the pill?' without interruption from the judge. As Catton (1975) has shown, merely asking such questions — without any answer — increases acquittal rates. Adler further discovered that sometimes the judge himself asked such questions. (See also Adler, 1985 for an analysis of recent case law.)

Concern about the application of section 2 was expressed by the Policy Advisory Committee to the Criminal Law Revision Committee (1984). The latter, however, was satisfied that, on the evidence before it, there were in fact no grounds for concern that either the letter or the spirit of the section was being disregarded. The nature of this 'evidence' bears examination. The Policy Advisory Committee asked members of the Bar, a predominantly male profession and made up of those who formed the subjects of Adler's criticisms, for their views. It is hardly surprising that they thought that the section was applied sensibly. Indeed, they complained more of the unfairness caused to *defendants* by the section than to unfairness caused to complainants. The Criminal Law Revision Committee stressed that what critics of this section did not understand was that previous sexual experience may be relevant to the issue of consent (1984: para. 2.87). Their evidence for this is the story of a woman who often went to public houses, met men and invited them to her flat for sexual intercourse. This would explain, according to the Committee, how the defendant came to be in her flat when she alleged he had raped her and would be relevant 'as it would tend to show that the complainant's denial of consent was unlikely to be true' (1984: para. 2.8). But as Wells (1985: 68) points out, 'there is no logic in this', rather 'it feeds into the dangerous prejudices which inform people's perceptions of rape'.[12]

Even if the moral character of the victim is not an issue at trial, it continues to be so at the pre-trial stages: police and prosecutorial decision-making. Certainly, women feel that the police make an assessment of whether or not they are an 'appropriate victim'. Hall's respondents who did not report an alleged sexual assault to the police gave the following reasons (1985: 110−11):

> They would have assumed I'd asked for it knowing that I was on the pill and not a virgin at 17.

> As I was travelling rough I expected they would say I 'asked for it'.

Clark and Lewis (1977) identified 116 rapes reported to the police in Toronto; the police decided that two-thirds were unfounded. Clark and Lewis had access to all the relevant information and documents. In their view, only 12 were unfounded. They further suggested that the decisions reached by the police were related to the victim's moral character rather than to evidential requirements. For example, all of the professional women making rape allegations had their allegations treated as founded; half the students and none of the women living on welfare had their allegations treated as founded. (See also Wright, 1980 in England; Chambers and Miller, 1983 in Scotland; Feldman-Summers and Palmer, 1980 in the United States.)

Prosecutors are also influenced by the character and credibility of the complaining witness. According to Stanko (1982), prosecutors make use of the concept of a 'solid case' and assess the victim in terms of his or her 'stand-up' qualities. They are unwilling to pursue a case if the victim's character is questionable and, therefore, conviction is unlikely. According to Stanko, in deciding this with respect to female victims, the prosecutors relied on assumptions about *proper* female behaviour and the degree of resistance a proper woman should put up. Wife abuse and acquaintance rape were not viewed as 'solid cases'. Stanko suggests that violence against women is inadvertently legitimized by this process and that prosecuting only certain convictions places female victims at a disadvantage. There is some support for this in Scottish research. Chambers and Miller found that almost a third of the sexual assault cases sent by police to the procurator fiscal were subsequently not proceeded with.

A variant of 'yes to one, then yes to all' is 'yes once means yes forever'. In those jurisdictions where evidence of prior sexual experience is generally restricted, prior sexual experience with the defendant is allowed. The most obvious example of this is wife rape, which in most jurisdictions is not an offence. Russell (1982) suggests from her interviews that at least one woman out of every seven who has been married had been raped by her husband. It may be more common than rape by other kinds of assailants (Gelles, 1977).

'The victim was asking for it'

In essence, this assumption implies that the victim should not have dressed like that (e.g. with no bra), behaved like that (e.g. hitch-hiked),[13] gone to places like that (e.g. singles' bars). Joe, a 19-year-old student, interviewed by Beneke, sums this up: 'I guess in any rape some of it's the woman's fault. Some of it has to be' (1982: 56). Amir, in his study of rape, developed the notion of victim precipitation. His definition is both extremely broad and stresses the *offender's* interpretation of the victim's behaviour, not the victim's. 'The victim actually — *or so it was interpreted by the offender* — agreed to sexual relations but retracted . . . *or did not resist strongly enough* when the suggestion was made by the offender. The term applies also to cases in which the *victim enters vulnerable situations* charged sexually' (1971: 266, my emphasis). Earlier, he seemed to define any form of female behaviour as rape-precipitating: 'A woman's behaviour, if passive, may be seen as worthy to suit action, and, if active, may be taken as an active promise of success to one's sexual intentions' (1971: 262). Despite this, only 19 per cent of the rapes in Amir's sample could be so 'explained'. MacDonald (1971: 78–9) also suggests that some women 'invite rape' and 'are rape-prone, as others are accident prone'. These views of women as seductive or inviting rape are widely held by both undetected 'rapists' (Ageton, 1983b) and convicted rapists, many of whom continue to deny their guilt (Gebhard et al., 1965).

They also underlie widely held attitudes. Voumvakis and Erikson (1984) analyzed newspaper accounts of attacks on women in three Toronto newspapers. Of the attributions of responsibility made in these articles, by far the largest category (almost half) related to the victim: for example, she had put herself in a perilous situation by using public transport at night or by taking a short cut. When comments of the police and criminal justice agencies were examined separately, the victim was blamed even more frequently, in over three-quarters of the cases. These views have little empirical basis. Curtis (1974), from a survey of police and court records in 17 American cities, found that victim precipitation was most characteristic in murder and assault, of some empirical importance in robbery and 'least relevant' in rape.

The underlying assumption here is that 'nice' girls do not get raped (reflecting the madonna/whore dichotomy) but anyone can become a rape victim. Even if women avoid so-called dangerous situations, this does not prevent rape (Bart, 1981). From the picture derived from reported rapes (Wright, 1980; Walmsley and White, 1979), around half take place in the daytime, in the women's own homes, and involve men they know. (See also Hall, 1985.)

This belief that the 'victim asked for it' does not tie in well with the profound and long-term effects which rape has on victims (nightmares, fear, shame, guilt, powerlessness, depression and the like). Kilpatrick et al. (1981) contrasted 20 victims, one, six and twelve months after the rape, with 20 matched non-victims. The victims were significantly more anxious, fearful, suspicious and confused than non-victims for at least one year after the assault. The work of rape crisis centres confirms this (Holmstrom and Burgess, 1978; London Rape Crisis Centre, 1984). Extreme reactions are especially likely to occur where the attack takes place in circumstances which the women defined as safe, for example, in their own homes (Scheppele and Bart, 1983). Ageton (1983b) stresses that reactions may in fact intensify with time. She found that her respondents were depressed and afraid of being alone two and three years after the assault. Shapland et al. (1985)

contrasted the effects suffered by victims of physical assault, sexual assault and robbery. Victims of sexual assault had both the highest level of effects at the first interview and the greatest tendency for the effects to persist.

In recent years women have been involved in 'take back the night' protests in many major cities. Shorter, however, blames increases in rape on this 'new mobilization for political action':

> Feminism has in the short run probably made women more likely to be raped because it legitimately encourages them to behave in a free autonomous manner . . . Responding to feminism, males may feel they want to mobilise for a sexual political struggle . . . so for many new style rapists . . . rape is merely to them a logical political response to a disturbing new challenge. (1977: 418)

Blaming the victim has taken a new direction.

'Rape is a cry for vengeance'

This belief has its origin in the seventeenth-century statement by Matthew Hale:[14] 'It is an accusation easily to be made and hard to be proved, and harder to be defended by the party accused though never so innocent' (quoted in Brownmiller, 1975: 413). Such warnings are still commonly found in discussions of police practice. Firth, for example, wrote:

> It should be borne in mind that except in the case of a very young child, the offence of rape is extremely unlikely to have been committed against a woman who does not immediately show signs of violence . . . watch out for the girl who is pregnant or late getting home one night; such persons are notorious for alleging rape or indecent assault. Do not give her sympathy. (1975: 1507)[15]

Rape victims certainly see the police as unsympathetic. For example, half of those interviewed by Chambers and Miller (1983) made negative comments about CID officers. These focused on their manner of questioning, the police officers' evident disbelief of the victim and the attribution of blame to the complainant (see also Hall, 1985).[16] A prevalent belief among the police in Chambers and Miller's survey was the existence of a high rate of false complaints among rape complainants.

Standard legal texts on evidence and procedure also warn of the danger of women contriving false charges of sexual offences. And as recently as 1984, the Criminal Law Revision Committee prefaced its report on sex offences with the words that 'by no means every accusation of rape is true' (1984: 5). Elliot provides a further recent example of this distrust of rape complainants. He believes that lying is more common in rape cases than in others because 'there *are* various and numerous causes for lying' (1984: 13, emphasis in the original). He cites these as getting pregnant, feeling guilty, blackmail, getting one's own back at an unfaithful lover, confusion of fantasies with reality, and selective recall. He also stresses that things are not always what they seem: bruises may result from a woman's taunts about a man's inadequate performance and 'alleged pack rape . . . may be a consensual frolic which has gone wrong only in that . . . the girl failed to reach home before her parents'. Because of all this, he argues, there must be special protections for the defendant. What's the evidence for all this?

In Clark and Lewis's (1977) study, only 7 out of 116 reported rapes were found to be false reports made by an alleged victim and in only two instances was there any threat to an innocent man; in the other cases, the victims quickly admitted the false claim. The Commander of New York City's rape analysis squad (quoted in Weinstein, 1977) believed that only about 2 per cent of all reports of rape and related sex offences were false, and that this was about the same as the rate of false charges in other serious offences. (See also Chambers and Miller, 1983.) Paradoxically, one of the points made by the rapists interviewed by Beneke (1982) was revenge as *their* motive for the rape. Chuck, for example, spoke of rape as getting back at the women who had hurt him in the past.

Nevertheless, this belief in revengeful women has led to special rules about corroboration in rape cases.[17] There are usually no witnesses to rape apart from the man and the woman. Physical evidence is, therefore, important; for example, semen (though this may have resulted from consensual intercourse) or bruises (though police advice is often not to resist for resistance may lead to greater injuries). In a number of American states, if there is no evidence of resistance, there is no rape. Hans and Brooks (1978), in an experimental study, found that mock juries which were given corroboration instructions tended to convict less than juries which did not hear them, although both were presented with the same evidence.

'Rape is a sexual act'

Historically, rape was a property offence (Clark and Lewis, 1977).[18] Women had limited property rights and were themselves viewed as the property of their fathers and, later, their husbands. In rape, the protected party was the male owner of the female property. The focus was on the trespass of that property and the penalty was compensation; the exact amount depended on the woman's economic position. Mitra (1979: 560) describes it thus:

> The evil that the law tried to prevent was the abduction of propertied virgins who, to the detriment of family rights in their disposal were thus compromised into marriage. The essence of the crime was theft of another man's property, and the victim's point of view was sometimes excluded to such an extent that the sexual aspect of the case might be found in the words: 'swived[19] against the will of her father'.

The popular conception now is that rape is sexually motivated: this is most apparent in accounts offered to excuse rape. Smart and Smart (1978: 98–9) provide examples of this from media coverage of rape:

> The pregnancy of B's wife may have been 'one of the reasons for his committing the offence'.
>
> R attacked her five days before his wife gave birth to their first child.
>
> Sex-starved window cleaner C. arrived at a young woman's house as she was having a bath . . . C. told police he had not had sex for eight months.
>
> Possibly at a difficult age (18) of your life you were overcome by your own sexual urges.

Many convicted rapists, however, have accessible female partners at the time of the rape and Groth and Birnbaum (1979), from a study of more than 500 rapists, describe rape as motivated by anger (involving an expression of hostility towards women and a desire to humiliate them) and power (involving the assertion of dominance over the woman). They described rape as a *pseudosexual* act: 'it is sexual behaviour in the primary service of non-sexual needs' (1979: 13). Holmstrom and Burgess (1980), on the basis of interviews with rape victims admitted to hospitals, agree that there are various social and psychological meanings attached to rape, most notably power, anger and male camaraderie. Herman (1979) uses homosexual rapes in prison to demonstrate that rape is really about domination. She argues that the objective is to control other men and, in fact, to transform them into women as this shows both to the rapist and to others in prison that the rapist is a real man. Herman quotes one prisoner who presents the alternatives graphically: fight or fuck. Most feminist writers (for example, Brownmiller, 1975; Clark and Lewis, 1977) see rape as a violent act. They argue that the use of force or physical coercion is the central feature of rape. At first sight, this seems wrong. Common sense tells us that date rape, and rape at knife-point by a stranger, are different kinds of experiences. But their point is as valid in date rapes as in rapes which involve the overt use of violence. Asserting dominance makes the sexual act possible in both.

'Rapists are grossly abnormal and psychologically disturbed'

Criminal justice professionals believe the main causes of rape to be mental illness, sexual frustration or poor judgement by the victim (Feldman-Summers and Palmer, 1980). Control samples and convicted rapists, however, are indistinguishable in both their sexual behaviour and other characteristics: there are more differences than similarities among rapists and more similarities than differences between rapists and controls (Ageton, 1983b). In Malamuth's (1981) study of college students, many indicated that they were likely to rape if they thought they could get away with it.[20] These students were similar to convicted rapists in their beliefs about rape and in their arousal by depictions of rape. Consequently, Malamuth suggested that many men have the proclivity to rape: husbands and acquaintances as well as strangers.

Russell (1982) also found that wife rape occurred in all social classes, in all racial and ethnic groups, in all religious groups and in a great range of age-groups. From this, she concluded that the social characteristics of husband rapists differed from men who rape women other than their wives and that the social characteristics of wife-rape victims differed from other rape victims. Her conclusion, however, is faulty. We know very little about non-apprehended rapists and unreported rape victims. Most of our knowledge about rapists comes from incarcerated samples; and most of our knowledge about rape victims comes from reported cases. These are likely to be quite biased samples. Russell's description of the husband rapist and the wife-rape victim may well reflect the characteristics of rapists and rape victims in general. We do not know. What we do know is that generalizations from convicted samples are highly suspect. The detection and conviction rates of rapists are low. Gilley (1974) calculated that the conviction rate for rape was less than 1 per cent and that consequently rape was a crime which did pay.

The consequences of rape myths

These assumptions about rape are widely held,[21] despite statutory changes in recent years. Burt (1980) found that over half of a representative sample of almost 600 residents of Minnesota believed the following: 'any healthy woman can resist a rapist'; 'in the majority of rapes, the victim was promiscuous or had a bad reputation' and 'if a girl engages in necking . . . and she lets things get out of hand, it is her fault if her partner forces sex on her'. Thornton et al. (1982) found that male students were more likely than female students to blame women for getting themselves raped. And there is some evidence that juries — laymen — are prone to believe these myths. At least, juries are more likely than a judge to acquit an accused rapist (Kalven and Zeisel, 1966). Acquittal rates are higher in rape trials than in other types of offences.

Assumptions about rape have at least three consequences. For potential offenders, they provide a social context in which rape is not only possible but encouraged (Field, 1978; Groth and Birnbaum, 1979). Burt (1980) goes further and suggests that culturally transmitted assumptions about men, women, violence and sexuality constitute a rape-supportive belief system. Clark and Lewis (1977: 148) quote an alleged rapist who sums up this view: 'I seduce. I don't rape.'

For victims, these assumptions create feelings of guilt and self-blame (Schwendinger and Schwendinger, 1980). Women do not report the incident to the police because they fear blame by their family, friends and the police. Paradoxically, we find the reverse of the ordinary situation: the victim feels on trial. Mills (1982) argues that rape results in quadruple victimization: the actual assault and then psychological assaults by the police, medical profession and criminal justice system. Some writers have taken a further step and blamed the mothers and wives of sex offenders for the offences. Their wives, for example, have been described as frigid (McCaldon, 1967; Albin, 1977).[22]

The major consequence of these assumptions, however, is for women generally. According to some feminist writers, rape is nothing more or less than a conscious process of intimidation by which *all* men keep *all* women in a state of fear;[23] it is the ultimate weapon which men use to exercise power over women (Griffin, 1971; Brownmiller, 1975; Hanmer, 1978). Such claims go too far. Some women are victimized more than others; we need to be able to explain this. Also, some men are victimized by men (for example, rape in prison). But rape and the fear of rape are part of all women's consciousness and operate as constraints on their freedom. Timothy Beneke writes that, after talking with women, he recognized for the first time that 'the threat of rape alters the meaning and feel of the night' (1982: 3). He went on to make a further important point: when one is raised without freedom, one may not recognize its absence. The fear of street crime also constrains the movements of such groups as the elderly. But one does not say to them: why do you go out alone? Why do you keep such sums of money in your purse? It is assumptions about rape victims which constrain women's behaviour as much as rape or the fear of rape. Bowker (1978) rejects this notion of rape as a mechanism of social control as rapists do not mention it as a motive, but this confuses cause and effect and intended and unintended effects. Whatever the motivation for rape, its effect is restrictive. In a poll of 1,000 women for the television programme 'Weekend World', a few years ago, the vast majority did not feel adequately protected by the law and most blamed the failure of the law for rape.

Rape is not natural and inevitable. Reeves Sanday (1981) reviewed the life-styles of 95 tribes: seventeen were rape-prone and these were characterized by male domination and sexual segregation; forty-five were rape-free; in these, women's reproductive and productive role was valued and women had prestige. There are lessons to be learned from such anthropological material, lessons about appropriate behaviour for men and women, especially expectations about men's and women's sexuality (Schwendinger and Schwendinger, 1981). In Young's words:

> Is it the *tyranny* of the discourse of sexuality that we can 'see' no alternative sexual relations for men and women, so that ultimately our own sexualities become our prisons . . . so the rhetoric of male – female sexuality, framed in terms of love, sex, marriage and pleasure, will produce, prohibit and constrain forms of sexual behaviour, the boundaries of which are watched and guarded by the laws of rape and sexual offences. (1986: 35)

It is this discourse which has to be changed to prevent rape. Human sexual behaviour though based on biological needs is the expression of cultural forces.

Some Parallels in Wife Abuse

Introduction

The extent of domestic violence is unknown. Ashley (1973) estimated that there were approximately 27,000 serious cases per year in England, but other writers have put the figure much higher. Borkowski et al. (1983: 27) speculate that something between one in five and one in three of all marriage experience physical violence at some point. (See also Marsden, 1978; Straus et al., 1980.) Domestic violence occurs within all age, cultural, racial, socio-economic and religious groups — there is no simple association with poverty, lack of education or psychological inadequacy — and it covers a wide range of activities: physical, psychological and sexual. Russell (1982) found that marital rape and battering frequently occur together.

The term 'domestic violence' is neutral; it gives no clue as to who beats and who is beaten. According to Strauss et al., both men and women are abusive. They developed a wife-beating and a husband-beating index and reported a rate of 3.8 per cent for wife-beating and 4.6 per cent for husband beating. From this, they concluded that 'some revision of the traditional view about violence seems to be needed' (1980: 41). I agree with Russell (1982) that this is an erroneous conclusion: Strauss et al. do not distinguish between offensive and defensive violence and they ignore the differences in strength and fighting skills between men and women. (See also Gelles and Cornell, 1985: 79–80; Pagelow, 1985.) In the vast majority of Russell's cases, the husband initiated the violence, and Dobash and Dobash (1979), in their analysis of over 1,000 cases of violence involving family members, found that three-quarters concerned husbands attacking wives; only ten cases involved assaults on husbands by wives.[24] The term 'domestic violence', therefore, obscures the issue; it is, in the main, women who are beaten by men.

Wife-assault is institutionalized and entrenched (Dobash and Dobash, 1979). Until the nineteenth century, English law gave husbands the right to beat their wives (Blackstone, 1765 reprinted 1966, vol. 1: 432). Consequently, the debate has often been about *how much* violence is appropriate (the original meaning of 'the rule of thumb' was that husbands could legitimately beat wives with a stick no thicker than the man's thumb) rather than whether violence is appropriate at all. Violence also begins early in marriages. Dobash and Dobash found that of the 109 women in their sample who had used refuges, 41 per cent had experienced their first attack within six months of the wedding. And the violence tends to be long-lasting. Almost half of Binney et al.'s (1981) sample (also drawn from women living in refuges) had experienced episodic violence for more than six years.

The police and wife abuse

Few women turn to the police for help (Walker, 1979). Pahl (1981) found that women sought help from friends or relatives before turning to formal agencies. The normal pattern was to contact doctors or social workers, lawyers and eventually the police. But even where women ask for help, the police do little. Parnas's (1972) observation of the Chicago police identified four categories of police action in domestic violence: 'talking down' the dispute, threatening the disputants and then leaving, asking one of the parties to leave the premises and, very rarely, making an arrest. (See also Brown, 1984; Roy, 1977; Langley and Levy, 1977.) In some areas, there are explicit policies against arrest. This stems from a variety of reasons: wife abuse is not seen as serious; the police think the family should stay together; they believe that the woman will withdraw the case the next day or they see the situation as a private or domestic matter and urge the woman to take civil action (McCabe and Sutcliffe, 1978). Battered women certainly complain about the inadequacy of police help (Pahl, 1978; Binney et al., 1981). Some of the women in Brown's (1984) sample saw the police as primarily concerned with their own safety, rude, and tending to blame the woman for the violence. One study (Evason, 1982) concluded that as a result of police reluctance to act, violent husbands believed they were above the law.

A common belief in the police is that the victim will not co-operate in the prosecution. Such claims are greatly exaggerated (Dobash and Dobash, 1979; McLeod, 1983; McCann, 1985). Wasoff (1982), for example, found in her Edinburgh sample that requests by the victim not to proceed occurred only twice out of 59 cases and both requests were refused. She asked why this belief was so tenacious and widespread. Her answer was that law-enforcement officials are faced with two conflicting social objectives: 'to punish violent criminal offenders or to adopt the non-interventionist stance in 'normal' family affairs that is the characteristic principle of family law' (1982: 199). Wasoff argues that it is adherence to the latter which makes the protection of women from domestic assault problematic. Russell (1982) goes further and believes that the primary reason for inaction is that most police officers are men and identify with the male assailant. Indirectly, this means that the police help to reinforce the control exercised by men over their families. Dobash and Dobash (1979) found that the police took action when the injuries were severe, when neighbours complained and when the husband contested the authority of the police.

But the reasons for inaction actually go deeper than this. Violence against a woman by her husband in the privacy of their home is, in our culture, viewed as a quite different crime from violence against a stranger in a public place, if, indeed, it is seen as a *real* crime at all. The Association of Chief Police Officers, for example, in its evidence to the Select Committee on 'Violence in Marriage' said: 'It is important to keep 'wife battering' in its correct perspective . . . We are, after all, dealing with persons 'bound in marriage', and it is important for a host of reasons to maintain the unity of the spouses' (1975: 366). This is echoed in Maynard's (1985) findings on social-work practice. In her research, social workers supported the nuclear family and did nothing which might threaten the continuance of a particular family unit even where battering was still occurring. Johnson (1985) examined the response of three agencies approached by battered women for help: the police, social workers and medical or paramedical personnel. He found that the request tended to be ignored or redefined and that there was a marked reluctance to become involved. The privacy of the family and of marriage was constantly stressed by the various agencies. Basically, state intervention in families was thought to be inappropriate.[25]

There are, however, two problems with this view. First, state intervention in families is viewed as appropriate where children are concerned and so the limits of familial freedom are already restricted. Secondly, as Pahl (1985) stresses, it is important to consider who is being protected by this view. It seems that the husband's right to privacy takes dominance over the wife's right to the protection of the law. Faragher (1985: 124) puts it quite simply: 'Whose privacy? Whose liberty?'

In some areas, the police have responded by becoming involved in mediation and counselling with a view to reuniting the family (Potter, 1978; Bard, 1970). Though this may be useful for some couples, domestic violence is not only, some (for example, Klein, 1982) would suggest not even, a personal problem. It reflects women's structural inequalities and lack of power. Women are often financially and emotionally dependent on the abusing spouse.

To change this requires long-term solutions, but, in the short term, there is some evidence that treating domestic violence as a *criminal* problem does work. Law suits in some American cities sought to compel the police to make arrests in cases of domestic violence. This approach was monitored in Minneapolis over six months in 1982 by the Police Foundation (Sherman and Berk, 1984) and they found that police arrests sharply reduced violence in the home. An increase in the arrest of husbands has also led to more favourable attitudes to the police among battered women (Bowker, 1982).

The trend in Britain, however, is in the opposite direction. The Commissioner of the Metropolitan Police in London recently suggested categorizing 'domestic disputes' with 'stranded people, lost property and stray animals' as tasks to be handed over to other agencies to relieve the police for 'crime prevention, detection and community policing — real crime work' (*The Times*, 4 October 1983). Similarly, Southgate and Ekblom report that the police define responses to requests for help with 'lost dogs, domestic disputes, rowdy youth and bothersome drunks' as 'rubbish work' (1984: 26).

Blaming the victim

The responses to wife abuse reflects many of the social attitudes raised in the discussion on rape. (See also Klein, 1979; Walker, 1979.) Women are often explicitly blamed for the violence: they must have been provocative, frigid, aggressive or whatever. Thus criminal justice and social-service professionals treat the women with suspicion and indifference. Maynard (1985), for example, found that social workers disbelieved what battered women said about their domestic situation, supported men's reasons for the violence and encouraged the women to understand these reasons. Brailey (1985) claims that local-authority housing departments make similar assumptions in denying women access to better housing.

While one could see this as part and parcel of orthodox victimology which assumes that victims are at least partly responsible for the resulting act through their own behaviour, most researchers in this area have ignored the importance of gender in understanding such interactions. Dobash and Dobash sum up what is wrong with this approach:

> If we claim that women in their position as wives 'cause' or 'precipitate' violence because they argue with their husbands over the injustice of their demands, fail to accept their authority or deny negative evaluations of them as wives and mothers, then we, like the violent husband, are guilty of simultaneously denying women a right to voice their own position and of blaming the victim and holding them accountable for the man's violence. (1984: 286)

Another aspect of victim-blaming is the belief that the woman wanted to be hit. Women are believed to be masochistic and to unconsciously encourage abuse. Psychiatrist Anthony Storr (1970), for example, wrote that nagging, aggressive women are often unconsciously demanding what they fear most. Pizzey and Shapiro (1981 and 1982) outraged many of their supporters when they suggested that some women repeatedly chose violent relationships for 'deep psychological reasons' of their own. Walker (1979) rejected these claims for the majority of women in her sample.

Victim-blaming is well summed up in the common question: why doesn't she leave?[26] Walker (1979: 45–7) adapted Seligman's concept of 'learned helplessness' to explain the psychological inability to do so. Seligman (1975) administered electric shocks to dogs in cages, at random intervals. The dogs quickly learned that no matter what response they made, they could not control the shock. When nothing they could do stopped the shocks, they became passive and submissive. According to Walker (1979: 47), this concept is useful in understanding why battered women do not free themselves from a battering relationship: 'Once the women are operating from a belief of helplessness, the perception becomes reality and they become passive, submissive, helpless.' The women need not actually be as helpless as they perceive themselves to be; it is their perception of what they can and cannot do which is crucial. Walker (1979: 51) argues that the very fact of being a woman, especially a married woman, automatically creates a situation of powerlessness.

But there are other reasons for a woman's inability to leave. Women are unable to leave relationships, for material and ideological reasons. The abused woman is likely to have no job, no house, no money and to have responsibility for her children (McCann, 1985; Brailey, 1985; Homer et al., 1985). She is also likely to accept traditional roles and expectations of marriage (Walker, 1979). Furthermore, *responses* to requests for help may prolong a woman's stay in an abusing relationship. For example, Binney et al. (1981) found that among the women they interviewed in refuges, the average number of agencies or individuals from whom they had sought help was five. They suggest that repeated failure to gain the type of help they needed left the women feeling demoralized. Requests for help can also go wrong. Bryan et al. (1985) cite the example of abused black women's children being taken into care after requests for help.

This question – why doesn't she leave? – may also be the wrong question to ask. Jones (1980) suggests that the question should rather be 'why don't the men let them go?' She presents case histories in which battered women who had left their husbands were sought out by them and killed. Russell (1982) presents similar case histories of husbands pursuing wives though it did not lead to the women's death. She interprets such actions on the husband's part as the continuance of the belief that the woman remains his property.

Various studies have described the characteristics of both the women who are abused and the men who abuse them (for example, Walker, 1979). However, the dark figure of wife assault is extensive. Research which has described the characteristics of particular samples (women in refuges, volunteers, apprehended men) is not likely to be generally valid. Wife abuse, like rape, is an extreme form of normality. Wilson describes it as 'an exaggeration of how society expects men to behave as the authority figure in the family' (1983: 95). She continues: 'The search for causation then becomes, in a sense, a wild goose chase, because it [wife abuse] is concerned with wider issues to do with the control of women by men, to do with power and inequality, and to do with how we perceive manhood.'

Some Parallels in the Sexual Abuse of Children

Introduction

Incest is a subject which has always fascinated, appalled and perplexed us. It does not, however, always arouse horror and revulsion. Webster Cory and Masters (1963: 3) wrote that: 'Ambivalence . . . has typically characterised human responses to the idea and practice of incest. The incestuous union ordinarily both attracts and repels.' Most societies have had incest taboos, but this did not mean that incest was entirely prohibited. Nor were punishments necessarily severe. Pollock and Maitland (1898, reprinted 1952), in *The History of the English Law before the time of Edward I*, wrote that the offence was sometimes punished in the ecclesiastical courts by whipping and other bodily penances, but that it was sometimes paid for with money. Incest only became a criminal offence in England in 1908.[27]

Despite the almost universal incest taboo, incest appears common and it occurs in all classes, ethnic and religious groups and at all educational levels. Sexual contact with family friends is similarly common. While no accurate statistics exist, the American Humane Society estimates that between 80,000 and 100,000 children are sexually abused each year and that in about a quarter of the cases it is by a relative. The National Society for the Prevention of Cruelty to Children reported recently that 11 per cent of all cases reported to it involved sexual abuse, usually by a natural or substitute father. A Canadian Commission (1984) found that about one in two women and one in three men had been the victim of at least one unwanted sexual act. About one in four assailants were family members or persons in a position of trust. (See also Kinsey et al., 1948 and 1953; Finkelhor, 1979; Nash and West, 1985.)

Finkelhor identifies what he calls the 'male monopoly' in sexual abuse (1979, 75: see also the Commission on Sexual Offences against Children in Canada, 1984). A consistent finding in the research is that the majority of offenders are male and the majority of victims are female. For example, Russell and Finkelhor (cited in Stark, 1984) estimate that women are responsible for 20 per cent of the sexual abuse of boys and only 5 per cent of the abuse of girls. The rest of this section concentrates on this disparity. Conventional literature makes little attempt to account for it. Russell and Finkelhor explain it by suggesting that men tend to sexualize their feelings of affection more than women do. Gebhard et al. (1965: 9–10) offer a different kind of explanation: the lower sex drive of women.

An alternative explanation, at least with respect to incest and sexual abuse within families, is that it is a product of patriarchal family relations. Like wife assault and rape, it tends to occur when traditional beliefs about the roles of man and woman, husband and wife, father and daughter are taken to extremes (Herman and Hirschman, 1977). Thus Armstrong (1978: 235) writes: 'The abusive father must have a sense of paternalistic prerogative in order to even begin to rationalise what he's doing . . . he must have a perception of his children as possessions, as objects. He must see his children as there to meet his needs rather than the other way around.' Such fathers may not feel that they have done anything wrong (Brady, 1979). They are aided in this by the assumptions we make about the sexual abuse of children.

Sexual abuse as fantasy

The sexual abuse of children reflects many of the themes and attitudes apparent in discussions of rape and wife abuse. Here too there is a reluctance to intervene. Rush (1974) cites a study in which 263 cases were reported to the police. Arrests were made in 173 cases. Almost half of these were dismissed for lack of proof. One of the main reasons for this was disbelief of the child. Children are said to have active imaginations and to make up stories for no apparent reason.[28] Freud was struck by the number of his patients who reported 'perverse acts by their father'. He presumed the reports to be fantasies and he saw them as a cause of hysteria. But Freud did not present any cases which demonstrated false accusations. Indeed, in the case history of Dora, in which the family alleged that Dora had lied about the incest, Freud subsequently validated it. Nevertheless, Freud's legacy is strong (MacDonald, 1971); the evidence for his views on fantasies of incest is not.

According to Piaget (1932), the ability to separate fantasy and reality is certainly apparent by the age of seven and so generally there is no reason to believe that children older than this are unable to distinguish the two. For children younger than this, it is difficult to imagine how they can describe sexual acts without having experienced them. Specifically with respect to sexual assault, Peters (1976) studied 64 children who were seen at a hospital emergency room with a complaint of sexual assault. In only four cases did the staff conclude that no sexual assault had occurred. And Goodwin et al.'s (1982) search of the psychological abstracts between 1968 and 1978 yielded only one paper on false accusations in incest. Their review of 88 psychiatric papers on incest published between 1973 and 1978 revealed only two papers on the historical importance of false accusations of incest and four on individual case reports of false retractions of valid incest accusations. They were unable to find a recent case report on the false accusation of incest. The Commission on Sexual Offences against Children in Canada (1984: 28—9) concluded both from a review of the literature and from empirical research that assumptions about the untrustworthiness of young children with respect to sex offences were largely unfounded.

Seduction by the child

Another reason for the rejection of reports by a child of sexual abuse is the belief in the seductive child.[29] Bender and Blau (1937: 54), for example, wrote that 'these children . . . do not deserve completely the cloak of innocence with which they have been endowed' and though they recognize the impact of fear and gifts, they continue: 'frequently we considered the possibility that the child might have been the actual seducer rather than the one innocently seduced'. They referred to the child playing an active or even initiating role. Other writers (Burton, 1968; Gibbens and Prince, 1963 and Maisch, 1973) echo this theme. Indeed, Maisch places quotation marks around the word 'victim' throughout his discussion. Virkkunen (1975) identified 31 cases of victim-precipitated paedophilia offences from 64 offenders seen by him for medical examination. This figure is probably explained by the fact that information on the victim's role in the offence was provided by the *offender*. Virkkunen also concluded that: 'The fact that each victim became several times the object of the act is *in itself* a proof that the victim cooperated in maintaining the situation' (1975: 179, my emphasis). There is no understanding of the possibility that the child acted from fear. Armstrong (1978) provides considerable evidence to rebut the claims of these writers. Many of the women interviewed by her were aged three, four and five when the abuse began and cannot be viewed as equal partners in the relationship.

No harm caused

Some writers have minimized the impact of sexual abuse. Klein (1932), for example, wrote that brother—sister incest might well be positive in alleviating the girl's anxiety about sex and developing her capacity for love. Burton (1968: 94) extended this to 'seductions' (her word) which did not entail violence and concluded that they may have afforded some emotional satisfaction to the child. Indeed, Constantine and Martinson (1981) argue that even exceptional experiences like incest are varied in impact and should not be categorically defined as negative. Batten further argues that sexual activity is 'eminently pleasurable for incestuous children' (1983: 246). (See also Lukianowicz, 1972; Schultz, 1975; West, 1983.) What these writers agree is harmful to the child is the parents' reaction to the discovery of sexual abuse. The 'helpful' object becomes, supposedly for the first time, bad. Kinsey et al., for example, wrote: 'It is difficult to understand why a child, except for its cultural conditioning, should be disturbed by having its genitalia touched . . . the emotional reactions of the parents, police and other adults . . . may disturb the child more seriously than the contacts themselves' (1953: 121). And Gibbens and Prince (1963) noted that legal procedures may be more harmful to the child than the original offence and 'may indeed be the *only* cause of serious upset' (1963: 3, my emphasis; see also, pp. 7–8). Such conclusions enable Maisch (1973: 216) to argue that: 'The basic motivation of today's laws will withstand neither critical nor rational examination, nor empirical testing by the medical and behavioural sciences. They appear to be a kind of ingrained prejudice.'

This minimization of harm contrasts sharply with the feelings of 'incest survivors' who talk of fear, revulsion, shame and guilt (Armstrong, 1978). In Herman's (1981) study of 40 incest victims, more than a third had attempted suicide. Nash and West (1985) found that some of their respondents still felt resentment and their attitudes to men were permanently affected. They noted two extremes of behaviour: sexual activity at an early age and withdrawal from adult sexual relationships.

Blaming the mother

It is also common to find references in the literature on sexual abuse to the responsibility of the mother for the abuse (Justice and Justice, 1979; McIntyre, 1982). For example, she must have been sexually frigid, castrating, domineering, out at work, or she must have *unconsciously* known yet did nothing to stop it. Often a role reversal between mother and daughter is referred to which involves the provision of sexual as well as domestic services to the father (Herman, 1981). Tormes (quoted in Rush, 1974) examined 20 cases of incest and reached 'the unavoidable conclusion' that the failure of the mother to protect the child against incestuous victimization is a crucial area of study. She concluded that the mother was the *only possible* agent of incest control within the family group. And Armstrong found, in her discussions with social workers, that it was axiomatic for them to say that 'the mothers always know — *on some level*' (1978: 55, emphasis in the original). 'The father rapes and brutalises' writes Rush (1974: 71) 'and it turns out to be the mother's fault and responsibility.' As Wilson (1983) remarks, these myths of the consenting or collusive mother explain nothing; ultimately it is the *man's* responsibility. While some of the incest victims interviewed by Armstrong (1978) were angrier at their mothers than their fathers, Armstrong interprets this not as showing how much at fault the mothers were, but rather how much more they needed from their mothers.

Because of this belief that incest is a symptom of family dysfunction, the current trend amongst practitioners is to attempt to reunite the family. Such action may be appropriate for some families. It does, however, reflect the ambivalence we have about incest and the sexual abuse of children. Nelson (1982: 72) sums this up nicely: 'It seems generally acceptable to imprison and remove from their families people who are not a danger to their families. It is not, apparently, acceptable to remove people who really are a danger to their families.'[30] Moreover, it is now becoming apparent that many girls who run away from home have been the victims of physical or sexual abuse (Phelps et al., 1982). Yet these girls are dealt with in the juvenile justice system as if *they* were the problem.

Conclusion

What links these three offences — rape, wife abuse and the sexual abuse of children — is men's dominance over women. In particular, the family is not the safe haven it is reputed to be; nor can women necessarily rely on the men they know for protection. Instances of all three kinds of assault are not rare occurrences and women are not responsible for them. Men — and patriarchal social forces — are.

Notes

Chapter 1 Criminology and Women

1 This is so in other disciplines too. See, for example, Carlson and Carlson (1960) and Gilligan (1982).
2 Generalizations from research on women, on the other hand, do not occur.
3 In the same way, Sutherland's (1939) work on white-collar crime fundamentally questioned criminological theories of that period.
4 For this, see, for example, Taylor, Walton and Young (1973).
5 The practical implications were clear and direct: the amelioration of living conditions, the reduction of unemployment and the creation of a sense of community. Indeed, the Chicago Area Project which grew out of Shaw and McKay's work is still in operation and similar community action programmes have been applied elsewhere. The theory is not, however, without criticism. Shaw and McKay ignored the likelihood that these areas were policed differently and that the high delinquency areas might have been created by police practices. Arrest rates do not reflect actual delinquency rates. Also, the high crime rates in some areas might have been created by a local housing policy in which problem families were grouped together (Gill, 1977).
6 Other criticisms are that delinquents share many values and attitudes with non-delinquents. It is also obvious that robbery, burglary and the like violate lower-class values as well as middle-class values. It is difficult to imagine a community or class so isolated that it is unaware of generally held values and concerns (through, for example, the influence of schools and television).
7 Research in England has consistently shown an association between low socio-economic status and crime. See Wadsworth (1979) and West and Farrington (1973). Social class differences in delinquency rates, however, are greater for boys than girls. Ouston's (1984) London data showed a range for boys extending from 17 per cent in non-manual occupations to 35 per cent in unskilled or semi-skilled occupations; the comparable figures for girls were 1.6 per cent and 7.5 per cent. Ouston seems

satisfied to note that the *pattern* of the relationships was broadly similar for boys and girls but these differences are considerable and require explanation.

8   It is not clear that the goals identified by Merton are as rigid or as fixed as he suggested or are as universally accepted. Also, the emphasis on crime as a utilitarian response to economic pressure makes the explanation of non-utilitarian, violent and sexual crimes problematic. Anomie theory both predicts too little crime (among the wealthy) and too much crime (among lower classes).

9   Recent research indicates not so much acceptance of these aspirations as an awareness of the lack of realistic alternatives to them (Lees, 1986). Sceptics may also suggest that marriage for women is a legitimate means of achieving *financial* goals.

10   This was less so for black women.

11   This perspective had a dramatic influence on theory, policy and practice throughout the 1970s. Moves towards decriminalization, diversion and deinstitutionalization all began at that time. The evidence for labelling theory, however, is contradictory and inconclusive. See, for example, Gold and Williams (1969), Ageton and Elliot (1974) and Mahoney (1974). Klein described it as 'our most widely accepted, untested formulation' (1972: 7).

12   It is remarkable how few men recognized this failure. One exception is Corrigan who acknowledged that 'many of the ladies (sic)' reading his book would be 'fairly irate' at his failure to mention girls (1979: 13). He recognized that he was following a 'male dominated sociological line of researching only into male adolescent activity'.

13   Bonger (1916) argued that women were less directly influenced by capitalism than men, and Leonard (1982) agrees. This does not seem to be right. Women experience *double* oppression — by the state and by men.

14   This is true in other areas, also; for example, research on the police. It is discussed in ch. 6.

15   Again, this is true of other disciplines. For a review, see Klein (1975).

16   Of course, it is not only women who are misrepresented. Stereotypical assumptions have also been made about male offenders: for example, the machismo of Cloward and Ohlin's (1961) gang member and the rational politicism of Taylor, Walton and Young's (1973) deviant.

17   Men, on the other hand, were seen as aggressive, independent, career-oriented, selfish, stable, unemotional, rational, determined, objective and serious.

18   These were, and are, also reflected in images of female victims. This is discussed in ch. 7.

19   There are parallels here with discussions about the existence or otherwise of a specifically feminist methodology. Clegg (1985) argues that there is no such thing as a coherent, unified set of practices and principles and that claims that particular methods, methodologies or epistemologies are uniquely feminist are both misguided and unfounded.

20 This is not as simple or simplistic as it sounds. As recently as 1982, in her British Sociological Association Presidential Address, Meg Stacey stated that women 'lack the terms to express the concepts which we as women understand. They are not in the literature or in the conceptualisations of a male dominated discipline' (1983: 7).

21 Some of the arguments in subsequent chapters apply to men too, but I do not consider them. That is not my purpose.

22 A caveat: although the amount of research on women has increased enormously in the past ten years, large gaps remain. It is difficult to obtain funding for research on women, including criminal women. Consequently, much of the research is small scale and at a doctoral level. Often, therefore, in subsequent chapters I can do no more than raise questions and speculate about answers.

Chapter 2   Gender Differences in Crime

1 An exception is the predominance of women among those accused of witchcraft (Demos, 1982). They outnumbered men by a ratio of about 4:1 and many of the men accused of witchcraft were members of the immediate family of the women so accused.

2 Research in particular areas finds much the same (Priestley et al., 1977; Baldwin and Bottoms, 1976).

3 A notifiable offence is broadly the same as what was called an indictable offence prior to 1978. It excludes most minor offences, but includes more than serious offences.

4 Indeed, Adam blamed women for increases in crime in the early twentieth century. He believed that this was due to their own crimes, their influence on men's crimes and the crimes of the children they neglected!

5 This suggestion has also been uncritically accepted by some feminist writers. See, for example, McIntosh, 1978.

6 These involve asking householders questions about whether or not they (or their family) have been victimized over a defined period.

7 When the sex of the victim was controlled for, however, there was no support for the thesis that *male* victims did not report female offenders. In fact, male victims reported female offenders more often than female victims did.

8 These involve asking respondents questions about whether or not they have committed offences over a defined period.

9 It is interesting that support roles are usually presented as inferior to active roles, yet they can be crucial to the eventual outcome.

10 Smart (1976) makes a similar distinction between 'sex-specific' and 'sex-related' crimes.

11 Flexner (1914: 108) presents the underlying rationale for this: 'The professional prostitute may be periodically punished without disturbing the usual course of society; no one misses her. The man, however, is

something more than a partner in an immoral act: he discharges important social and business relations, is as a father or brother responsible for the maintenance of others, has commercial or industrial duties to meet. He cannot be imprisoned without deranging society'.

12   33,892 women and 46,562 men were cautioned by the police or dealt with in the magistrates' or Crown Courts for thefts from shops in 1985. The equivalent figures for girls and boys were 24,347 and 42, 537.

13   Gelsthorpe (1986) demonstrates well how impressions of criminality can be at odds with reality. Police officers interviewed by her, for example, believed that more girls than boys were involved in shoplifting and that they stole different things; examination of local statistics showed this to be quite false. At a national level in 1985, only 36 per cent of juveniles cautioned for or found guilty of shoplifting were female.

14   The equivalent percentages for borstal girls and female prisoners were higher.

15   Statistics for the United States show much the same. See Leonard (1982) for a review.

16   Between 1965 and 1985 the male: female ratio for 10- to 14-year-olds moved from 7:1 to 3:1 and for 14- to 17-year-olds moved from 7:1 to 4:1; for the 17 to 21 age-group the ratio moved from 11:1 to 7:1.

17   Women's apparent invisibility in crime may indicate no more than the biases of male researchers (Campbell, 1984; Giordano, 1978).

18   This is not a particularly new approach. Lombroso and Ferrero (1895) sought to explain both women's criminality and their non-criminality.

Chapter 3   Theories of Women's Crime

1   It is not entirely a matter of history for men. Writers such as Jeffery (1979). Mednick and Christiansen (1977) and Wilson and Hernstein (1985) have contributed to a revival of interest in biological theories but the difference is that it is not an exclusive focus; it is viewed as one factor amongst many.

2   Freud's view, however, has often been misrepresented or misunderstood. He claimed that boys and girls initially demonstrated both masculine and feminine behaviours as a result of their bisexuality. Thus he did not view 'masculinity' and 'femininity' as innate, but rather as developing from the way the child *interpreted* the fact of biological sex differences. It was in this sense that he asserted 'anatomy is destiny'.

3   Sex chromosomal abnormalities exist and the presence of an extra Y chromosome in men has been linked to criminality. It was believed that the frequency of the XYY condition among criminals was greater than among men in the general population. This conclusion is now doubted. (See Owen, 1972 for a detailed review of this.) Recent studies of the actual rate of the XYY structure in the newborn show that it is not very

different from that found in prisoners. Also, the syndrome is exceedingly rare: most crimes are committed by chromosomally normal people and many XYY males are neither criminals nor mentally ill. Nevertheless Cowie et al. (1968) speculated that the female delinquent must have an abnormal chromosomal structure, for, to their mind, she demonstrated her 'maleness' by her delinquent activity. Further they noted in their sample of institutionalized girls 'markedly masculine traits' and described them as 'oversized, lumpish, uncouth and graceless' (1968: 171). There is, however, no evidence to support their claim of abnormal chromosomal structures among female delinquents. Some research has pointed to a greater prevalence of other chromosomal abnormalities among female prisoners than among the general population, but again, this was exceedingly rare and could not be an explanation for most criminal behaviour. See Widom, 1978 for a review.

4 Freeman (1984) is critical of Mead's work in Samoa but this does not detract from the general point of cultural diversity.

5 Mathilde and Mathias Vaerting (1923: 24) made much the same point from a historical viewpoint: 'There is not a single masculine quality which cannot be paralleled as a 'feminine' quality in the history of one race or another.'

6 Sayers also quotes examples of women being prohibited from certain jobs — breweries and wineries — on account of the potentially harmful effects of their menstruation. Women were also excluded from the temple — and hence from political and economic life — in traditional Jewish society.

7 The term 'premenstrual tension' was introduced by Frank in 1931. He described it as a feeling preceding menstruation of 'indescribable tension', irritability and a 'desire to find relief by foolish and ill-considered actions' (1931: 1054). A review of the literature on PMT (or PMS — 'premenstrual syndrome') reveals a much wider range of symptoms now. For example, Moos (1969) identified 150. It has now been defined so widely that it has incorporated, in Koeske's words: 'any troublesome or intense situation, emotion, behaviour or change, in body functioning which seemed to covary with the menstrual cycle' (1983: 10). A review of the literature also reveals a wider range of prevalence rates — from estimates of 15 per cent in 95 per cent — no doubt in part explained by the particular definition used by the researchers. For a review, see Nicholson and Barltrop, 1982.

8 This raises the issue of cycles in men too. These have been reported for weight, beard growth, pain thresholds, schizophrenia, manic-depression and epilepsy.

9 Pregnancy was also thought to lead to serious crime due to changes in the uterus and a considerable number of women were regarded as temporarily insane after childbirth. The Infanticide Act 1922 gave statutory force to such beliefs.

10 Craddock re-appeared in court in November 1981. A defence of PMT was rejected but the court accepted the reduced level of progesterone treatments as the explanation for her criminal behaviour and continued

the probation order. Counsel for Craddock subsequently appealed on the grounds that PMT should be a special defence. This was dismissed.

11 This kind of assumption has had obvious ramifications in criminal justice and penal policy. For example, when the new Holloway prison was being designed, it was explicitly designed with a view to becoming, at some later stage, a mental hospital.

12 See Busfield (1983) for an elaboration of this.

13 The precise definition of particular mental illnesses varies over time and place. For example, schizophrenia is used more broadly in the United States than in England, whereas the reverse is the case for manic depression (Busfield, 1983).

14 Attributions of madness can also be used to deny legitimacy to acts, both criminal and otherwise. For example, suffragettes were often described as mad and hysterical. Sir Almroth Wright wrote 'there is mixed up with the women's movement much mental disorder' (1913: 79).

15 See also the views of the Collingwood gang (Daniel and McGuire, 1972) and the bikers interviewed by Willis (1978). In Parker's (1974: 135 – 8) sample, girls were divided into three categories: 'somebody's tart', 'dirty tickets' and the 'not having any'. It is not only boys who make these distinctions; girls do too. See Cowie and Lees (1981) and Lees (1986).

16 Cohen saw the delinquent behaviour of lower-class boys as a protest against the norms and values of society. They endorsed the middle-class success ethic − the American dream − but they could not meet the 'middle-class measuring rod'. The working-class family had provided its children with poor socialization, poor speech and poor communication skills, and was described as easy-going, permissive and hedonistic. In school, working-class boys came into contact with middle-class standards: rationality, self-discipline, structured leisure, and the deferment of gratification. Failure to meet these standards led to conflict, frustration and failure. Because working-class boys could not succeed legitimately, they joined with others with similar problems of adjustment and formed a subculture with a value system in opposition to the larger society. Their behaviour, therefore, was described as non-utilitarian, malicious and negativistic.

17 Gilbert (1972) supports this line of reasoning. She argues that it was when girls were deprived of achieving such goals as wifehood and motherhood that they developed different ways of achieving these goals.

18 Cohen did accept in a later article with Short (1958: 35) the existence of gangs of girls 'strongly resembling the male hoodlum gang' but they continued to see the bulk of female delinquency as sexual. Even the female drug-addict subculture, according to them, exhibited 'a pathetic yearning for marriage to a stable, responsible, respectable man'.

19 Men's sexuality has not been explored as an explanation for men's criminality except in rape, but even there explanations point to anger

and hostility as potential motivations. See, for example, Groth and Birnbaum, 1979.

20 Revitch (1983) cites instances of orgasm by male offenders involved in burglary. This too is described as rare.

21 In quoting this, I am not agreeing with it. Men's gender role does not adequately explain rape, robbery or burglary.

22 Millett (1975) also referred to prostitution as the core of women's social condition.

23 The scale of attitudes towards feminism included the following items: (1) women should fight for equal rights with men; (2) it is not natural if a woman's career is as important to her as her husband and children; (3) if they feel like it, girls should ask boys for dates.

24 The black women in Glick and Neto's (1977) sample of prisoners came from more impoverished backgrounds than the white women and were more than twice as likely to have been on welfare when arrested. Further, black women in the United States act as household heads in almost 40 per cent of all black families as compared to less than 12 per cent of white families and Glick and Neto found that the black women in their sample were more likely to be living with, and be responsible for, their children than the white inmates.

25 Donzelot (1979) described the creation of the bourgeois family as a transition from a government of families to a government through families.

26 Larner's (1981) work on witches is relevant here. Eighty per cent of witches put to death were women. The stereotypical witch was an independent woman who did not conform to the idea of proper female behaviour. The peaks of witch-hunting coincided with law-and-order crises. Women became prime symbols of disorder and their punishment was a response to perceived threats to the social order. See also Erickson, 1966 and Demos, 1982. Hartmann (1977), in a different context and historical period, suggests that prosecutors and judges became harsher on women charged with crime as women became more assertive. In the Victorian period, she argues, middle-class women who committed offences were made into scapegoats by those frightened or resentful of social change. Another example is prostitution. According to Walkowitz (1980), nineteenth-century reformers attributed to prostitutes 'a wild impulsive nature, a restlessness, and a desire for independence' and viewed them as 'capable of independent and assertive behaviour rarely found among women of their own social class'.

27 Jensen and Eve (1976) analysed data from the same sample that Hirschi had drawn his data and found that the social bond variables were applicable to girls.

28 Hindelang did, however, report one surprising difference between his male and female respondents. He found that parental attachment was more of a deterrent to delinquency for boys than girls. He did not attempt to explain this.

Chapter 4   Women in the Criminal Justice System

1   Krohn et al. (1983) examined arrest data over the period 1948–76 in the United States and suggested that there was evidence that a bias in favour of women existed in the earlier period but that it was diminishing, at least with respect to adult women, in the later period. They believed the explanation lay in changes in women's demeanour: the police tended to deal more harshly with those women who were not deferential or submissive.

2   This does not mean that the police view men's and women's reasons for crimes to be the same. Police officers interviewed by Gelsthorpe (1986) viewed offending by girls as primarily stemming from pressures put on them to look attractive, and as planned. Boys, on the other hand, were viewed as acting for immediate reward or status, and impulsively.

3   The relevant factors in Landau's and Landau and Nathan's research were previous record, race and degree of parental control. These last two factors taken together indicate stereotypical beliefs about black families' (which, of course, means black women's) inability to control their children.

4   Overall, the rate of offending on bail is higher for men than for women. A Home Office (1981) survey found that about 8 per cent of men and 4 per cent of women re-offended while on bail during proceedings at magistrates' courts and that about 10 per cent of men and 2 per cent of women re-offended while on bail after committal for trial.

5   Salem (1982) makes the point that the absence of a medical recommendation does not necessarily mean the absence of mental disorder, but it is impossible to determine this one way or the other.

6   For men received into custody in 1984 and subsequently given a non-custodial penalty, the most common sentence was a probation order (25 per cent); suspended sentences and community service orders each accounted for a further 17 per cent and fines for about 14 per cent. Among women, probation was also the most common sentence (33 per cent) with suspended sentences the second most common (15 per cent). Fines and conditional discharges accounted for 12 per cent and 13 per cent of the sentences respectively. Figures for 1985 were not available at the time of going to press.

7   It is not officially permitted in England though Zander has argued that plea bargaining is an integral, necessary and, on the whole, beneficial part of the system: 'Well over 90 per cent of the two million or more cases dealt with by the criminal courts end with a guilty plea. If it were not so, the system would grind to a halt' (*The Guardian*, 12 July 1982). See also, Baldwin and McConville's (1977) controversial study of plea bargaining in Birmingham Crown Court.

8   Bishop et al. speculated why this might be so. First, they suggested that prosecutors are primarily influenced by the sufficiency of the evidence

rather than by social variables or the personal traits of offenders. Secondly, they point to the fact that the prime negotiators in plea bargaining are not the prosecutor and the defendant but the prosecutor and the defence counsel.

9   It is often also completely ignored as a factor. See, for example, Bottomley's review of research on sentencing (1973: ch. 4). The Home Office Research Unit's report on factors taken into account in sentencing (Softley, 1980), despite including men and women in its sample, did no separate analysis of them and this undoubtedly limits the validity of their results for female defendants.

10 Edwards (1984) also argues (from an analysis of the sentences of women who appeared before an English court on charges of violence against the person) that the women were frequently dealt with not merely according to a tariff system, but according to the degree to which their behaviour deviated from what was considered appropriate female behaviour. She concluded (1984: 182) that this often resulted in women being sentenced more harshly than men, but she presents no data to support this.

11 The Court of Appeal has since directed that judges should not distinguish between male and female defendants unless there are good reasons to do so: *R. v. Okaya and Nwaobi* (1984 6 Cr. App. RCS 253). In this case, the two male appellants had pleaded guilty to possessing a controlled drug with intent to supply and each was sentenced to five years' imprisonment. Their co-accused, Elliot, a woman, pleaded guilty to the same offence and was sentenced to two years' imprisonment. The sentencing judge found that all three were involved in the offence to a like degree but he drew a distinction between them for the purposes of sentencing on the basis that Elliot was a woman. Thus the only reason for the difference of three years between the sentences imposed on Elliot and on the appellants was Elliot's sex. The Appeal Court held that it was wholly wrong to make such a distinction unless there was a good reason, for example, where the woman acted under the influence of a man, and in the present case there was no good reason. Elliot had been sentenced leniently and this was wrong in principle. It was, however, insufficient ground for the appellants' sentences to be reduced. More recently, in *R. v. Hancock* (*Criminal Law Review*, 1986: 697) the court held, in sentencing a woman convicted of indecent assault, that in most cases female offenders should be dealt with on the same basis as male offenders.

12 Bedford (1974) found a similar relationship between the granting of parole in England and marital status. The proportion granted parole increased from 30 per cent for single women to 36 per cent for divorced, 40 per cent for separated and 55 per cent for married women. Within each category of mental status, the chances of parole increased for offenders with dependent children. Bedford does not, however, present comparable data on men and so the significance of this is not entirely clear.

13 Dominelli (1984), however, on the basis of discussions with magistrates

in West Yorkshire, believes that family responsibilities were more likely to operate as mitigating circumstances for male offenders than female. Taking care of the family was expected of a woman.

14 In an Alabama study (Alabama Law Review, 1975) the attitudes of a sample of criminal justice professionals towards women were tested. The researchers found that the sample was more concerned about women in their traditional roles as wives and mothers than about providing them with equality of treatment or fairness. Nearly a quarter of the judges agreed with the statement that women should be given suspended sentences more frequently than men and 56 per cent said that the existence of young children should weigh more heavily in sentencing a woman than a man.

15 There is a long history of concern about criminal women as mothers. Carpenter, for example, referred to female offenders' polluting influence; she referred to them as 'something fearfully rotten and polluted . . . undermining the very foundations of society' (1864: Vol. 11, 208). Not surprisingly, in the late nineteenth and early twentieth century, studies of 'cacogenic' families were common. These studies provided 'scientific' proof that women were the source of many social problems. Thus Dugdale (1910) believed that the degeneration of the Jukes family was transmitted through the female members of the family, not the male. For an elaboration, see Hahn (1980).

16 In a different context, that of family law and custody issues, Brophy and Smart make a similar point: 'It is not motherhood in isolation that is reviewed by the courts but motherhood within a family structure' (1981: 12).

17 Other groups identified for such special consideration were young adult offenders and those with no previous custodial experience if the sentence was to be of less than two years.

18 The Committee on the Mentally Abnormal Offender suggested that courts should also be particularly vigilant in looking for signs of mental disorder in female defendants (Butler Committee, 1975: 166).

19 Norland and Mann (1984) found similar thinking in their study of probation violation. Generally, few women were brought to court for breaches of their order; the sample included only 17 women as opposed to 322 men. This was said to be because prison was viewed by probation officers as unacceptable for women largely because of their parental obligations. To quote two probation officers (1984: 125):

> That is one of the big considerations, who is going to take care of the children when she's gone.

> It's not a big deal if a man has children, but, if a woman does, it is.

20 Eaton (1985 and 1986) suggests that the context of probation officers' reports also varies according to the sex of the defendant. Women are presented as responsible not just for the practical requirements of housework and childcare but also for the emotional situation in the

home. Probation officers also look to women in the construction of social inquiry reports on men.

21 DHSS (1983) statistics show that 73 per cent of those in care on the grounds of moral danger are female; only 15 per cent of those in care on offence grounds are female.

22 Social workers, too, have different attitudes towards sexual activity by male and female adolescents (Richardson, 1981).

23 This has a long history. Schlossman and Wallach (1978) argue that the practice of dealing differently with girls in America in the nineteenth century reflected the desire of reformers to purify society and to mould these young women into images of middle-class respectability. Young girls were punished for 'immorality' while similar behaviour by boys was ignored. For similar sentiments in England, see Carpenter (1857 and 1858).

24 This double-standard is international (Hancock and Chesney-Lind, 1982).

25 Adler's (1984) analysis of referral patterns to diversion programmes in the United States produced similar results. She found that about 40 per cent of participants were female and that more girls than boys were referred to the programmes for 'non offence' behaviour.

26 Other research projects in the United States present results which find no sex differences in dispositions. Teilmann and Landry (1981), for example, studied six areas. After controlling for offence-type and prior offences, they found no uni-directional gender bias present at any level of the system. Similarly, Horwitz and Wasserman (1980) found that sex did not have an impact on the severity of disposition; the main factor was the number of previous arrests. There are a number of possible explanations for these contradictory results: juvenile court practice may have changed in the last ten years (see also Curran, 1984); the methodology of earlier projects may not have been as rigorous or as sophisticated as later research; or, simply, different courts adhere to different sentencing approaches.

27 As an aside, Quinton (1910: vii) describes how many of the younger women in prison when he was governor 'revelled in their Swedish drill' and that a lady instructress 'soon imparted to them a martial step and bearing'.

28 Gelsthorpe (1981) traced the sentencing of juvenile offenders between 1965 and 1979. Despite claims by criminal justice professionals about the special needs of female offenders, she argues that sentencing patterns are not as differentiated as we might expect.

29 Rossi et al. (1985) present data which indicate that their sample generally viewed female offenders with less severity than male offenders. This is not explored further, and could be due to assumptions made about the seriousness of those crimes committed by men and women, even when labelled similarly.

30 Feminist research indicates that other areas of law (for example, employment, welfare and family) share this ideology about appropriate roles for women (Smart and Brophy, 1985).

31   The move towards sentencing guidelines in many jurisdictions in the United States is a step in this direction. In theory, sex is not a factor to be taken into account by judges in sentencing. It has resulted in more women being sent to prison (Sarri, 1981).

32   Johnson (1977: 9) proposed that girls should be treated as boys. 'After all, the delinquent girl like the delinquent boy is human too.'

33   It was argued by some at the Conference that there was no equality between men and women elsewhere in society and that, therefore, it was questionable whether one should strive for it within the criminal justice system, where at least some women benefited from lenient treatment. But the point is, it is only where women accept their traditional status that lenient treatment results.

Chapter 5   Women in Prison

1   Dominelli (1984) did find that the content of community service differed. The bulk of the placements for women involved domestic labour; none of the men were given such tasks.

2   See Matthews, 1981 for a summary of the evidence presented.

3   See Smith, 1962 for a detailed history of women's prisons.

4   One of the main concerns at the time was the ease of sexual contact between the sexes even where there were separate quarters.

5   The British Society of Ladies for Promoting the Reformation of Female Prisoners was founded by Mrs Fry in 1821 and they produced guidelines for adoption by local associations.

6   Some reforms directed sepcifically towards women did occur from about 1864 onwards when 'refuges' (minimum-security institutions) were established in which women could serve the last nine months of their sentence. In addition, female prisoners were given £4 instead of £3 on discharge (the sum male prisoners were given) and were entitled to one-third remission rather than one-quarter.

7   Women peace campaigners in the 1980s have also written about their experiences. See, for example, Benn, 1983; Tansy and Sear, 1985.

8   She was the first female Assistant Commissioner. The Prison Commission felt that since female offenders were very different from male offenders they needed a female Commissioner who could pay special attention to the needs of female prisoners (Commissioners of Prisons, 1936: 43).

9   Holloway was opened in 1852 but at that time took both men and women (120 men and 27 women on opening). The architect's brief, according to Camp (1974), was the provision of accommodation for 400 in separate cells to be capable of housing men, women and children. It was not until 1902 that it received only women.

10   For an earlier discussion of designing a women's prison, see Rotner, 1962.

11 This was not a new idea. Mary Size, the first governor at Askham Grange prison near York, recorded in her memoirs that the plan was 'to live together as a family and behave in every way as a decent family should' (1957: 146).

12 The view of the sherriffs whom Carlen (1983) interviewed was that Cornton Vale was a combination of a rest-home, maternity home, hospital and domestic-science college.

13 According to Carlen (1983), this model is quite meaningless for the majority of the women passing through Cornton Vale: they have already either had their family lives impaired by previous terms of imprisonment or have rejected conventional family life altogether.

14 The Prison Department set up a Holloway Project Committee. It was highly critical of the building design and made a wide range of recommendations in its report in July 1985 which, if implemented, are likely to improve conditions for both prisoners and officers.

15 In the United States, women currently make up about 7 per cent of the jail population, 6 per cent of federal prisoners and about 4 per cent of state prisoners. The largest number of incarcerated women is in the south, though California tends to have more women in penal institutions than any other state. As of February, 1984, there were 14 women (compared with 1,298 men) awaiting execution in the United States. In November 1984, the first woman was executed there since 1962.

16 The number of women in prison in the United States increased by 182 per cent between 1974 and 1984.

17 91,456 men and 4,733 women were received into prison under sentence in 1985. In addition, just over 19,100 men and over 1,300 women were received into prison in default of payment of a fine, about 52,100 men and 2,680 women were received as untried prisoners and about 16,900 men and 1,120 women were received as convicted unsentenced prisoners (Home Office, 1986c, table 1.3).

18 As of 1984, there were two federal institutions for women and two co-correctional federal institutions (compared with 31 federal prisons for men) in the United States. Most states operate only one prison for women (eight have more). In 1984, there were 61 state institutions for women and 460 for men. Two states (New Hampshire and West Virginia) have no separate prisons for women. It is common for women in the United States to be imprisoned in separate units within men's prisons or jails.

19 The picture is less clear in the United States. Among convicted female felons, violent offences were the major category (43 per cent) in Glick and Neto's (1977) survey, followed by property offences (29 per cent) and drug offences (22 per cent). The majority of convicted misdemeanants were property offenders (41 per cent). Among the unsentenced, violent offenders and property offenders each made up 30 per cent and drug offenders 22 per cent.

20 During the first decade of this century, two-thirds of Holloway's prisoners were serving sentences for prostitution or drunkenness. As

recently as 1950, 17 per cent of female prison receptions were sentenced for drunkenness.

21 This remains so despite the recent decarceration of soliciting. Prostitutes continue to go to prison in default of payment of fines.

22 A comparison of male and female prisoners received under sentence of imprisonment in 1985 showed that women had committed fewer offences of violence against the person (9 per cent compared with 14 per cent), burglaries (6 per cent compared with 22 per cent) and robberies (2 per cent compared with 3 per cent). The largest offence group amongst women was theft, handling, fraud and forgery, which accounted for 59 per cent of female prisoners compared with 32 per cent of male prisoners (Home Office 1986c, tables 5.4 and 4.4). The *1983 Jail Census* for the United States (*Bureau of Justice Statistics Bulletin*, 1985) shows that in the United States women were less likely than men to be in jail for violence offences in general (they made up 21 per cent and 31 per cent of inmates respectively) and robbery in particular (6 per cent and 11 per cent respectively); women, on the other hand, were more likely to be there for larceny and almost four times as likely to be there for fraud, forgery or embezzlement.

23 This represents a marked change. An early analysis of Holloway prisoners in the first decade of the century (quoted in Camp, 1974: 61) indicates that 75 per cent of the women admitted during 1910 had previously served prison sentences. Many of these previous convictions were for drunkenness.

24 A more recent figure is not available.

25 It has been suggested in England that women are more likely to be sentenced to imprisonment than men for a first offence (Fitzgerald and Sim, 1979; Mawby, 1977). This is, however, false and, indeed, the criminal statistics show quite the opposite. The percentage of female first-offenders who receive an immediate prison sentence is one-fifth of the male percentage (about 1 per cent and 5 per cent respectively). The false impression is created by using statistics on prison receptions which do indicate that a higher proportion of female than male receptions have no previous offences. But these figures tell us nothing about the proportions between imprisonment rates of 'first-offenders'.

26 In Glick and Neto's (1977) survey in the United States the women with the most extensive involvement in the criminal justice system were petty offenders, prostitutes, drug users and shoplifters.

27 This general picture is confirmed in studies of individual states. See, for example, Sarri, 1981; French, 1977.

28 Black incarceration rates generally in the United States are about 8.5 times that of whites. In Glick and Neto's (1977) survey, black women made up 10 per cent of the adult female population in those states studied, but were half of those incarcerated.

29 For recent autobiographical accounts in different countries, see Celima (1985), el Sa'adawi (1985) and Peckham (1985) and the 'Women in Prison' sections in *The Abolitionist* (the magazine of Radical Alternatives to Prison).

30 This has been possible since 1968. Women serving long sentences receive an annual clothing grant. This privilege, not available to male prisoners, is, however, double-edged. The Prison Department noted in its 1969 report that it led not only to improvements in self respect but in attitudes to authority (1970: 21, para 41).

31 Many of the points which follow are also relevant for some men.

32 The average length of stay would have been about 12 months.

33 Glick and Neto (1977) noted that more than half of their sample had dependent children living with them prior to their imprisonment.

34 Some institutions in the United States allow weekend visits; others have nurseries or children's centres where children can visit their mothers. A few prisons also provide periods of leave so that inmates can spend time off the grounds with their families and children. Michigan, for example, allows inmates mothers two days a year to visit children. See Baunach (1985) for a review of the American situation.

35 In 85 per cent of the cases surveyed by Glick and Neto (1977), the woman's family maintained custody of the children during the mother's incarceration; in 10 per cent of the cases, the husband provided the care and, in the remaining cases, the child was placed in foster care.

36 In the early American reformatories for women, children could be kept with their mothers until they were two years old (Lekkerkerker, 1931). Bedford Hills Correctional Facility in New York is now the only prison in the United States with a nursery where infants may live with their mothers until the age of one.

37 This policy was to be challenged in the High Court in 1986 but the Home Secretary avoided it by allowing a 19-year-old prisoner to keep her baby despite a three and a half year sentence for fraud.

38 The original intention in the redeveloped Holloway was for babies to remain until the age of five years (Kelley, 1970).

39 Cf. Sack et al. (1976) found that fathers' incarceration led to problematic behaviour, especially for children in ages ranging from 5 to 14.

40 In *R.* v. *Ouless and Ouless* (Criminal Law Review, 1986: 702) the female appellant, wife of the male appellant, pleaded guilty to five counts of robbery or attempted robbery. She had assisted in the planning of the robberies and had waited for her husband in the car while he committed them, but had not directly participated in the actual robberies. She was given five years' youth custody, he fifteen years' imprisonment. The woman gave birth to a child after sentence and it was argued that the sentence should be reduced so that the child could remain with its mother rather than be separated under normal Home Office practice. It was held that the function of the court was to assess the proper sentence for the offence and the offender. The treatment of the child was a matter for the Home Office. Though the fact that the appellant had a young child could not be ignored, the sentence of five years was right.

41 In one case the hearing took place six months before the mother's release. The mother wished to retain custody and the child had been placed in six foster homes in four years. Despite the poor quality of this substitute care, the judge severed parental rights as the woman could

not be realeased immediately. This decision was upheld on appeal. Similarly an Oregon statute permitted the state to assume custody of the inmate's children and place them for adoption if the parent was to be imprisoned for a minimum of three years. There are, however, also cases in which it was stated that terminating the women's rights as a mother would be vindictive and that incarceration *per se* was not sufficient evidence of unfitness.

42 In fact, it is deliberate policy in England to mix female adult prisoners and female young offenders between the ages of 15 and 20. Male young offenders, on the other hand, are kept separate from male adult prisoners on the grounds of contamination. It is believed that it is more likely that the majority of older women will influence the young for good rather than the other way round. For example, para. 120 of the *Report of the Work of the Prison Department for 1983* (Prison Department, 1984) states that there is a more stable atmosphere if adult women and young female prisoners are held together.

43 This again is not a recent phenomenon. Dr Mary Gordon was critical at the beginning of this century of 'the criminal, feeble-minded, drunken, the early dement, the paranoic, the senile, the crippled and the young offender' all gathered together under one prison system (quoted in Camp, 1974).

44 On the other hand, a greater proportion of female prisoners are held in open conditions: 22 per cent compared with 7 per cent of male prisoners in 1985 (Home Office, 1986c, table 1.2).

45 In September 1986, 38 women were held there; only four are graded category A prisoners (category A is the highest security rating).

46 A survey of 47 men's prisons and 15 women's prisons in the United States cited by Simon (1975) revealed that the average number of vocational programmes in men's prisons was ten; the average in women's was three. Similarly, the average number of industries in men's prisons was 3.2; in women's prisons it was 1.2. Further, women's choices were mainly limited to cosmetology, clerical training, food services and nurses' aid training. Glick and Neto (1977) found that sewing employed the largest number of women in prison and, in Giallombardo's (1966) study of Alderson, half the population were involved in cooking, sewing, weaving, farm and dairy work, gardening, baking and maintenance. Glick and Neto describe the training in women's prisons as 'technologically useless' due to antiquated equipment. A few states offer more. For example, women in the Oregon Women's Correctional Centre can participate in training programmes available at the nearby facility for male prisoners. These include business education courses and computer programming (Sobel, 1980).

47 On the other hand, women in English prisons have not been involved in large-scale disturbances as have male prisoners, though the women in 'H' wing at Durham staged a 35-day hunger strike in protest at their conditions.

48 This is not so in the United States.

49 Hoghughi (1978: 104) described the girls in his institutions as 'by far the more complex and extreme . . . most of the boys, by comparison, pale into insignificance'. More girls than boys were described as 'seriously aggressive' (1978: 114); they were also described as having severe mood swings, high levels of anxiety, low self esteem and as having attempted suicide.

50 The 1985–6 report of the work of the Prison Department (Prison Department, 1986) records that 692 men and 619 women were involved in incidents of self injury without apparent suicidal intent.

51 Glick and Neto (1977) found that in California at least half of the female inmates in jails were receiving tranquilizers.

52 Of course, the pains of imprisonment will differ for different women, just as they do for different men, because of differences in background and differences in pre-institutional experience. Some categories of prisoners, for example, vagrants and alcoholics, experience little sense of deprivation.

53 The Younger Committee (Advisory Council on the Penal System, 1974) considered this and rejected it.

Chapter 6 Women as Criminal Justice Professionals

1 Following the 1833 Factory Act women replaced children in the factories and the long hours and dangerous conditions continued for some years.

2 This is, of course, a complicated issue. Women may not seek promotion for various reasons, personal and cultural. The situation is also changing though men are still over-represented in these posts.

3 'Ann' the student who was top of the class, was described negatively by 65 per cent of the female students; when this role was occupied by 'John', he was described negatively by only 10 per cent of the male students. But see the discussion of more recent research in ch. 3.

4 The Equal Pay Act 1970 and the Sex Discrimination Act 1975 in England and the Civil Rights Act 1964 and the Equal Employment Opportunity Act 1972 in the United States. Further, the Supreme Court in the United States in *Reed* v. *Reed* (1971) decided that distinctions based on sex had to be carefully scrutinized. The state of Idaho had allowed fathers automatic preference over mothers in the administration of the estate of a minor child. In that case, the court held that such a distinction was invalid. In *Frontiero* v. *Richardson* (1973) some members of the court took the view that sex should be treated as an inherently 'suspect' classification: 'What differentiates sex from such nonsuspect states as intelligence or physical disability, and aligns it with the recognised suspect criteria, is that the sex characteristic frequently bears no relation to ability to perform or contribute to society.'

5 The phrase used in England is that sex must be a 'genuine occupational qualification'; in the United States it must be 'a bona fide occupational qualification'.

6   In the United States women can work in men's prisons. This was thought to be not possible in Great Britain. Section 7(2)(d) of the Sex Discrimination Act explicitly refers to prisons containing men as institutions in which being a man might be a genuine occupational qualification. In a case before an industrial tribunal in 1983 involving a female catering officer in a male prison, it was established that on the facts of that particular case a genuine occupational qualification was not made out. More recently, in September 1986, the Home Office announced plans to allow senior officers of both sexes to work in opposite sex prisons. I will discuss this further later in the chapter.

7   These figures are considerably higher than they were ten years ago. Over the period 1975 – 85, the number of female police officers in England and Wales increased by 94 per cent, compared with an 8 per cent increase in the number of male officers. (Chief Inspector of Constabulary, 1976 and 1986).

8   An exception to this may be probation. Certainly, there are caring aspects to it (and this may be the reason why there are more female probation officers than female police officers), but there are also aspects of control (for example, proceedings for breach of the order). There is also some American research (Norland and Mann, 1984) which indicates that male probation officers dislike working with female clients because the women expect the relationship to be caring. Social work, on the other hand, does attract women. Nevertheless, an analysis by Popplestone (1980) showed that the majority of higher-status posts were held by men. Richardson (1981) believes this in part reflects the attitudes of male-dominated selection committees.

9   In England, the physical requirements for entry to the police are different for men and women.

10   It is impossible to date this precisely but Sarah Peters is described by Hinde (1951) as visiting Newgate prison in October 1748.

11   This is not always apparent in texts on the police. Two examples demonstrate this. The title of Cain's (1973) book is *Society and the Policeman's Role* (my emphasis). Policewomen are not discussed, though police wives are. In Black's (1980) text, *The Manners and Customs of the Police*, there are two references to the existence of women in the police. One is in parenthesis and the other is a footnote.

12   The first American policewoman, Alice Stebbins Wells, was appointed in 1910 in Los Angeles. By 1915, 25 cities in the United States employed policewomen.

13   Bland (1985) argues, however, that these patrols were often used by the authorities to control women in order to protect *men* from venereal disease which it was believed was spread by women.

14   In 1922 the number of women employed by the Metropolitan Police was cut from 112 to 24.

15   Lillian Wyles was amongst the original 25 women employed by the Metropolitan Police in 1919 and her autobiography (1952) makes interesting and revealing reading. The women patrolled in pairs and were followed everywhere by two uniformed male police officers who

were under orders never to let them out of their sight. She also refers to the 'downright malice and vindictive spirit' of some of the men.

16 The highest rank a woman could reach, however, regardless of ability was Superintendent.

17 There now exist programmes where female officers take an active and supervisory role — for example 'Cagney and Lacey', 'The Gentle Touch' and 'Juliet Bravo' — but these remain exceptions.

18 Chapter headings in books on the police convey these messages. For example, in McNee's (1983) book on his five years in the Metropolitan Police, the headings include 'Order and Disorder', 'Race and Riots', 'Terrorism and Crime'. There is little on police work as a social service.

19 Research, on the other hand, indicates that women make good leaders. Price (1974) compared the scores of 26 female police executives to 227 male police executives on the Dynamic Personality Inventory. Eleven traits associated with leadership were studied: five were equal for men and women, but six showed significant differences and on five of these six it was women who exhibited the stronger leadership. Women were more flexible, showed greater emotional independence, more self-assertion and greater initiative. The male officers were more submissive, more authoritarian, more prejudiced and less creative. Though the sample of women was small, this research questions the validity of the belief that women lack leadership skills.

20 Sexual harassment occurs in all occupational spheres. See, for example, Evans, 1978.

21 Gudjonsson and Adlam (1985) looked at stress among British police officers but did not deal separately with men and women. Long hours and shift work were the most common stress factors.

22 He argues that the existence of an informal quota, that not more than 10 per cent of police officers should be female, is in breach of the Sex Discrimination Act 1975.

23 These attitudes seem slow to change. Golden (1981) surveyed students in the United States who were planning careers in law enforcement. Their attitudes were generally more favourable than current officers to the use of women as police officers. But when attitudes about specific capabilities were examined — for example, physical ability, strength, emotional stability — the attitudes of the male students were similar to the negative attitudes expressed by current officers.

24 Women do seem to join the police for different reasons than men. Perlstein (1972) found that the desire for security motivated men while women tended to join because of a desire to help people. This is also reflected in prior job experiences. Perlstein found that 37 per cent of his sample of policewomen had been employed in 'helping' professions (nursing, social work and teaching) while the men had been employed as clerks, salesmen, blue collar workers or semi-professionals.

25 Women working in the Prison Service have a different social profile from the men; this is especially apparent when prison officers are contrasted. Less than a third of female officers are married, compared with virtually all male officers (Marsh et al., 1985). Correspondingly,

fewer female officers have dependent children and they are also younger. In addition, female prison officers have stayed in full-time education longer than male officers and have usually worked previously in 'white collar' rather than manual occupations. This means that they are likely to bring different skills and experiences to their jobs and may be the reason why female prison officers express greater job satisfaction than male officers (Marsh et al., 1985). Levels of stress, however, were much the same for both groups and were considerably higher than for men and women in other grades within the Prison Service.

26 There seems to be equality of opportunity in appointment to the governor grade. In 1984 – 85, 14 men and 11 women were appointed to the Governor grade from open competitions.

27 Women now work as guards in men's prisons in every state but the percentage varies from state to state. *Corrections Compendium* in 1982 reported a survey of the percentage of female officers in men's institutions. Oklahoma was highest with 23 per cent. In contrast to this, it is not uncommon to find large numbers of male officers in women's prisons in the United States. Potler (1985), for example, writing of Bayview Correctional Centre (for women) in New York states that most officers were male.

28 This conclusion was reached from references in the evidence to an attack on a female clerical worker in an Alabama prison and to an incident involving a female student who was taken hostage during a visit to one of the maximum-security institutions there.

29 The English case of the female catering officer in a male detention centre provides some anecdotal support for this. She felt that inmates were more careful with their manners, appearance and language when a woman was present. She had also had only two disciplinary matters in the previous 12 months. One involved a minor scuffle between two inmates which was not reported. Both apologized to her subsequently. The other was more serious and involved a knifing. The industrial tribunal did not view the incident as having anything to do with her being female; nor was she inhibited in dealing with it because she was female.

Chapter 7   Women as Victims

1 Other groups experience similar restrictions, for example, the elderly, but that is not my concern here.

2 When respondents were asked about whether they ever worried about the possibility that other household members might be the victim of a crime, those with families and especially those with children emerged as more concerned, and the differences between the sexes were less marked. Men, therefore, may be unwilling to admit to personal fear, but willing to express concern about their families.

3 Women are also worried about, and victims of, other kinds of offences but not much information is available on, for example, burglary which has addressed these issues (cf. Shapland et al., 1985).

4 Graham (1983) makes a general methodological point that women's experiences in a sexist society and within male-dominated language may be literally unspeakable. Kelly (1984) makes much the same point explicitly with reference to sexual abuse: that is, women may not have the words to describe what happened. She also suggests women 'forget' these events as a survival strategy.

5 Polk (1985) contrasted American and English 'attrition rates' and found that the probability of receiving a custodial sentence in each jurisdiction was relatively similar but that attrition took place at different points in the two systems.

6 Plea bargaining is an important factor in the American context and rape charges are commonly bargained down to assault with intent to ravish or to simple assault and battery. Wright (1984) suggests that this is so in England, too.

7 Legal definitions vary from jurisdiction to jurisdiction. In England and Wales the essential elements are penetration of the vagina with a penis against the will of the woman, knowing that the woman does not consent to intercourse, or reckless as to whether or not she consents to it. An honest but unreasonable belief that the woman was consenting can lead to an acquittal (section 1(1)a of the Sexual Offences (Amendment) Act 1976). But whatever the definition, the law is moulded by men, both as legislators and judges.

8 The Lord Chief Justice in *R. v. Roberts and Roberts* (1982, 4 Cr. App. R (s) 8) identified several factors which aggravated the crime of rape and which led to heavy sentences. These included: the presence of a weapon, serious injury, sexual indignities, abuse of a position of trust, the involvement of more than one offender, the extreme youth or age of the victim and intrusion of the victim's home. More recent guidelines were set out by him in Billam 1986 1ALL.E.R. 985. He said that five years in prison should be the minimum sentence for an adult pleading not guilty and with no mitigating circumstances and that eight years should be the minimum for two or more rapists acting together, for men who rape victims in their own homes, for those who abused positions of responsibility and for rape involving abduction. Those who conduct 'campaigns of rape' should get not less than 15 years and perverted or psychopathic offenders should get life sentences. He went on to say that where there are 'aggravating features' which included excessive violence, a planned attack, the use of weapons, further degrading sexual acts, attacks on the very young and very old, and repeated rapes, the sentences should be substantially higher. However, such statements *indirectly* have the effect of minimizing rapes which occur in other circumstances.

9 The reason for this difference seems to have been that the female students felt that it was the *woman's* duty to stop foreplay at this point.

10   Victimology has generally focused on the role of victims in explaining criminal behaviour and has supposedly identified certain crime-prone victims. Thus there are victims of assault who have been previously assaulted. But the issue is different here. In rape, discussions refer not to prior sexual *victimization* but to prior sexual *activity*.

11   There is an interesting parallel in Hartman's (1977: 8) analysis of Victorian women accused of murder: 'in ten of the twelve cases false beliefs about a sexual issue prompted either the verdict of the jury, that of the public or both'.

12   The moral character of the victim is also considered relevant in sentencing. For example, Lord Justice Watkins reduced the prison sentences of six men convicted of indecency against a female soldier because the victim was 'dissolute and sexually depraved' (*Guardian*, 28 February 1986).

13   Thomas (1979) referred to such victims as guilty of contributory negligence. In the 2nd edition of his text, reference to this was omitted but judges continue to quote him.

14   Simpson (1985) argues that Hale was generally quite sympathetic to rape victims (cf. Geis, 1978) and that the statement reflects a prevalent belief at that time that rape charges were motivated by attempts at monetary gain. Simpson shows, however, that what was later categorized as 'extortion' was no more than an honest attempt by genuine victims to use the criminal courts as civil courts. The small sums usually paid to victims merely compensated them for the cost of the prosecution. A combination of public apology and compensation was a recognized policy of the courts.

15   Blair (1985: 10), a detective inspector, stresses that he has not met a police officer who agrees with this view. However, the film of the Thames Valley police questionning a rape victim broadcast on 18 January 1982 did reveal questionable tactics. Home Office guidelines were sent in March 1983 to chief officers of police emphasizing the need to treat rape complainants with tact and understanding. In a number of police areas there are now special training courses for police officers, often female, in investigating rape, and some police stations have separate facilities for rape victims. This may lead to increases in reported rapes. For example, the number increased in London from 68 in the first three months of 1984 to 107 in the same period in 1985 (*Sunday Times*, 18 August 1985). In Sao Paulo, Brazil, a police department was set up for women and run by women. On average, 200 women go there every day. This resulted in a considerable increase in allegations of rape, wife and child abuse.

16   Shapland et al.'s (1985) findings contradict these. Sexual assault victims in their sample were more satisfied with the police than physical assault or robbery victims. The sample, however, contains only victims whose assaults were recorded as crimes by the police.

17   Corroboration means evidence from some other independent source implicating the accused in a material particular and tending to support the accuracy of evidence already given. Corroborative evidence is

required in certain situations, for example, perjury and the unsworn evidence of a child of tender years. Though not required by law, it is expected in practice in other situations, for example, the sworn evidence of a child of tender years, and in rape cases. Juries are warned that it is unsafe to convict on the evidence of the victim unless he or she is corroborated.

18　Schwendinger and Schwendinger (1982) argue that it is still the case.

19　'Swived' means to lie with, copulate, be dishonoured.

20　On a 5-point scale from 1 (not likely at all) to 5 (very likely) 35 per cent rated themselves at 2, and 20 per cent at 3.

21　Sexual harassment at work reflects similar widely held assumptions (Tysoe, 1982).

22　Wives have been blamed in other situations too. Seddon (1981), in her discussion of the so-called Yorkshire Ripper murders, refers to this as 'the Sonia syndrome'. Sonia, Peter Sutcliffe's wife, was described in newspaper accounts as having dominated him and as not providing a satisfying sex life. The implication was that if she had acted otherwise, the murders would not have occurred.

23　Such beliefs lead some feminists to discuss men in stereotypical terms (Brownmiller, 1975; Clark and Lewis, 1977) and to call for harsh sentences for rapists. For a more measured discussion of sentencing, see Pitch (1985).

24　Bates (reported in *New Society*, 27 August 1981: 355) argues that men are less likely than women to report incidents to the police, but few women report their assaults to the police. In the Dobash's study, only 2 per cent were reported.

25　Such beliefs are widespread. Darryl and Sandra Benn conducted an experiment to see whether strangers would come to the help of a woman who was being physically and verbally abused by a man on the street (cited in Walker, 1979). Passers-by at different times saw two men in an argument, two women in an argument and a man and a woman in an argument. The severity of the abuse was the same in all three instances. The strangers intervened with the two women and the two men far more often than with the man and the woman. When asked about this, the strangers said that they did not feel they had the right to interfere in a marital dispute.

26　There are civil remedies short of divorce or seperation available to wives. In England, for example, the Domestic Violence and Matrimonial Proceedings Act 1976 empowers the County Court to grant various kinds of injunctions. Protections are also contained in the Matrimonial Homes Act 1983 and the Domestic Proceedings and Magistrates Courts Act 1978. Women, however, complain of difficulties in the implementation and enforcement of these orders. See Maidment (1985) for an elaboration of this. She argues that the law alone cannot change deep-seated attitudes. McCann's (1985) analysis of the judicial interpretation of those Acts supports this view.

27　It was already an offence in many states in the United States by this time and it had been a criminal offence in Scotland since 1567.

28   In the debates preceding the Incest Act in 1908, fears were expressed about blackmail and false accusations. Corroboration, therefore, was necessary to prevent this.

29   In the English case of *R. v. Moores* (1980 2 Cr. App. R (s) 317) the defendant had intercourse with his 15-year-old daughter when his marriage was breaking down. The original four-year sentence was reduced on appeal to immediate release on the grounds of the girl's promiscuity. See also *R. v. Wilbourne* (1982 4 Cr. App. R (s) 163). In contrast, a sentence of two years' imprisonment was upheld where the defendant had intercourse with his married daughter whom he had not seen for 20 years: *R. v. Bedford* (1979 1 Cr. App. R (s) 231).

30   In England, the proportion of men sentenced to imprisonment for incest is considerably lower than that for rape. A Home Office study of sex offenders convicted between 1973 and 1976 found that 69 per cent of incest offenders were sentenced to imprisonment compared with 91 per cent of rapists (Walmsley and White, 1979).

Bibliography

Acton, N. (1870) *Prostitution considered in its moral, social and sanitary aspects in London and other large cities*. London: John Churchill and sons.

Adam, H. (1914) *Women and Crime*. London: Werner Lourie.

Adler, C. and Polk, K. (1982) Diversion and hidden sexism, *ANZJ of Criminology*, 15, 100.

Adler, C. (1984) Gender bias in juvenile diversion, *Crime and Delinquency*, 30, 400.

Adler, F. (1975) *Sisters in Crime*. New York: McGraw-Hill.

Adler, F. (1977) The interaction between women's emancipation and female criminality: a cross cultural perspective, *International Journal of Criminology and Penology*, 5, 101.

Adler, F. (1983) *Nations not Obsessed with Crime*. Littleton: Rothman.

Adler, Z. (1982) The reality of rape trials, *New Society*, 4 February, 190.

Adler, Z. (1985) The relevance of sexual history evidence in rape: problems of subjective interpretation, *Criminal Law Review*, 769.

Advisory Council on the Penal System (1968a) Interim report of the Detention Centre sub-committee: *Detention of girls in a detention centre*. London: HMSO.

Advisory Council on the Penal System (1968b) Report: *The regime of long term prisoners in conditions of maximum security*: Chairman, Sir Leon Radzinowicz. London: HMSO.

Advisory Council on the Penal System (1974) Report: *Young adult offenders*: Chairman, Sir Kenneth Younger. London: HMSO.

Ageton, S. (1983a) The dynamics of female delinquency, 1976 – 1980, *Criminology*, 21, 555.

Ageton, S. (1983b) *Sexual assault among adolescents*. Lexington: D. C. Heath and Co.

Ageton, S. and Elliot, D. (1974) The effects of legal processing on delinquent orientations, *Social Problems*, 22, 87.

Alabama Law Review (1975) Alabama Law Review summer project 1975: a study of differential treatment accorded female defendants in Alabama criminal courts. *Alabama Law Review*, 27, 676.

Albin, R. (1977) Psychological studies of rape, *Signs*, 3, 2, 423.

218 *Bibliography*

Al-Issa, I. (1980) *The Psychopathology of Women*. Englewood Cliffs: Prentice Hall.
Allen, D. (1980) Young male prostitutes: a psychosexual study, *Archives of Sexual Behaviour*, 9, 399.
Almquist, E. (1977) Women in the labour force, *Signs*, 2, 843.
Alper, T. (1974) Achievement motivation in college women, *American Psychology*, 29, 194.
American Bar Association (1983) Women in the law, *American Bar Association Journal*, 69, 1383.
Amir, M. (1971) *Patterns in Forcible Rape*. Chicago: The University of Chicago Press.
Archer, J. (1976) Biological explanations of psychological sex differences. In Lloyd, B. and Archer, J. (eds) *Exploring Sex Differences*. London: Academic Press.
Arditi, R. et al. (1973) The sexual segregation of American prisons, *Teydale Law Journal*, 82, 6, 1229.
Argenent, H. (1981) Shoplifting: a review, *Criminology and Penology Abstracts*, 21, 3, i.
Armstrong, L. (1978) *Kiss Daddy Goodnight: a speak out on incest*. New York: Hawthorne Books, Inc.
Ashley, J. (1973) House of Commons Debates, Hansard, vol. 860, col-218.
Astor, S. (1971) Shoplifting survey, *Security World*, 8, 3, 34.
Austin, R. (1981) Liberation and female criminality in England and Wales, *British Journal of Criminology*, 21, 371.
Avery, J. (1981) *Police – force or service?* Sydney: Butterworths.
Baird Committee (1920) Report: *The employment of women on police duties*. London: HMSO.
Baldwin, J. and McConville, M. (1977) *Negotiated justice: pressures to plead guilty*. London: Martin Robertson.
Baldwin, J. and McConville, M. (1979) *Jury Trials*. Oxford: Clarendon Press.
Baldwin, J. and Bottoms, A. E. (1976) *The Urban Criminal: a study in Sheffield*. London: Tavistock.
Bambridge, F. (1979) Intermediate treatment: children at risk of being in trouble. BA dissertation University of Warwick. Unpublished.
Bandura, A., Grusec, J. and Menlove, F. (1966) Observational learning as a function of symbolization and incentive set, *Child Development*, 37, 3, 499.
Bard, M. (1970) *Training Police as Specialists in Family Crisis Intervention*. Washington: US Department of Justice, Government Printing Office.
Bartell Associates (1978) *The Study of Police Women Competency in the Performance of Sector Police Work in the City of Philadelphia*. Philadelphia: State College.
Barrett, M. and McIntosh, M. (1982) *The Anti-Social Family*. London: Verso.
Bart, P. (1981) A study of women who both were raped and avoided rape, *Journal of Social Issues*, 37, 4, 123.
Bartlett, H. and Rosenblum, A. (1977) *Policewomen Effectiveness*. Denver: Civil Service Commission and Denver Police Department.

Batten, D. (1983) Incest — a review of the literature, *Medicine, Science and Law*, 23, 4, 245.

Baunach, P. (1985) *Mothers in Prison*. New Brunswick: Transaction Books.

Baunach, P. and Rafter, N. (1982) Sex-role operations: strategies for women working in the criminal justice system. In Rafter, N. and Stanko, E. (eds) *Judge, Lawyer, Victim, Thief*. Boston: Northeastern University Press.

Beattie, J. (1975) The criminality of women in 18th century England, *Journal of Social History*, 8, 80.

Becker, H. (1963) *Outsiders: studies in the sociology of deviance*. New York: Free Press.

Bedford, A. (1974) Women and parole, *British Journal of Criminology*, 14, 106.

Bell, D. (1982) Policewomen: myths and reality, *Journal of Police Science and Administration*, 10, 1, 112.

Bender, L. and Blau, A. (1937) The reaction of children to sexual relations with adults, *American Journal of Orthopsychiatry*, 7, 500.

Beneke, T. (1982) *Men on Rape*. New York: St Martin's Press.

Benn, M. (1983) Women in prison . . . breaking the silence, *Spare Rib*, November, 51.

Bernstein, I. et al. (1977) Charge Reduction: an intermediary stage in the process of labelling criminal defendants, *Social Forces*, 56, 1, 362.

Binney, V. et al. (1981) *Leaving Violent Men: a study of refuges and housing for battered women*. London: Women's Aid Federation.

Bishop, D. et al. The effects of gender on charge reduction. Paper presented at the American Society of Criminology, November 1983.

Black, D. (1980) *The Manners and Customs of the Police*. New York: Academic Press.

Black, D. and Reiss, A. (1970) Police control of juveniles, *American Sociological Review*, 35, 1, 63.

Blackstone, W. (1966) *Commentaries on the laws of England*. (first published 1765) London: Dawsons.

Blagg, H. and Wilson, C. (1912) *Women and Prisons*. London: Fabian Society.

Blair, I. (1985) *Investigating Rape*. London: Croom Helm.

Bland, L. (1985) In the name of protection: the policing of women in the First World War. In Brophy, J. and Smart, C. (eds) *Women in Law*. London: Routledge and Kegan Paul.

Bloch, H. and Geis, G. (1970) *Man, Crime and Society*. (2nd ed.) New York: Random House.

Bloch, P. and Anderson, D. (1974) *Policewomen on Patrol*. Washington: Police Foundation.

Block, A. (1979) Aw! Your mother's in the Mafia: women criminals in progressive New York. In Adler, F. and Simon, R. (eds) *The Criminology of Deviant Women*. Boston: Houghton Mifton Co.

Blos, P. (1957) Pre-oedipal factors in the aetiology of female delinquency, *Psychoanalytic Studies of the Child*, 12, 229.

Blos, P. (1969) Three typical constellations in female delinquency. In Pollak, O. and Friedman, A. (eds) *Family Dynamics and Female Sexual*

Delinquency. Palo Alto: Science and Behaviour Books.

Bonger, W. (1916) *Criminality and Economic Conditions*. London: Heinemann.

Borkowski, M. Murch, M. and Walker, V. (1983) *Marital Violence: the community response*. London: Tavistock.

Bottomley, A. K. (1970) *Prison before trial*. London: Bell.

Bottomley, A. (1973) *Decisions in the Penal Process*. London: Macmillan.

Bottoms, A. E. and Pratt, J. (1985) Intermediate treatment for girls in England and Wales: a preliminary paper, European Working Papers Series, European University Institute, University of Florence. Revised version forthcoming in Cain, M. (ed.) *Growing Up Good: policing the behaviour of girls in Europe*. London: Sage (in press).

Bottoms, A. E. (1986) *Intermediate treatment evaluation project*. (Research Bulletin no. 2.) Cambridge: Institute of Crominology.

Bowersox, M. (1981) Women in corrections: competence, competition and the social responsibility norm, *Criminal Justice and Behaviour*, 8, 491.

Bowker, L. (1978) A scream in the night: women as victims. In Bowker, L. (ed.) *Women, Crime and the Criminal Justice System*. Lexington: D. C. Heath and Co.

Bowker, L. (1982) Police services to battered women: bad or not so bad? *Criminal Justice and Behaviour*, 9, 476.

Bowser Petersen, C. (1982) Doing time with the boys. In Raffel Price, B. and Sokoloff, N. (eds) *The Criminal Justice System and Women*. New York: Clark Boardman Co. Ltd.

Box, S. (1971) *Deviance, Reality and Society*. London: Holt, Rinehart and Winston.

Box, S. (1981) *Deviance, Reality and Society*. London: Holt, Rinehart and Winston.

Box, S. (1983) *Power, Crime and Mystification*. London: Tavistock Publications.

Box, S. and Hale, C. (1983) Liberation and female criminality in England and Wales, *British Journal of Criminology*, 23, 35.

Brady, K. (1979) *Father's day: a true story of incest*. New York: Dell Publishing Co. Inc.

Brailey, M. (1985) Making the break. In Johnson N. (ed.) *Marital Violence*. London: Routledge and Kegan Paul.

Bridgeman Committee (1924) Report: *The employment of policewomen*. London: HMSO.

Bromberg, W. (1965) *Crime and the Mind*. New York: The Macmillan Company.

Brophy, J. and Smart, C. (1981) From disregard to disrepute: the position of women in family law, *Feminist Review*, 9.

Broverman, I. et al. (1970) Sex role stereotypes and clinical judgments of mental health, *Journal of Consulting and Clinical Psychology*, 34, 1, 1.

Broverman, I. et al. (1972) Sex role stereotypes: a current appraisal, *Journal of Social Issues*, 28, 2, 59.

Brown, G. and Harris, T. (1978) *Social Origins of Depression: A study of psychiatric disorder in women*. London: Tavistock.

Brown, S. (1984) Police responses to wife beating: neglect of a crime of violence, *Journal of Criminal Justice*, 12, 277.

Brownmiller, S. (1975) *Against our Will: men, women and rape.* Harmondsworth: Penguin Books Ltd.

Bryan, J. (1973) Apprenticeships in prostitution and occupational ideologies and individual attitudes of call girls. In Rubington, E. and Weinberg, M. (eds) *Deviance: the interactionist perspective.* London: Macmillan.

Bryan, B. Dadzie, S. and Scafe, S. (1985) *The Heart of the Race.* London: Virago.

Buckle, A. and Farrington, D. (1984) An observational study of shoplifting, *British Journal of Criminology*, 24, 63.

Bureau of Justice Statistics Bulletin (1985) *The 1983 jail census.* Washington: US Department of Justice, Bureau of Statistics.

Burt, M. (1980) Cultural myths and supports for rape, *Journal of Personality and Social Psychology*, 38, 217.

Burton, L. (1968) *Vulnerable Children.* New York: Schocken Books.

Busfield, J. (1983) Gender, mental illness and psychiatry. In Evans, M. and Ungerson, C. (eds) *Sexual Divisions: patterns and processes.* London: Tavistock.

Butler Committee (1975) Report: *Mentally abnormal offenders.* London: HMSO.

Cain, M. (1973) *Society and the Policeman's Role.* London: Routledge and Kegan Paul.

Cain, M. and Hunt, A. (eds) (1979) *Marx and Engels on Law.* London: Academic Press.

Cameron, M. (1964) *The Booster and the Snitch.* London: Collier Macmillan.

Camp, J. (1974) *Holloway Prison: the place and the people.* Newton Abbot: David and Charles.

Campbell, A. (1981) *Girl Delinquents.* Oxford: Basil Blackwell.

Campbell, A. (1984) *The Girls in the Gang: a report from New York City.* Oxford: Basil Blackwell.

Campbell, A. (1986) Self-report of fighting by females, *British Journal of Criminology*, 26, 28.

Caplan, P. (1975) Sex differences in antisocial behaviour: does research methodology produce or abolish them?, *Human Development*, 18, 444.

Carey, K. (1979) Police policy and the prosecution of women. Unpublished paper.

Carlen, P. (1983) *Women's Imprisonment: a study in social control.* London: Routledge and Kegan Paul.

Carlen, P. (ed.) (1985) *Criminal Women.* Cambridge: Polity Press.

Carlson, E. and Carlson, R. (1960) Male and female subjects in personality research, *Journal of Abnormal and Social Psychology*, 41, 482.

Carpenter, M. (1857) Reformatories for convicted girls, *Transactions of the National Association for the Promotion of Social Science*, 338.

Carpenter, M. (1858) On the disposal of girls from reformatory schools, *Transactions of the National Association for the Promotion of Social Science*, 413.

Carpenter, M. (1864) *Our Convicts*, vol. I and II. London: Longman, Green,

Longman, Roberts and Green.

Casburn, M. (1979) *Girls will be Girls*. London: Explorations in Feminism, WRRC.

Catton, K. (1975) Evidence regarding the prior sexual history of an alleged rape victim: its effect on the perceived guilt of the accused, *University of Toronto Faculty of Law Review*, 33, 165.

Cawson, P. (1981) *Young Offenders in Care*. London: DHSS Social Research Branch.

Celima, H. (1985) *Women in Soviet Prisons*. New York: Paragon.

Cernkovich, S. and Giordano, P. (1979) Delinquency, opportunity and gender, *Journal of Criminal Law, Criminology and Police Science*, 70, 145.

Cernkovich, S and Giordano, P. (1979) A comparative analysis of male and female delinquency, *Sociological Quarterly*, 20, 131.

Chambers, G. and Miller, A. (1983) *Investigating Sexual Assault*. Edinburgh: HMSO.

Chandler, S. and Torney, M. (1981) The decisions and the processing of rape victims through the criminal justice system, *California Sociologist*, 4, 155.

Charles, M. (1982) Women in policing: the physical aspect, *Journal of Police Science and Administration*, 10, 194.

Chatterton, M. (1983) Police work and assault charges. In Punch, M. (ed.) *Control in the Police Organisation*, Cambridge: MIT Press.

Chesler, P. (1972) *Women and Madness*. New York: Avon Books.

Chesney-Lind, M. (1973) The judicial enforcement of the female sex role: the family court and the delinquent, *Issues in Criminology*, 8, 51.

Chief Inspector of Constabulary (1976) *Report*. London: HMSO.

Chief Inspector of Constabulary (1986) *Report*. London: HMSO.

Chief Inspector of Prisons (1982) Report: *HM Prison Durham*. London: Home Office.

Choisy, M. (1962) *Psychoanalysis of the Prostitute*. London: Peter Owen.

Christiansen, K. and Jensen, S. (1972) Crime in Denmark — a statistical history, *Journal of Criminal Law, Criminology and Police Science*, 63, 82.

Clark, L. and Lewis, D. (1977) *Rape: the price of coercive sexuality*. Toronto: The Women's Press.

Clegg, S. (1985) Feminist methodology — fact or fiction?, *Quality and Quantity*, 19, 83.

Clinard, M. (1978) *Cities with Little Crime: the case of Switzerland*. Cambridge: Cambridge University Press.

Cloward, R. and Ohlin, L. (1961) *Delinquency and Opportunity*. London: Routledge and Kegan Paul.

Cohen, A. and Short, J. (1958) Research in delinquent subcultures, *Journal of Social Issues*, 14, 3, 20.

Cohen, A. (1955) *Delinquent Boys*. Glencoe: The Free Press.

Commission on sexual offences against children in Canada (1984): *Report: Summary*. Ottawa: Ministry of Supply and Services.

Commissioner of Police of the Metropolis (1978) *Report for the year 1977*. London: HMSO.

Commissioners of Prisons (1936) *Report for the Year 1934*. London: HMSO.
Commissioners of Prisons (1947) *Report for the Year 1945*. London: HMSO.
Committee of Inquiry on the Police (1978) *Report*. London: HMSO.
Constantine, L. and Martinson, F. (1981) (eds) *Children and Sex*. Boston: Little, Brown and Co.
Cooke, W. (1945) The differential psychology of the American woman, *American Journal of Obstetrics and Gynaecology*, 49, 457.
Cooper, H. (1979) Woman as terrorist. In Adler, F. and Simon, R. (eds) *The Criminology of Deviant Women*. Boston: Houghton Mifflin Co.
Corrigan, P. (1979) *Schooling the Smash Street Kids*. London: Macmillan.
Cowie, C. and Lees, S. (1981) Slags and drags, *Feminist Review*, 9, 17.
Cowie, J., Cowie, V. and Slater, E. (1968) *Delinquency in Girls*. London: Heinemann.
Crawford, J. (1980) Two losers don't make a winner: the case against the co-correctional institution. In Smykla, J. (ed.) *Co-ed Prison*. New York: Human Sciences Press.
Crepault, C. and Couture, M. (1980) Men's erotic fantasies, *Archive of Sexual Behaviour*, 9, 5, 565.
Criminal Law Revision Committee (1984) *15th Report: Sex Offences*. London HMSO.
Critchley, T. (1967) *A History of Police in England and Wales 1900 – 1966*. London: Constable.
Crouch, B. and Alpert, G. (1982) Sex and occupational socialisation among prison guards, *Criminal Justice and Behaviour*, 1982, 159.
Crowther Committee (1959) *Fifteen to eighteen*. London: HMSO.
Curran, D. (1984) The myth of the 'new' female delinquent, *Crime and Delinquency*, 30, 3, 386.
Curtis, L. (1974) Victim precipitation and violent crime, *Social Problems*, 21, 594.
Dalton, K. (1960a) Effect of menstruation on schoolgirls' weekly work, *British Medical Journal*, 1, 326.
Dalton, K. (1960b) Schoolgirls' behaviour and menstruation, *British Medical Journal*, 2, 1647.
Dalton, K. (1961) Menstruation and crime, *British Medical Journal*, 2, 1752.
Dalton, K. (1977) *The Premenstrual Syndrome and Progesterone Therapy*. London: Heinemann.
Daniel, S. and McGuire, P. (eds) (1972) *The Painthouse: words from an East End gang*. Harmondsworth: Penguin.
Datesman, S. Scarpitti, F. and Stephenson, R. (1975) Female Delinquency: an application of self and opportunity theories, *Journal of Research in Crime and Delinquency*, 12, 107.
Datesman, S. and Scarpitti, F. (1980) Unequal protection for males and females in the juvenile court. In Datesman, S. and Scarpitti, F. (eds) *Women, Crime and Justice*. Oxford: University Press.
Davis, K. (1971) Prostitution. In Merton, R. and Nisbet, R. (eds) *Contemporary Social Problems*. (3rd edn.) New York: Harcourt, Brace Jovanovich.

Deaux, K. (1976) *The Behaviour of Women and Men*. Belmont: Wadsworth Publishing Co.

De Crow, K. (1975) *Sexist Justice*. New York: Vintage Books.

De Fleur, L. (1975) Biasing influence on drug arrest records: implications for deviance research. *American Sociological Review*, 40, 88.

Dell, S. (1971) *Silent in Court*. Occasional Papers on Social Administration, no. 42. London: Bell.

Demos, J. (1982) *Entertaining Satan*. Oxford: Oxford University Press.

Department of Health and Social Security (1984) *In-patient statistics from the mental health inquiry for England 1979*. London: HMSO.

Department of Health and Social Security (1983) *Children in Care of Local Authorities, Year ending 31 March 1983 England*, London: DHSS.

Deutsch, H. (1944) *The Psychology of Women*. vol. 1. New York: Grune and Stratton.

Dobash, R. and Dobash, R. (1979) *Violence against Wives: a case against patriarchy*. New York: The Free Press.

Dobash, R. and Dobash R. (1984) The nature and antecedents of violent events, *British Journal of Criminology*, 24, 269.

Dobash, R., Dobash, R. and Gutteridge, S. (1986) *The Imprisonment of Women*. Oxford: Basil Blackwell.

Dominelli, L. (1984) Differential justice: domestic labour, community service and female offenders, *Probation Journal*, 31, 3, 100.

Donzelot, J. (1979) *The Policing of Families*. London: Hutchinson.

D'Orban, P. (1971) Social and psychiatric aspects of female crime, *Medicine, Science, and the Law*, 11, 104.

Downes, D. (1966) *The Delinquent Solution: a study of subcultural theory*. London: Routledge and Kegan Paul.

Downes, D. (1978) Promise and performance in British criminology, *British Journal of Sociology*, 29, 4, 483.

Dugdale, R. (1910) *The Jukes: a study in crime, pauperism, disease and heredity*. (4th ed) New York: G. P. Putnam's Sons.

Dumaresq, D. (1981) Rape-Sexuality in the Law, *M/F*, no. 5 – 6, 41.

Eaton, M. (1983) Mitigating circumstances: familiar rhetoric, *International Journal of Sociology of Law*, 11, 385.

Eaton, M. (1985) Documenting the defendant: placing women in social inquiry report. In Brophy, J. and Smart, C (eds) *Women in Law*. London: Routledge and Kegan Paul.

Eaton, M (1986) *Justice for Women?*. Milton Keynes: Open University Press.

Edwards, S. (1981) *Female Sexuality and the Law*. Oxford: Martin Robertson.

Edwards, S. (1982) Premenstrual tension, *Justice of the Peace*, 7, August, 476.

Edwards, S. (1984) *Women on Trial*. Manchester: Manchester University Press.

Ehrhardt, A. (1985) The psychobiology of gender. In Rossi, A. (ed.) *Gender and the Life Course*. New York: Aldine.

Eichler, M. (1980) *The Double Standard*. New York: St Martin's Press.

Ekblom, P. and Heal, K (1982) *The Police Response to Calls from the Public*. (Research and Planning Unit Paper 9) London: Home Office.

Elliot, D. (1984) Rape complainants' sexual experience with third parties, *Criminal Law Review*, 4.

Elliott, D. and Ageton, S. (1980) Reconciling race and class differences in self-reported and official estimates of delinquency, *Journal of Research in Crime and Delinquency*, 16, 3.

Ellis, A. (1945) The sexual psychology of human hermaphrodites, *Psychosomatic Medicine*, 7, 108.

Ellis, D. and Austin, P. (1971) Menstruation and criminal behaviour in a correctional centre for women, *Journal of Criminal Law Criminology and Police Science*, 62, 3, 388.

Ellis, H. (1894) *Man and Woman*. London: Walter Scott.

Epps, P. (1962) Women shoplifters in Holloway Prison. In Gibbens, T. and Prince, J. (eds) *Shoplifting*. London: ISTD.

Erickson, M. and Smith, W. (1974) On the relationship between self-reported and actual deviance, *Humboldt Journal of Social Relations*, 2, 106.

Erikson, K. (1966) *The Wayward Puritans*. Englewood Cliffs: John Wiley.

Evans, L. (1978) Sexual harassment: women's hidden occupational hazard. In Chapman, J. and Gates, M. (eds) *The Victimization of Women*. Beverley Hills, California: Sage.

Evason, E. (1982) *Hidden Violence: a study of battered women in Northern Ireland*. Belfast: Farset Co-operative Press.

Expenditure Committee (1978 – 9) *Women and the Penal System*. (Education, arts and Home Office sub-committee: oral audience and written submissions. Vols 61 – i to 61 – xiv) London: House of Commons.

Eysenck, S. and Eysenck, H. (1973) The personality of female prisoners, *British Journal of Psychiatry*, 122, 693.

Faragher, T. (1985) The police response to violence against women in the home. In Pahl, J. (ed.) *Private Violence and Public Policy*. London: Routledge and Kegan Paul.

Farrington, D. (1981) The prevalence of convictions, *British Journal of Criminology*, 21, 173.

Farrington, D. and Kidd, R. (1977) Is financial dishonesty a rational decision? *British Journal of Social and Clinical Psychology*, 16, 139.

Farrington, D. and Knight, B. (1979) Two non-reactive field experiments on stealing from a 'lost' letter, *British Journal of Social and Clinical Psychology*, 18, 277.

Farrington, D. and Knight, B. (1980) Stealing from a 'lost' letter: effects of victim characteristics, *Criminal Justice and Behaviour*, 7, 423.

Farrington, D., Knapp, W., Erickson, B. and Knight, B. (1980) Words and deeds in the study of stealing, *Journal of Adolescence*, 3, 35.

Farrington, D. and Morris, A. (1983) Sex, sentencing and reconvictions, *British Journal of Criminology*, 23, 3, 229.

Faulkner, D. (1971) The development of Holloway prison, *Howard Journal*, 13, 2, 122.

Faust, B. (1982) *Women, Sex and Pornography*. Aylesbury: Pelican Books.

Feldman, M. P. (1977) *Criminal Behaviour: a psychological analysis*. London:

John Wiley and Sons.

Feldman-Summers, S. and Lindner, K. (1976) Perceptions of victims and defendants in criminal assault cases, *Criminal Justice and Behaviour*, 3, 2, 135.

Feldman-Summers, S. and Palmer, G. (1980) Rape as viewed by judges, prosecutors and police officers, *Criminal Justice and Behaviour*, 7, 19.

Field, H. (1978) Attitudes towards rape: a comparative analysis of police, rapists, crisis counsellors and citizens, *Journal of Personality and Social Psychology*, 36, 158.

Figueira-McDonough, J. (1980) A reformulation of the 'equal opportunity' explanation of female delinquency, *Crime and Delinquency*, 333.

Finkelhor, D. (1979) *Sexually Victimized Children*. New York: The Free Press.

Finkelhor, D. and Yllo, K. (1982) Forced sex in marriage: a preliminary report, *Crime and Delinquency*, 28, 459.

Firth, A. (1975) Interrogation, *Police Review*, LXXXIII, 1507.

Fisher, C. and Mawby, R. (1982) Juvenile delinquency and police discretion in an inner city area, *British Journal of Criminology*, 22, 63.

Fitzgerald, M. and Sim, J. (1979) *British Prisons*. Oxford: Basil Blackwell.

Fitzgerald, M. and Sim, J. (1982) *British Prisons*. (2nd edn) Oxford: Basil Blackwell.

Flexner, A. (1914) *Prostitution in Europe*. New York: The Centenary Co.

Flynn, E. (1982) Women as criminal justice professionals: a challenge to change traditions. In Rafter, N. and Stanko, E. (eds) *Judge, Lawyer, Victim, Thief*. Boston: Northeastern University Press.

Fortune, E., Vega, M. and Silverman, I. (1980) A study of female robbers in a southern correctional institution, *Journal of Criminal Justice*, 8, 317.

Foucault, M. (1977) *Discipline and Punish: the birth of the prison*. London: Allen Lane.

Fox, Sir L. (1952) *The English Prison and Borstal Systems*. London: Routledge and Kegan Paul.

Fox, J. and Hartnagel, T. (1979) Changing social roles and female crime in Canada, *Review of Canadian Sociology and Anthropology*, 16, 96.

Frank, R. (1931) The hormonal causes of premenstrual tension, *Archives of Neurology and Psychiatry*, 26, 1053.

Franklin, A. (1979) Criminality in the work place: a comparison of male and female offenders. In Adler, F. and Simon, R. (eds) *The Criminology of Deviant Women*. Boston: Houghton Mifflin Co.

Frazier, C. et al. (1983) The role of probation officers in determining gender differences in sentencing severity, *The Sociological Quarterly*, 24, 305.

Freeman, D. (1984) *Margaret Mead and Samoa*. Harmondsworth: Penguin.

French, L. (1977) An assessment of the black prisoner in the south, *Signs*, 3, 483.

Freud, S. (1924) The dissolution of the Oedipus complex. In *Standard Edition of the Complete Psychological Works of Sigmund Freud*, vol. 19. London: Hogarth Press.

Freud, S. (1925) Some psychical consequences of the anatomical distinction between the sexes. In *The Standard Edition of the Complete Psychological*

Works of Sigmund Freud, vol. 19. London: Hogarth Press.

Freud, S. (1933) The psychology of women (lecture 33). In *New Introductory Lectures on Psychoanalysis*. New York: W. W. Norton & Co.

Friedland, M. (1965) *Detention before Trial*. Toronto: University of Toronto.

Galvin, J. and Polk, K. (1983) Attrition in case processing: is rape unique?, *Journal of Research in Crime and Delinquency*, 20, 126.

Gebhard, P. (1969) Misconceptions about female prostitutes, *Medical Aspects of Human Sexuality*, 24.

Gebhard, P., Gagnon, J., Pomeron, W. and Christenson, C. (1965) *Sex Offenders: an analysis of types*. New York: Harper and Row.

Geis, G. (1978) Lord Hale, witches and rape, *British Journal of Law and Society*, 5, 26.

Gelles, R. (1977) Power, sex and violence: the case of marital rape, *The Family Coordinator*, 26, 339.

Gelles, R. (1979) *Family Violence*. London: Sage.

Gelles, R. and Cornell, C. (1985) *Intimate Violence in Families*. Beverley Hills: Sage Publications.

Gelsthorpe, L. (1981) *Girls in the Juvenile Court: defining the terrain of penal policy*. London: Justice for Children.

Gelsthorpe, L. (1986) Towards a sceptical look at sexism, *International Journal of Sociology of Law*, 14, 125.

Genders, E. and Player, E. (1986) Women's imprisonment, *British Journal of Criminology*, 26, 357.

Giallombardo, R. (1966) *Society of Women*, New York: Wiley.

Gibbens, T. (1957) Juvenile prostitution, *British Journal of Delinquency*, 8.

Gibbens, T. (1971) Female offenders. *British Journal of Hospital Medicine*, (Sept.), 279.

Gibbens, T. and Prince, J. (1962) *Shoplifting*. London: ISTD.

Gibbens, T. and Prince, J. (1963) *Child Victims of Sex Offences*. London: ISTD.

Gibbens, T., Soothill, K. and Pope, P. (1977) *Medical Remands in the Criminal Court*. Oxford: Oxford University Press.

Gibbons, D. (1977) *Society, Crime and Criminal*. (3rd edn) Englewood Cliffs, New York: Prentice Hall.

Gibbs, C. (1971) The effect of the imprisonment of women upon their children, *British Journal of Criminology*, 11, 113.

Gibson, E. and Klein, S. (1961) *Murder*. Home Office Research Unit Report, 4. London: HMSO.

Gibson, E. and Klein, S. (1969) *Murder 1957 to 1968*. London: HMSO.

Gilbert, J. (1972) Delinquent (approved school) and non-delinquent (secondary-modern school) girls, *British Journal of Criminology*, 12, 325.

Gill, O. (1977) *Luke Street: housing policy, conflict and the creation of the delinquency area*. London: Macmillan.

Gilley, J. (1974) How to help the raped, *New Society*, 27 June, 756.

Gilligan, C. (1982) *In a Different Voice*, Cambridge: Harvard University Press.

Giordano, P. (1978) Girls, guys and gangs: the changing social context of female delinquency, *The Journal of Criminal Law and Criminology*, 69, 126.

Gladstone Committee (1895) *Report of the Departmental Committee on Prisons*. London: HMSO.

Glaser, D. (1972) *Adult Crime and Social Policy*. Englewood Cliffs, New York: Prentice Hall.

Glick, R. and Neto, V. (1977) *National study of women's correctional programs*. Washington: Government Printing Office.

Glueck, S. and Glueck, E. (1934) *Five Hundred Delinquent Women*. New York: Alfred Knopf.

Gold, M. and Williams, J. (1969) National study of the aftermath of apprehension, *Prospectus*, 3, 3.

Gold, M. (1970) *Delinquent Behaviour in an American City*. California: Brooks/Cole.

Gold, M. and Reimer, D. (1975) Changing patterns of the delinquent behaviour among Americans 13 through 16 years old: 1967 −72, *Crime and Delinquency Literature*, 7, 483.

Golden, K. (1981) Women as patrol officers: a study of attitudes, *Police Studies*, 4, 3, 29.

Golden, K. (1982) Women in criminal justice: occupational interests, *Journal of Criminal Justice*, 10, 147.

Goodman, N. and Price, J. (1967) *Studies of Female Offenders*. (Studies in the causes and treatment of offenders, no. 11.) London: HMSO.

Goodwin, J., Sahd, D and Rada, R., (1982) False accusations and false denials of incest: clinical myths and clinical realities. In Goodwin, J. (ed.) *Sexual Abuse: incest victims and their families*. Massachusetts: John Wright.

Gordon, M. (1922) *Penal Discipline*. London: George Routledge and Sons.

Gove, W. (1985) The effect of age and gender on deviant behaviour: a biopsychosocial perspective. In Ross, A. (ed.) *Gender and the Life Course*. Hawthorne, New York: Aldine Publishing.

Gove, W. and Tudor, J. (1972) Adult sex roles and mental illness, *American Journal of Sociology*, 78, 812.

Graham, H. (1983) Do her answers fit his questions? Women and the survey method. In Gamarnikov, E., Morgan, D., Purvis, J and Taylorson, D. (eds) *The Public and the Private*. London: Heinemann.

Green, E. (1961) *Judicial Attitudes in Sentencing*. New York: St Martin's Press.

Greenberg, D. (1981) *Crime and Capitalism*. Palo Alto: Mayfield.

Greenwald, H. (1958) *The Call Girl*. New York: Ballantine.

Greenwood, V. (1981) The myth of female crime. In Morris, A. and Gelsthorpe, L. (eds) *Women and Crime*. Cambridge: Institute of Criminology.

Griffin, S. (1971) Rape: the all American crime, *Ramparts*, September, 26.

Griffiths, A. (1884) *The Chronicles of Newgate*. London: Chapman and Hall.

Grinder, R. (1961) New techniques for research in children's temptation behaviour, *Child Deviance*, 32, 679.

Groth, N. and Birnbaum, H. (1979) *Men Who Rape: the psychology of the offender.* New York: Plenum Press.

Group 4 (1972) Are Britons four times more honest than Yankees? Paper submitted to the Home Office working party on internal shop security. Cited in Buckle, A. and Farrington, D. (1984).

Gudjonsson, G. and Adlam, J. (1985) Occupational stresses among British police officers, *The Police Journal*, 58, 1, 73.

Gunn, J. et al. (1978) *Psychiatric Aspects of Imprisonment.* London: Academic Press.

Hagan, J., Simpson, J. and Gillis, A. (1979) The sexual stratification of social control: a gender-based perspective on crime and delinquency, *British Journal of Sociology*, 30, 25.

Hahn, N. (1980) Too dumb to know better: cacogenic family studies and the criminology of women, *Criminology*, 18, 1, 3.

Hall, R. (1985) *Ask Any Woman.* Bristol: Falling Wall Press.

Hall, S. and Scraton, P. (1981) Law, class and control, in Fitzgerald, M., McLennan, G. and Pawson, J. (eds) *Crime and Society*, London: Routledge and Kegan Paul.

Hancock, L. and Chesney-Lind, M. (1982) Female status offenders and justice reforms: an international perspective, *ANZJ of Criminology*, 15, 109.

Hanmer, J. (1978) Violence and the social control of women. In Littlejohn, G., Smart, B and Wakeford, J. (eds) *Power and the State.* London: Croom Helm.

Hans, V. and Brooks, N. (1978) Effects of corroboration instructions in a rape case on experimental juries, *Osgood Hall Law Journal*, 15, 701.

Hardiker, P. (1977) The role of probation officers in sentencing. In Parker, H. (ed.) *Social Work and the Courts.* London: Edward Arnold.

Harris, A. (1977) Sex and theories of deviance: towards a functional theory of deviant typescripts, *American Sociological Review*, 42, 3.

Harris, M. (1936) *I knew them in prison.* New York: Viking Press.

Hartman, M. (1977) *Victorian Murderesses.* Guernsey: Robson Books.

Hartmann, H. (1981) The unhappy marriage of marxism and feminism: towards a more progressive union. In Sargent, L. (ed.) *Woman and Revolution.* London: Pluto Press.

Heffernan, E. (1972) *Making it in Prison: the square, the cool and the life.* New York: John Wiley and Sons.

Heidensohn, F. (1985) *Women and Crime.* Basingstoke: Macmillan.

Herman, D. (1979) The rape culture, Freeman, J. (ed.). In *Women: a feminist perspective.* Palo Alto: Mayfield Publishing Co.

Herman, J. (1981) *Father-Daughter Incest.* Cambridge: Harvard University Press.

Herman, J. and Hirschman, L. (1977) Father daughter incest, *Signs*, 2, 4, 735.

Herskovitz, H. (1969) A psychodynamic view of sexual promiscuity. In Pollak, O. and Friedman, A. (eds) *Family Dynamics and Female Sexual Delinquency.* Palo Alto: Science and Behaviour Books.

Hewitt, M. (1958) *Wives and Mothers in Victorian Industry.* London: Barry and Rockcliffe.

Hicks, J. and Boyle, S. (1983) Like living in a submarine, *The Abolitionist*, no. 15, 8.

Higgins, L. (1951) Historical background of policewomen's service, *Journal of Criminal Law and Criminology*, 41, 822.

Hiller, A. (1982) Illness, crime and the female role. Unpublished paper presented at British Sociological Association, Manchester.

Hilton, J. (1976) Women in the police service, *The Police Journal*, 49, 93.

Hinde, R. (1951) *The British Penal System, 1773–1950*. London: Duckworth.

Hindelang, M. (1971) Age, sex and versatility of delinquent involvement, *Social Problems*, 18, 522.

Hindelang, M. (1973) Causes of delinquency: a partial replication and extension, *Social Problems*, 21, 471.

Hindelang, M. (1974) Decisions of shoplifting victims to involve the criminal justice process, *Social Problems*, 21, 580.

Hindelang, M. (1979) Sex differences in criminal activity, *Social Problems*, 27, 143.

Hirschi, T. (1969) *Causes of Delinquency*. Berkeley: University of California Press.

Hoffman-Bustamente, D. (1973) The nature of female criminality, *Issues in Criminology*, 8, 117.

Hoghughi, M. (1978) *Troubled and Troublesome*. London: Burnett.

Holland, T. et al. (1979) Preferences of prison inmates for male versus female institutional personnel, *Journal of Applied Psychology*, 64, 564.

Holloway Project Committe (1985) *Report*, London: Home Office, HM Prison Service.

Holman, M. and Krepps-Hess, B. (1983) Women correctional officers in the California Department of Corrections. Research Unit, California Department of Corrections.

Holmstrom, L. and Burgess, A. (1978) *The Victim of Rape: institutional reactions*. New York: John Wiley.

Holmstrom, L. and Burgess A. (1980) Sexual behaviour of assailants during reported rape, *Archives of Sexual Behaviour*, 9, 5, 427.

Home Office (1966) *Inquiry into prison escapes and security*. (The Mountbatten Report) London: HMSO.

Home Office (1968) *Social Inquiry Reports before Sentence*. (Home Office Circular no. 188/1968) London: Home Office.

Home Office (1970) *Treatment of Women and Girls in Custody*. London: HMSO.

Home Office (1971) *Reports to the Courts on Accused Persons*. (Circular no. 59/1971) London: Home Office.

Home Office (1978) *Criminal Statistics England and Wales, 1977*. London: HMSO.

Home Office (1979) *Committee of Inquiry into the U.K. Prison Services* (the May Committee Report) London: HMSO.

Home Office (1981) *Estimates of offending by those on bail.* (Statistical Bulletin 22/81) Surbiton: Home Office Stastical Department.

Home Office (1982) *Prison Statistics, England and Wales, 1981,* London: HMSO.

Home Office (1984a) *Managing the Long Term Prison System* (the Report of the Control Review Committee) London: HMSO.

Home Office (1984b) *Criminal Justice: a working paper.* London: HMSO.

Home Office (1984c) *Criminal Statistics England and Wales 1983.* London: HMSO.

Home Office (1986a) *Criminal Statistics England and Wales, 1985.* London: HMSO.

Home Office (1986b) *Criminal Statistics England and Wales, 1985 Supplementary vols 1 and 4.* London: HMSO.

Home Office (1986c) *Prison Statistics England and Wales, 1985.* London: HMSO.

Home Office Statistical Bulletin (1983) *Crime Statistics for the Metropolitan Police District Analysed by Ethnic Group.* Surbiton: Government Statistical Services (Statistical Bulletin 22/83).

Home Office Statistical Bulletin (1985) *Criminal Careers of those Born in 1953, 1958 and 1963.* (Statistical Bulletin 7/85.) Surbiton: Government Statistical Services.

Home Office Statistical Bulletin (1986a) *Previous Offences of Persons Convicted in 1982.* (Statistical Bulletin 2/86.) Surbiton: Government Statistical Services.

Home Office Statistical Bulletin (1986b) *The Ethnic Origin of Prisoners.* Surbiton: Government Statistical Services.

Homer, M., Leonard, A and Taylor, P. (1985) The burden of dependency. In Johnson, N. (ed.) *Marital Violence.* London: Routledge and Kegan Paul.

Horne, P. (1980) *Women in Law Enforcement.* Springfield: C. Thomas.

Horne, P. (1985) Female correction officers, *Federal Probation,* 49, 46.

Horner, M. (1970) Femininity and successful achievement: a basic inconsistency. In Bardwick, J. et al. (eds) *Feminine Personality and Conflict.* Belmont, California: Brooks Cole.

Horney, K. (1926) The flight from womanhood. Reprinted in Miller, J. (ed.) (1973) *Psychoanalysis and Women.* Harmondsworth: Penguin.

Horney, K. (1932) The dread of woman, *International Journal of Psychoanalysis,* 13, 348.

Horney, K. (1937) *The Neurotic Personality of our Time.* London: Routledge and Kegan Paul.

Horwitz, A. (1977) The pathways into psychiatric treatment: some differences between men and women, *Journal of Health and Social Behaviour,* 18, 169.

Horwitz, A. and Wasserman, M. (1980) Some misleading conceptions in sentencing research: an example and a reformulation in the juvenile court, *Criminology,* 18, 3, 411.

Hough, M. and Mayhew, P. (1983) *The British Crime Survey.* (Home Office

Research Study no. 76.) London: HMSO.

Hough, M. and Mayhew, P. (1985) *Taking Account of Crime: key findings from the 1984 British Crime Survey.* (Home Office Research Study no. 85.) London: HMSO.

Howard, J. (1780) *The State of Prisons in England and Wales.* London: William Eyres.

Hudson, B. (1979) What the nice girls do. In *Nice Girls Aren't Naughty.* Papers from a conference on female deviance. Colchester: University of Essex.

Huff, D. and Geis, I. (1954) *How to Lie with Statistics.* New York: Norton.

Hunt, J. (1984) The development of rapport through the negotiation of gender in fieldwork among police, *Human Organisation*, 43, 4, 283.

Hunter, S. (1986) On the line: working hard with dignity, *Corrections Today*, June, 12.

Hutter, B. and Williams, G. (1981) *Controlling Women.* London: Croom Helm.

ILEA Inspectorate (1982) *Equal Opportunities for Girls and Boys.* London: ILEA.

Imperato-McGinley, J. et al., (1979) Androgens and the evolution of male-gender identity among pseudohermaphrodites with S-reductase deficiency, *New England Journal of Medicine*, 300, 1233.

Ingram, G. (1980) The role of women in male federal correctional institutions, *American Correctional Association*, 275.

James, J. (1976) Motivations for entrance into prostitution. In Crites, L. (ed.) *The Female Offender.* Lexington: D. H. Heath and Co.

James, J. and Thornton, W. (1980) Women's liberation and the female delinquent, *Journal of Research in Crime and Delinquency*, 17, 230.

Jeffery, C. (ed.) (1979) *Biology and Crime.* Beverley Hills: Sage Publications Inc.

Jensen, G. and Eve, R. (1976) Sex differences in delinquency: an examination of popular sociological explanations, *Criminology*, 13, 427.

Jespersen, A. (1986) Rachel has the last laugh, *Police Review*, 4 July, 1394.

Johnson, A. (1980) On the prevalence of rape in the United States, *Signs*, 6, 1, 136.

Johnson, H. (1986) *Women and Crime in Canada.* Ottawa: Solicitor General, Canada.

Johnson, N. (1977) Special problems of the female offender, *Juvenile Justice*, 28, 3, 3.

Johnson, N. (1985) Police, social work and medical responses to battered women. In Johnson, N. (ed.) *Marital Violence.* London: Routledge and Kegan Paul.

Jones, A. (1980) *Women who Kill.* New York: Holt, Rinehart and Winston.

Jones, S. (1983) Community policing in Devon and Cornwall: some research findings on the relationship between the public and the police. In Bennett, T. (ed.) *The Future of Policing.* Cambridge: Institute of Criminology.

Jones, T. Maclean, B and Young, J. (1986) *The Islington Crime Survey.* Aldershot: Gower.

Jurik, N. (1985) An officer and a lady: organisational barriers to women working as correctional officers in male prisons, *Social Problems*, 32, 4, 375.

Jurik, N. and Halemba, G. (1984) Gender, working conditions and job satisfaction of women in a non-traditional occupation: female correctional officers in men's prisons, *The Sociological Quarterly*, 25, 551.

Justice, B. and Justice, R. (1979) *The Broken Taboo*. New York: Human Sciences Press.

Kalvan, H. and Zeisel, H. (1966) *The American Jury*. Boston: Little Brown.

Kanin, E. (1982) Female rape fantasies — a victimization study, *Victimology*, 7, 1,

Katz, S. and Mazur, M. (1979) *Understanding the Rape Victim: a synthesis of research findings*. New York: John Wiley and Sons.

Kelley, J. (1970) The new Holloway, *Prison Service Journal*, 10, 37, 2.

Kelly, L. (1984) Some thoughts on feminist experience in research on male sexual violence in Butler, O. (ed.) *Feminist Experience in Feminist Research*. Manchester: University of Manchester, Department of Sociology.

Kilpatrick, D., Resick, P and Veronen, L. (1981) Effects of a rape experience: a longitudinal study, *Journal of Social Issues*, 37, 4, 105.

Kinsey, A. Pomeroy, W. and Martin, C. (1948) *Sexual Behaviour in the Human Male*. Philadelphia: W. B. Saunders & Co.

Kinsey, A., Pomeroy, W., Martin, C. and Gebhard, P. (1953) *Sexual Behaviour in the Human Female*. Philadelphia: W. B. Saunders & Co.

Kissel, P. and Katsampes, P. (1980) The impact of women correction officers on the functioning of institutions housing male inmates, *Journal of Offender Counselling and Rehabilitation*, 4, 213.

Klein, D. (1973) The etiology of female crime: a review of the literature, *Issues in Criminology*, 8, 3.

Klein, D. (1979) Can this marriage be saved?: battery and sheltering, *Crime and Social Justice*, Winter, 19.

Klein, D. (1982) The dark side of marriage: battered wives and the domination of women. In Rafter, N. and Stanko, E. (eds) *Judge, Lawyer, Victim, Thief*. Boston: Northeastern University Press.

Klein, D. and Kress, J. (1976) Any woman's blues: a critical overview of women, crime and the criminal justice system, *Crime and Social Justice*, 5, 34.

Klein, M. (1932) *Psychoanalysis of Children*. London: Hogarth.

Klein, M. (1972) *On the Front End of the Juvenile Justice System*. Los Angeles Regional Criminal Justice Planning Board.

Klein, V. (1975) *The Feminine Character*. Urbana: University of Illinois Press.

Koeske, R. (1983) The politics of PMS. Unpublished paper presented to the American Psychological Association, Anaheim.

Konopka, G. (1966) *The Adolescent Girl in Conflict*. Englewood Cliffs, New Jersey: Prentice Hall.

Koser Wilson, N. (1982) Women in the criminal justice professions: an analysis of status conflict. In Rafter, N. and Stanko, E. (eds) *Judge,*

Lawyer, Victim, Thief. Boston: Northeastern University Press.

Koss, M. and Oros, C. (1982) Sexual experience survey: a research instrument investigating sexual aggression and victimization, *Journal of Consulting and Clinical Psychology*, 50, 455.

Kozuba-Kozubska, J. and Turrel, D. (1978) Problems of dealing with girls, *Prison Service Journal*, 29, 4.

Kramer, H. and Sprenger, J. (1971) (first published 1484), *Malleus Malificarum*. New York: Dover Books.

Kreuz, L. and Rose, R. (1972) Assessment of aggressive behaviour and plasma testosterone in a young criminal population, *Psychosomatic Medicine*, 34, 321.

Krohn, M., Curry, J. and Nelson-Kilger, S. (1983) Is chivalry dead?, *Criminology*, 21, 3, 417.

Kruttschnitt, C. (1982a) Respectable women and the law, *The Sociological Quarterly*, 23, 2, 221.

Kruttschnitt, C. (1982b) Women, crime and dependency, *Criminology* 19, 4, 495.

LaFree, G. (1980) The effect of sexual stratification by race on official reactions to rape, *American Sociological Review*, 45, 842.

Landau, S. (1974) Rape: the victim as defendant, *Trial*, July/August, 19.

Landau, S. (1981) Juveniles and the police, *British Journal of Criminology*, 21, 1, 27.

Landau, S. and Nathan G. (1983) Selecting delinquents for cautioning in the London Metropolitan area, *British Journal of Criminology*, 23, 2, 128.

Langley, R. and Levy, R. (1977) *Wife Beating: the silent crisis*. New York: E. P. Dutton.

Larner, C. (1981) *Enemies of God: the witchhunt in Scotland*. Baltimore: Johns Hopkins University Press.

Laub, J. and McDermott, M. (1985) An analysis of serious crime by young black women, *Criminology*, 23, 81.

Lees, S. (1986) *Losing Out*. London: Hutchinson.

Lekkerkerker, E. (1931) *Reformatories for Women in the United States*. Groningen: J. B. Wolters.

Lemert, E. (1951) *Social Pathology*. New York: McGraw Hill.

Lemert, E. (1972) *Human Deviance: social problems and social control*. Englewood Cliffs, New Jersey: Prentice Hall.

Leonard, E. (1982) *Women, Crime and Society*. New York: Longman.

Leonard, E. (1983) Judicial decisions and prison reform: the impact of litigation on women prisoners, *Social Problems*, 31, 1, 45.

Lewis, D. (1975) The black family: socialisation and sex roles, *Phylon*, 36, 221.

Lewis, D. (1981) Black women offenders and criminal justice: some theoretical considerations. In Warren, M. (ed.) *Comparing Female and Male Offenders*. Beverley Hills: Sage Publications Inc.

Lombroso, C. and Ferrero, W. (1895) *The Female Offender*. London: Fisher Unwin.

London Rape Crisis Centre (1984) *Sexual Violence: the reality for women*.

London: Women's Press.

Lorenz, K. (1969) *On Aggression*. New York: Bantam.

Lucas, N. (1926) *London and its Criminals*. London: Williams and Norgate.

Lukianowicz, N. (1972) Incest, *British Journal of Psychiatry*, 120, 301.

Lytton, Lady C. (1914) *Prisons and Prisoners*. London: Heinemann.

Maccoby, E. (1967) *The Development of Sex Differences*. London: Tavistock.

Maccoby, E. and Jacklin, C. (1975) *The Psychology of Sex Differences*. Oxford: Oxford University Press.

MacDonald, J. (1971) *Rape: offenders and their victims*. Springfield: C. C. Thomas.

McCabe, S. and Sutcliffe, F. (1978) *Defining Crime*. Oxford: Basil Blackwell.

McCaldon, R. J. (1967) Rape, *Canadian Journal of Corrections*, 9, 37.

McCann, K. (1985) Battered women and the law: the limits of the legislation. In Brophy, J. and Smart, C. (eds) *Women in Law*. London: Routledge and Kegan Paul.

McClintock, F. (1963) *Crimes of Violence*. London: Macmillan.

McClintock, F. and Avison, N. (1968) *Crime in England and Wales*. London: Heinemann.

McConville, S. (1981) *A History of English Prison Administration*, vol. 1. London: Routledge and Kegan Paul.

McCord, J. and Otten, L. (1983) A consideration of sex roles and motivators for crime, *Criminal Justice and Behaviour*, 10, 3.

McIntosh, M. (1978) The state and the oppression of women. In Kuhn, A. and Wolpe, A. (eds) *Feminism and Materialism*. London: Routledge and Kegan Paul.

McIntyre, K. (1982) Roles of mothers in father-daughter incest, *Social Work*, 26, 463.

McLeod, E. (1982) *Working Women: prostitution now*. London: Croom Helm.

McLeod, M. (1983) Victim non co-operation in the prosecution of domestic assault, *Criminology*, 21, 395.

McNee, Sir D. (1983) *McNee's Law*. London: Collins.

McRobbie, A. and Garber, J. (1976) Girls and subcultures. In Hall, S. and Jefferson, T. (eds) *Resistance through Rituals*. London: Hutchinson.

Madsen, C. (1968) Nurturance and modelling in preschoolers, *Child Development*, 39, 221.

Maguire, M. and Shapland, J. (1980) Is he the villain, she the victim? *New Society*, 18–25 December, 54, xiv.

Mahoney, A. (1974) The effects of labelling upon youths in the juvenile justice system: a review of the evidence, *Law and Society Review*, 8, 583.

Maidment, S. (1985) Domestic violence and the law: the 1976 Act and its aftermath. In Johnson, N. (ed.) *Marital Violence*. London: Routledge and Kegan Paul.

Maisch, H. (1973) *Incest*. London: Andre Deutsch.

Malamuth, N. (1981) Rape proclivity among males, *Journal of Social Issues*, 37, 138.

Mandaraka-Sheppard, A. (1986) *The Dynamics of Aggression in Women's*

Prisons in England. Aldershot: Gower.
Mannheim, H. (1965) *Comparative Criminology*. London: Routledge and Kegan Paul.
Mansfield, C. (1979) A new role for women police, *Police Review*, 11 May, 737.
Mapes, C. (1917) Sexual assault, *The Urologic and Cutaneous Review*, 21, 8, 430.
Mark, Sir R. (1978) *In the Office of Constable*. London: Collins.
Marks, D. (1975) Retail store security in Ireland, *Top Security*, September, 204.
Marsden, D. (1978) Sociological perspectives on family violence. In Martin, J. (ed.) *Violence in the Family*. Chichester: Wiley.
Marsh, A., Dobbs, J., Monk, J with White, A. (1985) *Staff Attitudes in the Prison Service*. London: HMSO.
Marsh, T. (1981) *Roots of Crime: a biophysical approach to crime prevention and rehabilitation*. New Jersey: Nellen Co. Ltd.
Martin, M., Gelfand, D. and Hartmann, D. (1971) Effects of adult and peer observers on boys' and girls' responses to an aggressive model, *Child Development*, 42, 1271.
Martin, S. (1980) *Breaking and Entering: policewomen on patrol*. Berkeley: University of California Press.
Matthews, J. (1981) *Women in the Penal System*. London: NACRO Briefing.
Matza, D. and Sykes, G. (1961) Juvenile delinquency and subterranean values, *American Sociological Review*, 26, 712.
Maudsley, H. (1874) Sex in mind and education, *Fortnightly Review*, 15, 466.
Mawby, R. (1977) Sexual discrimination and the law, *Probation Journal*, 24, 2, 38.
Mawby, R. (1980) Sex and crime: the results of a self-report study, *British Journal of Sociology*, 31, 525.
Mawby, R. (1982) Women in prison, *Crime and Delinquency*, 28, 24.
Maxfield, M. (1984) *Fear of Crime in England and Wales*. (Home Office Research Study no. 78.) London: HMSO.
May, D. (1981) What price equality? *Police Review*, 6 March, 458.
Mayhew, H. and Binny, J. (1862) *The Criminal Prisons of London and Scenes of Prison Life*. London: Griffin, Bihn & Co.
Maynard, M. (1985) The response of social workers to domestic violence. In Pahl, J. (ed.) *Private Violence and Public Policy*. London: Routledge and Kegan Paul.
Mays, J. (1954) *Growing up in the City*. Liverpool: Liverpool University Press.
Mead, M. (1935) *Sex and Temperament in Three Primitive Societies*. New York: William Morrow.
Medinnus, G. (1966) Age and sex differences in conscience development, *Journal of Genetic Psychology*, 109, 117.
Mednick, S. and Christiansen, K. (1977) *Biosocial Bases of Criminal Behaviour*. New York: Gardner.

Mendelsohn, B. (1974) The origin of the doctrine of victimology. In Drapkin, I. and Viano, E. (eds) *Victimology*. Lexington: D. C. Heath and Co.

Merton, R. (1938) Social structure and anomie, *American Sociological Review*, 3, 672.

Merton, R. (1959) *Social Theory and Social Structure*. Glencoe: The Free Press.

Miller, W. (1958) Lower class culture as a generating milieu of gang delinquency, *Journal of Social Issues*, 14, 5.

Millett, K. (1971) *Sexual Politics*. London: Hart-Davis.

Millett, K. (1975) *The Prostitution Papers*. St Albans: Paladin.

Millman, M. (1975) She did it all for love: a feminist view of the sociology of deviance. In Millman, M. and Moss Kanter, R. (eds) *Another Voice*. New York: Anchor Books.

Mills, C. W. (1940) Situated actions and vocabularies of motive, *American Sociological Review*, 5, 904.

Mills, E. (1982) One hundred years of fear: rape and the medical profession. In Rafter, N. and Stanko, E. (eds) *Judge, Lawyer, Victim, Thief*. Boston: Northeastern University Press.

Mitra, C. (1979) For she has no right or power to refuse her consent, *Criminal Law Review*, 558.

Money, J. et al. (1955) An examination of some basic sexual concepts: the evidence of human hermaphroditism, *John Hopkin Hospital Bulletin*, 97, 301.

Moorehead, C. (1985) The strange events at Holloway, *New Society*, 11 April, 72, 40.

Moos, R. (1969) Typology of menstrual cycle symptoms, *American Journal of Obstetrics and Gynaecology*, 103, 3, 390.

Morris, A. and Gelsthorpe, L. (1981) False clues and female crime. In Morris, A. and Gelsthorpe, L. (eds) *Women and Crime*. Cambridge: Institute of Criminology.

Morris, A. and Wilkinson, C. (1983) Secure care: just an easy answer?, *Community Care*, 8 December, 22.

Morris, R. (1964) Female delinquency and relational problems, *Social Forces*, 43, 82.

Morris, R. (1965) Attitudes towards delinquency by delinquency, non-delinquents and their friends, *British Journal of Criminology*, 5, 249.

Morris, T. (1957) *The Criminal Area*. London: Routledge and Kegan Paul.

Morris, T. and Morris, P. (1963) *Pentonville: a sociological study of an English prison*. London: Routledge and Kegan Paul.

Moulds, E. (1980) Chivalry and paternalism: disparities of treatment in the criminal justice system. In Datesman, S. and Scarpitti, F. (eds) *Women, Crime and Justice*. Oxford: Oxford University Press.

Moyer, I. (1981) Demeanour, sex and race in police processing, *Journal of Criminal Justice*, 9, 235.

NACRO (1985) *Mothers and Babies in Prison*. London: NACRO Briefing.

Naffin, N. (1985) The masculinity-femininity hypothesis: a consideration of gender-based personality theories of female crime, *British Journal of*

Criminology, 25, 365.

Nagel, I. (1981) Sex differences in the processing of criminal defendants. In Morris, A and Gelsthorpe, L. (eds) *Women and Crime*. Cambridge: Institute of Criminology.

Nagel, S. and Weitzman, L. (1971) Women and litigants, *The Hastings Law Journal*, 23, 171.

Nash, C. and West, D. (1985) Sexual molestation of young girls. In West, D. (ed.) *Sexual Victimisation*. Aldershot: Gower.

National Advisory Commission on Criminal Justice Standards and Goals (1973) *Corrections*. Washington DC: Government Printing Office.

Nelson, S. (1982) *Incest: fact and myth*. Edinburgh: Strathmullion.

Newsom Committee (1963) *Half our Future*. London: HMSO.

Nicholson, J. and Barltrop, K. (1982) Do women go mad every month?, *New Society*, 11 February, 59, 226.

Norland, S. and Mann, P. (1984) Being troublesome: women on probation, *Criminal Justice and Behaviour*, 11, 115.

Oakley, A. (1972) *Sex, Gender and Society*. London: Temple Smith.

Oakley, A. (1981) *Subject Women*. Oxford: Martin Robertson.

Ouston, J. (1984) Delinquency, family background and educational attainment, *British Journal of Criminology*, 24, 2.

Owen, D. (1972) The 47, XYY male: a review, *Psychological Bulletin*, 18, 209.

Owings, C. (1969) *Women Police*. New Jersey: Patterson Smith.

Pagelow, M. (1985) The 'battered husband syndrome': social problem or much ado about little?. In Johnson, N. (ed.) *Marital Violence*. London: Routledge and Kegan Paul.

Pahl, J. (1978) *A Refuge for Battered Women: a study of the role of a woman's centre*. London: HMSO.

Pahl, J. (1981) *A Bridge Over Troubled Waters: a longitudinal study of women who went to a refuge*. Report to DHSS.

Pahl, J. (1985) Introduction. In Pahl, J. (ed.) *Private Violence and Public Policy*. London: Routledge and Kegan Paul.

Parker, H. (1974) *View from the Boys*. Newton Abbot: David and Charles.

Parker, H., Casburn, M. and Turnbull, D. (1981) *Receiving Juvenile Justice*. Oxford: Basil Blackwell.

Parlee, M. (1982) Changes in moods and activation levels during the menstrual cycle in experimentally-naive subjects, *Psychology of Women Quarterly* 7, 2, 119.

Parnas, R. (1972) The police response to domestic disturbance. In Radzinowicz, L. and Wolfgang, M. (eds) *The Criminal in the Arms of the Law*. New York: Basic Books.

Pearson, G. (1983) *Hooligan: a history of respectable fears*. London: Macmillan.

Pearson, R. (1976) Women defendants in magistrates' courts, *British Journal of Law and Society*, 3, 265.

Peckham, A. (1985) *A Woman in Custody*. Glasgow: Fontana.

Perlstein, G. (1972) Policewomen and policemen: a comparative look, *Police Chief*, 34, 3, 74.

Peters, J. (1976) Children who are victims of sexual assault and the psychology of offenders, *American Journal of Psychotherapy*, 30, 3, 398.

Phelps, R. J. et al. (1982) *Wisconsin Female Juvenile Offender Project*. Wisconsin: Youth Policy and Law Center, Wisconsin Council on Juvenile Justice.

Piaget, J. (1932) *The Moral Judgment of the Child*. London: Kegan Paul.

Pike, L. (1876) *A History of Crime in England*. London: Smith, Elder and Co.

Piliavin, I. and Briar, S. (1964) Police encounters with juveniles, *American Journal of Sociology*, 70, 206.

Pitch, T. (1985) Critical criminology, the construction of social problems and the question of rape, *International Journal of the Sociology of Law*, 13, 35.

Pitts, J. (1986) Black young people and juvenile crime: some unanswered questions. In Matthews, R. and Young, J. (eds) *Confronting Crime*. London: Sage.

Pizzey, E. and Shapiro, J. (1981) Choosing a violent relationship, *New Society*, 23 April, 56, 133.

Pizzey, E. and Shapiro, J. (1982) *Prone to Violence*. Feltham: Hamlyn.

Platt, A. (1978) *The Child Savers*. (2nd edn) Chicago: University Press.

Polk, K. (1985) A comparative analysis of attrition in rape cases, *British Journal of Criminology*, 25, 280.

Pollak, O. (1961) *The Criminality of Women*. New York: A. S. Barnes.

Pollock, Sir F. and Maitland, F. (1898, reprinted 1952) *The History of the English Law before the time of Edward I*. Cambridge: Cambridge University Press.

Popplestone, R. (1980) Top jobs for women: are the cards stacked against them, *Social Work Today*, 23 September, 12.

Posen, I. (1979) A survey of women in Holloway with children under five. Psychology Unit, Holloway prison.

Potler, C. (1985) *A neglected population: women prisoners at Bayview*. New York: The Correctional Association of New York.

Potter, J. (1978) The police and the battered wife: the search for understanding, *Police Magazine*, 1, 40.

Price, B. (1974) A study of leadership strength of female police executives, *Journal of Political Science and Administration*, 11, 2, 219.

Priestley, P., Fears, D. and Fuller, R. (1977) *Justice for Juveniles*. London: Routledge and Kegan Paul.

Prison Department (1970) *Report on the Work of the Prison Department, 1969*. London: HMSO.

Prison Department (1980) *Report on the Work of the Prison Department, 1979*. London: HMSO.

Prison Department (1984) *Report on the Work of the Prison Department 1983*. London: HMSO.

Prison Department (1986) *Report on the Work of the Prison Department, 1985 – 6*. London: HMSO.

Procek, E. (1981) Psychiatry and the social control of women. In Morris, A. and Gelsthorpe, L. (eds) *Women and Crime*. Cambridge: Institute of

240 *Bibliography*

Criminology.
Prochaska, E. (1980) *Woman and Philanthropy in the Nineteenth Century.* Oxford: Clarendon Press.
Pugh, M. (1983) Contributory fault and rape convictions: loglinear models for blaming the victim, *Social Psychology Quarterly*, 46, 233.
Pugh, R. (1968) *Imprisonment in Medieval England.* Cambridge: Cambridge University Press.
Quinton, R. (1910) *Crime and Criminals.* London: Longmans, Green & Co.
Radford, J. (1983) Violence against women: women speak out. Wandsworth Policing Campaign.
Rafter, N. (1985) *Partial Justice: women in state prisons 1800 – 1935.* Boston: Northeastern University Press.
Reckless, W. (1961) *The Crime Problem.* New York: Appleton Century Crofts.
Reckless, W., Dinitz, S. and Murray, E. (1957) The 'good' boy in a high delinquency area, *Journal of Criminal Law, Criminology and Police Science*, 48, 18.
Reckless, W. and Kay, B. (1967) The female offender (Consultants' paper), President's Commission on Law Enforcement, Washington, DC, mimeo.
Reeves, Sanday, P. (1981) The socio-cultural context of rape: a cross cultural study, *Journal of Social Issues*, 37, 4, 5.
Reige, M. (1972) Parental affection and juvenile delinquency in girls, *British Journal of Criminology*, 12, 55.
Reiner, R. (1978) *The Blue-Coated Worker: a sociological study of police unionism.* Cambridge: Cambridge University Press.
Reiss, A. (1971) *The Police and the Public.* New Haven: Yale University Press.
Remington, P. (1981) *Policing: occupation and the introduction of female officers.* Washington: University Press of America.
Revitch, E. (1983) Burglaries with sexual dynamics. In Schlesinger, L. and Revitch, E. (eds) *Sexual Dynamics of Anti-social Behaviour.* Springfield, Illinois: Charles C. Thomas.
Rich, A. (1976) *Of Woman Born.* New York: W. W. Norton & Co. Inc.
Richardson, D. (1981) Sexism in social work, *Community Care*, 5 November, 16.
Richardson, H. (1969) *Adolescent Girls in Approved Schools.* London: Routledge and Kegan Paul.
Riger, S. and Gordon, M. (1981) Fear of rape: a study in social control, *Journal of Social Issues*, 37, 4, 71.
Riley, D. and Shaw, M. (1985) *Parental Supervision and Juvenile Delinquency.* (Home Office Research Study no. 83) London: HMSO.
Riley, D. (1986) *Sex differences in teenage crime: the role of lifestyle.* (Home Office Research and Planning Unit Research Bulletin no. 20, 34) London: HMSO.
Rittenmeyer, S. (1981) Of battered wives, self defence and double standards of justice, *Journal of Criminal Justice*, 9, 389.
Roberts, J. and Palermo, J. (1958) A study of the administration of bail in

New York, *University of Pensylvania Law Review*. 106, 685.

Robin, G. (1977) Forcible rape: institutionalized sexism in the criminal justice system, *Crime and Delinquency*, 23, 136.

Robins, D. and Cohen, P. (1978) *Knuckle Sandwich*. Harmondsworth: Penguin.

Rock, P. (1977) Review Symposium on *Women, Crime and Criminology* (Smart, C.) *British Journal of Criminology*, 17, 392.

Rodmell, S. (1981) Men, women and sexuality: a feminist critique of the sociology of deviance, *Women's Studies International Quarterly*, 4, 145.

Rolph, C. (1955) *Women of the Streets*. London: Secker and Warburg.

Rose, H. et al. (1971) Plasma and testosterone, dominance, rank and aggressive behaviour in male rhesus monkeys, *Nature*, 231, 366.

Rose, H. et al. (1972) Plasma testosterone levels in the male rhesus: influences of sexual and social stimuli, *Science*, 178, 643.

Rosenblum, K. (1975) On being sane in insane places, Science, 179, 250.

Rosenhan, N. (1973) Female deviance and the female sex role: a preliminary investigation, *British Journal of Sociology*, 26, 169.

Rossi, P. et al. (1985) Beyond crime seriousness: fitting the punishment to the crime, *Journal of Quantitative Criminology*, 1, 1.

Rotner, S. (1962) Design for a women's prison, *Howard Journal*, 11, 134.

Roy, M. (1977) *Battered Women: a psycho-sociological study of domestic violence*. London: Van Nostrand Reinhold.

Royal Commission on Police Powers (1929) *Report*. London: HMSO.

Ruck, S. (1951) *Paterson on Prisons*. London: Frederick Muller Ltd.

Rush, F. (1974) The sexual abuse of children: a feminist point of view. In Connell, N. and Wilson, C. (eds) *Rape: the first sourcebook for women*. New York: New American Library.

Russell, C. and Miller, B. (1978) Profile of a terrorist. In Elliott, J. and Gibson, L. (eds) *Contemporary Terrorism*. Garthersburg: International Association of Chief of Police.

Russell, D. (1982) *Rape in Marriage*. New York: Collier Books, McMillan Publishing Co.

Russo, N. and Sobel, S. (1981) Sex differences in the utilization of mental health facilities, *Professional Psychology*, 12, 1, 7.

Rutter, M. and Giller, H. (1983) *Juvenile Delinquency: trends and perspectives*. Harmondsworth: Penguin Books.

el Sa'adawi, N. (1986) *Memoirs from the Women's Prison*. London: The Women's Press.

Sachs, A. and Wilson, J. (1978) *Sexism and the Law: a study of male beliefs and judicial bias*. Oxford: Martin Robertson.

Sack, W., Seidler, J. and Thomas, S. (1976) The children of imprisoned parents: a psychosocial exploration, *American Journal of Orthopsychiatry*, 46, 618.

Salem, S. (1982) Draft of the final report of the Psychiatric Remands Research Project: The psychiatric remands process in magistrates' courts, Cambridge. Unpublished.

Sargent, L. (1981) (ed.) *Women and Revolution*. London: Pluto Press.

Sarri, R. (1981) Michigan prisons for women: a brief historical view. In Figuera-McDonogh, J. et al. (eds) *Women in Prison – Michigan: 1968 – 78*. The University of Michigan School of Social Work.

Sarri, R. (1983) Gender issues in juvenile justice, *Crime and Delinquency*, 29, 3, 381.

Sayers, J. (1982) *Biological Politics*. London: Tavistock.

Scarpitti, E., Murray, E., Dinitz, S. and Reckless, W. (1960) The 'good' boy in a high delinquency area: four years later, *American Sociological Review*, 25, 555.

Scheppele, K. and Bart, P. (1983) Through women's eyes: defining danger in the wake of sexual assault, *Journal of Social Issues*, 39, 2, 63.

Schlossman, S. and Wallach, S. (1978) The crime of precocious sexuality: female delinquency in the progressive era, *Harvard Educational Review*, 48, 65.

Schofield, M. (1968) *The Sexual Behaviour of Young People*. Harmondsworth: Penguin.

Schultz, L. (1975) Child sex victims: socio-legal perspectives. In Schultz, L. (ed.) *Rape Victimology*. Springfield, Illinois: Charles C. Thomas.

Schultz, L. and De Savage, J. (1975) Rape and rape attitudes on a college campus. In Schultz, L. (ed.) *Rape Victimology*. Springfield, Illinois: Charles C. Thomas.

Schwartz, I., Jackson-Beeck, M., Anderson, R. (1984) The hidden system of juvenile control, *Crime and Delinquency*, 30, 3, 371.

SchWeber, C. (1982) The government's unique experiment in salvaging women criminals. In Rafter, N. and Stanko, E. (eds) *Judge, Lawyer, Victim, Thief: women, gender roles and criminal justice*. Boston: Northeastern University Press.

SchWeber, C. (1984) Beauty marks and blemishes: the co-ed prison as a microcosm of integrated society, *The Prison Journal*, 46, 1, 3.

Schwendinger, J. and Schwendinger, H. (1974) Rape myths: in legal, theoretical and everyday practice, *Crime and Social Justice*, Summer, 4.

Schwendinger, J. and Schwendinger, H. (1981) Rape, sexual inequality and levels of violence, *Crime and Social Justice*, Winter, 3.

Schwendinger, J. and Schwendinger, H. (1982) Rape, the law and private property, *Crime and Delinquency*, 28, 271.

Sealy, A. and Wain, C. (1980) Person perception and jurors' decisions, *British Journal of Social and Clinical Psychology*, 19, 7.

Seddon, V. (1981) Violence against women: male power in action, *Marxism Today*, August, 14.

Seear, Baroness N. and Player, E. (1986) *Women in the Penal System*. London: Howard League.

Select Committee (1975) *Violence in Marriage*, 553, London: HMSO.

Seligman, M. (1975) *Helplessness: on depression, development and death*. San Fransisco: Freeman.

Shacklady-Smith, L. (1978) Sexist assumptions and female delinquency: an empirical investigation. In Smart, C. and Smart, B. (eds) *Women, Sexuality and Social Control*. London: Routledge and Kegan Paul.

Shapland, J., Willmore, J. and Dubb, P. (1985) *Victims in the Criminal Justice System*. Aldershot: Gower.

Sharpe, S. (1976) *Just Like a Girl – How girls learn to be women*. Harmondsworth: Penguin.

Shaw, C. and McKay, H. (1942) *Juvenile Delinquency and Urban Areas*. Chicago: Chicago Press.

Shaw, C. and McKay, H. (1969) *Juvenile Delinquency and Urban Areas*. Chicago: University of Chicago Press.

Sherman, L. (1975) An evaluation of policewomen on patrol in a suburban police department, *Journal of Police Science and Administration*, 3, 4, 434.

Sherman, L. and Berk, R. (1984) The Minneapolis domestic violence experiment, Police Foundation Reports 1, Washington DC.

Short, J. and Nye, F. (1958) Extent of unrecorded juvenile delinquency, *Journal of Criminal Law, Criminology and Police Science*, 49, 296.

Shorter, E. (1977) On writing the history of rape, *Signs*, 3, 2, 471.

Shover, N., Norland, N., James, J. and Thornton, W. (1979) Gender roles and delinquency, *Social Forces*, 58, 162.

Sichel, J. et al. (1978) *Women on Patrol: a pilot study of police performance in New York City*. Washington DC: Government Printing Office.

Silbert, M. and Pines, A. (1982) Victimization of street prostitutes, *Victimology*, 7, 122.

Simon, R. (1975) *Women and Crime*, Lexington: D. C. Heath and Co.

Simpson, A. (1985) Rape and the malicious prosecutor. Paper presented at ASC, *Journal of Criminal Law and Criminology*, forthcoming.

Size, M. (1957) *Prisons I have Known*. London: George Allen and Unwin.

Smart, C. (1976) *Women, Crime and Criminology*. London: Routledge and Kegan Paul.

Smart, C. (1977) Reply to Paul Rock, *British Journal of Criminology*, 17, 397.

Smart, C. (1979) The new female criminal: reality or myth? *British Journal of Criminology*, 19, 1, 50.

Smart, C. (1981) Comment on paper by Greenwood, V. (1981). In Morris, A. and Gelsthorpe, L. (eds) *Women and Crime*. Cambridge: Institute of Criminology.

Smart, C. (1985) Legal subjects and sexual objects: ideology, law and female sexuality. In Brophy, J. and Smart, C. (eds) *Women in Law*. London: Routledge and Kegan Paul.

Smart, C. and Brophy, J. (1985) Locating law: a discussion of the place of law in feminist politics. In Brophy, J. and Smart, C. (eds) *Women in Law*. London: Routledge and Kegan Paul.

Smart, C. and Smart, B. (1978) Accounting for rape: reality and myth in press reports. In Smart, C. and Smart, B. (eds) *Women, Sexuality and Social Control*. London: Routledge and Kegan Paul.

Smith, A. (1962) *Women in Prison*. London: Stevens and Son.

Smith, D. (1983) A survey of police officers. In *Police and People in London* Vol. 3 London: Policy Studies Institute.

Smith, D. and Visher, C. (1980) Sex and involvement in deviance/crime: a quantitative review of the empirical literature, *American Sociological Review*, 45, 691.

Smykla, J. (1979) Co-ed Corrections in the United States: a look at theory, operations and research issues, *Howard Journal*, 18, 44.

Smykla, J. (1980) *Co-ed Prison*. New York: Human Sciences Press.

Snortum, J. and Beyers, J. (1983) Patrol activities of male and female officers as a function of work experience, *Police Studies*, 6, 1, 36.

Sobel, S. (1980) Women in prison: sexism behind bars, *Professional Psychology*, April, 331.

Softley, P. (1980) Sentencing practice in magistrates' courts, *Criminal Law Review*, 161.

Southgate, P. (1981) Women in the Police, *The Police Journal*, 54, 2, 157.

Southgate, P. and Ekblom, P. (1984) *Contacts between police and public*. (Home Office Research Study no. 77.) London: HMSO.

Spender, D. (1981) *Men's Studies Modified*. Oxford: Pergamon Press.

Stacey, M. (1983) Social science and the state: fighting like a woman. In Gamarnskow, E., Morgan, D., Purvis, J. and Taylorson, D. (eds) *The Public and the Private*. London: Heinemann.

Stanko, E. (1982) Would you believe the woman?: prosecutorial screening for 'credible' witnesses and a problem of justice. In Rafter, N. and Stanko, E.(eds) *Judge, Lawyer, Victim, Thief*. Boston: Northeastern University Press.

Stark, E. (1984) The unspeakable family secret, *Psychology Today*, March, 38.

Steffensmeier, D. (1978) Crime and the contemporary woman: an analysis of changing levels of female property crime 1960−75, *Social Forces*, 57, 2, 566.

Steffensmeier, D. (1980) Assessing the impact of the women's movement on sex-based differences in the handling of adult defendants, *Crime and Delinquency*, 26, 3, 344.

Steffensmeier, D. and Cobb, M. (1981) Sex differences in urban arrest patterns, 1934−79, *Social Problems*, 29, 1, 37.

Steffensmeier, D. and Steffensmeier, R. (1980) Trends in female delinquency, *Criminology*, 18, 1, 62.

Steffensmeier, D., Steffensmeier, R. and Rosenthal, A. (1979) Trends in female violence, 1960−77, *Sociological Focus*, 12, 3, 217.

Stevens, P. and Willis, C. (1979) *Race, Crime and Arrests*. (Home Office Research Study no. 58.) London: HMSO.

Stewart, C. and Shine, J. (1984) Disturbed Women in Holloway. Psychology Department, HM Prison Holloway. Unpublished.

Storr, A. (1970) *Human Aggression*. Harmondsworth: Penguin Books.

Straus, M. et al. (1980) *Behind Closed Doors*. New York: Anchor Press/Doubleday.

Sullivan, P. (1979) The role of women in the police service. *Police Journal*, 52, 336.

Sulton, C. and Townsey, R. (1981) *A Progress Report on Women in Policing*. Washington DC: The Police Foundation.

Sutherland, E. (1939) *Principles of Criminology*. (3rd edn) Chicago: Lippincott.

Sutherland, E. and Cressey, D. (1960) *Principles of Criminology*. (6th edn) Chicago: Lippincott.

Sykes, G. (1958) *The Society of Captives*. Princeton: Princeton University Press.

Tansy, K. and Sear, J. (1985) A short report on our experiences at Styal prison, *The Abolitionist*, no. 2, 16.

Taylor, I., Walton, P. and Young, J. (1973) *The New Criminology*. London: Routledge and Kegan Paul.

Taylor, I., Walton, P. and Young, J. (1975) *Critical Criminology*. London: Routledge and Kegan Paul.

Taylor, R. and Dalton, K. (1983) Premenstrual syndrome: a new criminal defence?', *California Western Law Review*, 19, 2, 269.

Teilmann, K. and Landry, P. (1981) Gender bias in juvenile justice, *Journal of Research in Crime and Delinquency*, 18, 1, 47.

Terry, R. (1970) Discrimination in the handling of juvenile offenders by social control agencies. In Garabedian, P. and Gibbons, D. (eds) *Becoming Delinquent*. Chicago: Aldine Press.

Thomas, D. (1979) *Principles of Sentencing*. London: Heinemann.

Thornton, B. et al. (1982) The relationships of observer characteristics to beliefs in the causal responsibility of victims of sexual assault, *Human Relations*, 35, 4, 321.

Thornton, W. and James, J. (1979) Masculinity and delinquency revisited, *British Journal of Criminology*, 19, 225.

Trasler, G. (1965) Criminology and the socialisation process, *Advancement of Science*, 545.

Turk, A. (1969) *Criminality and the Legal Order*. Chicago: Rand McNally and Co.

Turner, T. and Tofler, D. (1986) Indicators of psychiatric disorder among women admitted to prison, *British Medical Journal*, 292, 651.

Tysoe, M. (1982) The sexual harassers, *New Society*, 4 November, 62, 212.

US Department of Justice (1984) *Sourcebook of Criminal Justice Statistics – 1983*. Washington DC: Bureau of Justice Statistics.

US Department of Justice (1986) *Criminal Victimization in the United States, 1984*. Washington DC: Bureau of Justice Statistics.

Vaerting, M. and Vaerting, M. (1923) *The Dominant Sex: a study in the sociology of sex differences*. London: Allen and Unwin.

Vega, M. and Silverman, I. (1982) Female officers as viewed by their male counterparts, *Police Studies*, 5, 1, 31.

Virkkunen, M. (1975) Victim precipitated pedophilia offences, *British Journal of Criminology*, 15, 2, 175.

Visher, C. (1983) Gender, police, arrest decisions and notions of chivalry, *Criminology*, 21, 5.

Von Hentig, H. (1940) The criminality of the negro, *Journal of Criminal Law, Criminology and Police Science*, 30, 662.

Voumvakis, S. and Erikson, R. (1984) *News Accounts of Attacks on Women: a comparison of 3 Toronto newspapers*. Research Report of the Centre of Criminology, University of Toronto.

Wadsworth, M. (1979) *Roots of Delinquency: infancy, adolescence and crime*. Oxford: Martin Robertson.

Walker, L. (1979) *The Battered Woman*. New York: Harper Colophon Books.

Walker, M. (1985) Statistical anomalies in comparing the sentences of males and females, *Sociology*, 19, 3, 446.

Walker, N. (1965) *Crime and Punishment in Britain*. Edinburgh: Edinburgh University Press.

Walker, N. (1977) *Behaviour and Misbehaviour: explanations and non-explanations*. Oxford: Basil Blackwell.

Walker, N. (1981) Feminists' extravaganzas, *Criminal Law Review*, 379.

Walkowitz, J. (1980) *Prostitution and Victorian Society*. Cambridge: Cambridge University Press.

Walmsley, R. and White, K. (1979) *Sexual Offences, Consent and Sentencing*. (Home Office Research Unit Study No. 54.) London: HMSO.

Ward, D. and Kassebaum, G. (1965) *Women's Prison: sex and social structure*. Chicago: Aldine.

Ward, J. (1982) Telling tales in prison. In Frankenberg, R. (ed.) *Custom and Conflict in British Society*. Manchester: Manchester University Press.

Wasoff, F. (1982) Legal protection from wife beating, *International Journal of the Sociology of Law*, 10, 2.

Webb, D. (1984) More on gender and justice: girl offenders on supervision, *Sociology*, 18, 367.

Webster Cory, D. and Masters, R. (1963) *Violation of Taboo: incest in the great literature of the past and present*. New York: Julian Press Inc.

Weinstein, M. (1977) Implications of New York's new rape law. In Neary, M. and Patai, F. (eds) *Rape: the violent crime*. New York: The Americam Academy for Law Enforcement.

Weis, K. and Borges, S. (1973) Victimology and rape: the case of the legitimate victim, *Issues in Criminology*, 8, 71.

Weisstein, N. (1971) Psychology constructs the female. In Gornick, V. and Moran, B. (eds) *Women in Sexist Society*. New York: Basic Books.

Wells, C. (1985) Law Reform, rape and ideology, *Journal of Law and Society*, 12, 1, 63.

West, D. (1967) *The Young Offender*. Harmondsworth: Penguin.

West, D. (1983) Sex offences and offending. In Tonry, M. and Morris, N. (eds) *Crime and Justice: an annual review of research, vol. 5*. Chicago: University of Chicago Press.

West, D. and Farrington, D. (1973) *Who Becomes Delinquent?*. London: Heinemann.

Wexler, J. and Logan, D. (1983) Sources of stress among women police officers, *Journal of Police Science and Administration*, 11, 1, 46.

Widom, C. (1978) Toward an understanding of female criminality, *Progress in Experimental Personality Research*, 8, 245.

Widom, C. (1981) Perspectives of female criminality: a critical examination of assumptions. In Morris, A. and Gelsthorpe, L. (eds) *Women and Crime*. Cambridge: Institute of Criminology.

Wiener, C. (1975) Sex roles and crimes in late Elizabethan Hertfordshire, *Journal of Social History*, 8, 38.

Wiles, P. (1970) Criminal statistics and sociological explanations of crime. In Wiles, P. and Carson, W. (eds) *Crime and Delinquency in Britain*. Oxford: Martin Robertson.

Williams, L. (1984) The classic rape: when do victims report?, *Social Problems*, 31, 4, 459.

Willis, P. (1978) *Profane Culture*. London: Routledge and Kegan Paul.

Willmott, P. (1966) *Adolescent Boys of East London*. London: Routledge and Kegan Paul.

Wilson, E. (1983) *What is to be done about: Violence against women*. Harmondsworth: Penguin Books.

Wilson, J. (1968) *Varieties of Police Behaviour: the management of law and order in eight communities*. Cambridge: Harvard University Press.

Wilson, J. Q. and Hernstein, R. (1985) *Crime and Human Nature*. New York: Simon and Schuster.

Wisan, G. (1979) The treatment of rape in criminology textbooks, *Victimology*, 4, 1, 86.

Wise, N. (1967) Juvenile delinquency among middle-class girls. In Vas, E. (ed.) *Middle-class Delinquency*. New York: Harper Row.

Wolfendon Committee (1957) Report: *Homosexual Offences and Prostitution*, (Cmnd. 247.) London: HMSO.

Wootton, B. (1959) *Social Science and Social Pathology*. London: Allen and Unwin.

Worrall, A. (1981) Out of place: female offenders in the court, *Probation Journal*, 28, 90.

Worrall, A. and Pease, K. (1986) Personal crime against women: evidence from the 1982 British Crime Survey, *Howard Journal*, 25, 2, 118.

Worsley, H. (1849) *Juvenile Depravity*. London: Gilpin.

Worth, J. (1981) Characteristics of female lifers, *Prison Medical Journal*, no. 22, 16.

Wright, Sir A. E. (1913) *The Unexpurgated Case against Woman Suffrage*. London: Constable.

Wright, D. and Cox, E. (1971) Changes in moral belief among sixth-form boys and girls over a seven year period in relation to religious belief, age and sex difference, *British Journal of Sociology and Clinical Psychology*, 10, 332.

Wright, R. (1980) Rape and physical violence. In West, D. (ed.) *Sex Offenders in the Criminal Justice System*. Cambridge: Institute of Criminology.

Wright, R. (1984) A note on the attrition of rape cases. *British Journal of Criminology*, 24, 399.

Wyles, L. (1952) *A Woman at Scotland Yard*. London: Faber and Faber.

Young, A. (1986) Feminism and the rape laws, *The Abolitionist*, no. 21, 34.

Young, J. (1981) Thinking seriously about crime: some models of criminology. In Fitzgerald, M., McLennan, G. and Pawson, J. (eds) *Crime and Society*. London: Routledge and Kegan Paul.

Young, V. (1980) Women, race and crime, *Criminology*, 18, 26.

Zavitzianos, G. (1983) The kleptomanias and female criminality. In Schlesinger, L. and Revitch, E. (eds) *Sexual Dynamics of Anti-Social Behaviour*. Springfield: Charles Thomas.

Zimmer, L. (1982) Female guards in men's prisons: creating a role for themselves. Cornell University, doctoral dissertation. Unpublished.

Zimmer, L. (1986) *Women Guarding Men*. Chicago: University of Chicago Press.

Index